Modern Hypnosis

Edited and Compiled by

LESLEY KUHN

Editor *Your Mind: Psychology Digest*

AND

SALVATORE RUSSO, Ph.D.

Director, Veterans Service Bureau, Trenton, N. J.

Foreword by Melvin Powers

Introduction by André Weitzenhoffer, Ph.D.

Published by
Melvin Powers
WILSHIRE BOOK COMPANY
12015 Sherman Road
No. Hollywood, California 91605
Telephone: (213) 875-1711

Copyright 1958
by
WILSHIRE BOOK COMPANY

Kuhn, Lesley, 1904— *ed.*

Modern hypnosis, ed. and comp. by Lesley Kuhn and Salvatore Russo. New York, Psychological Library, 1947. Hollywood, Wilshire Book Company, 1958

349 p.   24 cm.

1st ed.
Bibliography: p. 338-349.

2nd edition

1. Hypnotism.   I. Russo, Salvatore, 1906—   joint ed.
II. (Title)
BF1141.K95   134.082   Med. 47—2471
U. S. Armed Forces   Medical Library
for Library of Congress   [a53e1]†

Printed by
HAL LEIGHTON PRINTING COMPANY
P.O. Box 3952
North Hollywood, California 91605
Telephone: (213) 983-1105

ISBN 0-8-7980-100-X

CONTENTS

FOREWORD

The manifold phenomena of hypnosis are being utilized in many professional fields today, but the press and other mediums of mass communication have dwelled almost entirely on those aspects which feature the spectacular. The result has been that the public is largely unfamiliar with the true scope of this valuable medical and psychological tool.

Undoubtedly, nearly everybody knows now that relatively painless childbirth may be achieved by hypnotherapy, but how many know that it is equally valuable in treating speech disorders or reorienting the personality so that it may function more efficiently in a world in which anxiety increases daily?

In MODERN HYPNOSIS, recognized authorities in all the uses of hypnosis have contributed chapters to afford both lay and professional people a panoramic view of this fascinating and rapidly expanding modality. Most of them are illustrated with carefully documented case histories, which remove the subject matter from the realm of theoretical abstractions to reality.

Despite the increasing use of hypnosis, little headway has been made in the removal of misconceptions. Hypnotherapists report that most of their patients feel that they will have to relinquish their will power and be "under the spell" of the operator rather than partners in a mutual endeavor that cannot succeed without their cooperation. Indeed, the fact is slowly emerging that patients hypnotize themselves, rather than the other way around.

Public knowledge of some of the uses of hypnosis has not eradicated the prevalent viewpoint that patients can be forced to commit acts they would not ordinarily consider. To discuss this serious problem, MODERN HYPNOSIS has called on Dr. Milton Erickson, the outstanding authority in the field. Readers will find his answers most illuminating.

Millions of people still think of hypnosis as sleep or unconsciousness, but nothing could be further from the truth. Dr. Wesley Raymond Wells, a Harvard University researcher, discusses this important point in detail and concludes that hypnosis is much more akin to the waking state—a state, in fact, in which the subject is hyperacute rather than somnolent.

These are only a few of the subjects which are discussed in this much needed book. Although the reading matter is primarily of a practical nature, readers possessed of intellectual curiosity will find a variety of theories pertaining to those aspects of hypnosis which are still being disputed by the various schools of thought.

This book should be read by all who are just becoming acquainted with hypnosis, and particularly by those whose information has been gleaned from sources which can only lead to misconceptions. Hypnosis is a powerful force for good, but it can only reach its potential through an informed public. MODERN HYPNOSIS contains that information.

Melvin Powers
Publisher

12015 Sherman Road
No. Hollywood, California 91605

INTRODUCTION

In 1841 James Braid, a surgeon of Manchester, England, published a book which introduced the world to the science of hypnotism. The title of this book was "Neurypnology" and in it, Braid introduced our own modern expressions "hypnotism," "hypnotic," "hypnotist," and so forth. It is interesting to see just what he had in mind when he wrote this famous work and herewith are some of his definitions:

"Neurypnology:" meaning "the rationale or doctrine of nervous sleep," denotes "a peculiar condition of the nervous system, into which it can be thrown by artificial contrivance: or thus, a peculiar condition of the nervous system, induced by a fixed and abstracted attention of the mental and visual eye, on one object, not of an exciting nature."

And more precisely, "neuro-hypnotism" or "hypnotism" for short was used by Braid to denote this nervous sleep. Today we tend to speak of "hypnosis" rather than hypnotism in this connection and for the most part we no longer accept the notion of hypnosis as a form of sleep.

The story of how hypnosis came to be discovered by James Braid is simply told. Having witnessed an exhibition of mesmeric phenomena, and being convinced both of the reality of these phenomena and of the incorrectness of the prevalent explanation which ascribed these to the influence of a mysterious vital fluid otherwise known as animal magnetism or mesmeric fluid, he rapidly proceeded to track down the real cause which, as we just saw, he thought was a matter of intense concentration combined with visual fixation. And there it remained for a while.

Although hypnotism had its start in England, Germany and especially France very early became the leaders in the study and applications of hypnosis. This state of affairs persisted until around 1910 when all interest in the phenomenon died down to practically nothing both here and abroad. Right from the start various controversies arose in connection with the nature of hypnosis as well as the kind of things it could do. One of the most famous and important of these controversies is the one which raged between a group of investigators who came to be known as the Paris School and another group referred to as the Nancy School. Charcot, a famous French neurologist, and really a far better scientist than Mr. Blankfort would have us believe in the last chapter of this book, did erroneously conclude that all hypnotic phenomena were pathological, that is, that they were the product of a diseased nervous system and that as such they had an abnormal physical basis.

He and his students were the ones who made up the Paris School. On the other hand, Bernheim, another French physician, who headed the Nancy group, believed that all hypnotic phenomena, including hypnosis, were perfectly normal effects which were brought about entirely by suggestions, hence were strictly mental in origin. Charcot and Bernheim fought very bitterly over these issues with the latter eventually winning. Today it is largely held that suggestion plays a very important part in the production of hypnotic phenomena, and some individuals, like Bernheim, even believe that there is not hypnosis but only suggestion.

The years extending roughly between 1900 and 1930 were rather dull and depressing years insofar as hypnosis is concerned. For sure some investigators still studied it and some therapists still made use of it, but for reasons which need not be examined here interest in this subject matter became pretty much relegated to nightclubs and the stage, and its main function became that of being a source of amusement.

In the year 1933 a most important work written by a Yale University psychologist made its appearance. This was Clark L. Hull's now classic: "Hypnosis and Suggestibility." This work not only was able to shed considerable light on various aspects of suggestion and hypnosis and did much toward clearing the proverbial cobwebs away from this topic, but above all it showed in a very definitive manner that hypnosis was a fit subject for scientific study. Hull's book is indeed the first truly modern (20th century) scientific book in this field. It did much toward making a respectable field out of hypnotism and with its publication America also became definitely established as the center for scientific hypnotism. We remain to this date the leaders in this area. It should not be thought, however, that the new rise of hypnotism went unhampered from 1933 on. It was indeed a slow and arduous rise. But by 1949 hypnotism was sufficiently well established that a small group of investigators and practitioners were able to found the Society for Clinical and Experimental Hypnosis, which in 1953 began to publish its official journal, the Journal of Clinical and Experimental Hypnosis. Somewhat earlier the British Society of Medical Hypnotists had been organized in England, and it too has been publishing a small scientific journal since late 1948. Very recently a second professional society, The American Society of Clinical Hypnosis, has come into being and it will soon also be publishing a scientific journal. But perhaps the most significant events to date have been the formal recognition of hypnosis some time ago by the British Medical Association, and very recently by the American Medical Association.

This very brief and sketchy account of the history of hypnotism will, I hope, make it clear that science has by no means abstained from studying and using hypnosis as seems to be the common belief. As I have already intimated, during the last quarter of the nineteenth century the spotlight of science was very much turned upon hypnotic phenomena. Some individuals in recent years have deplored the dirth of information and the lack of experimentation in this area. I find this lament rather strange because there are around 10,000 books and articles in print dealing with hypnotism and animal magnetism. There are roughly 1000 scientific treatises and lesser scientific works on hypnotism alone, and about 8000 scientific articles on this same topic dealing with both its nature and applications. Not all are in English, it is true, and many are difficult to obtain. These various writings are of course not all equally good. Indeed, some should never have seen print. But even discounting these and considering only such material as is readily available in the English language one quickly passes the 1000 mark!

In the pages which follow you will find a very small but select sample of what is available in the scientific literature on hypnotism. Nearly every author whose article has been included in this book is a modern pioneer in hypnotism as well as a well-known investigator and authority on hypnotic phenomena. Each of these men has made important contributions to this field of inquiry and nearly every one of the articles you will read has left a permanent impression. It is hoped that, small as this sample is, it and the excellent appended bibliography will help to dispel the notion that no one has done anything worth telling about or that information is unavailable in this most interesting field of inquiry. But best of all, as you read this book you will read what scientists have had to say to each other about their research and ideas, for each of these articles was originally written by scientists for other scientists. And as you read them not only will you come to know these men at their work but you will come to realize that fundamental research in hypnotism is no child's play and can only be carried out by well trained individuals.

It is perhaps fitting to conclude this introduction with a note of congratulation to the editors of this work for having compiled as useful and significant a collection of articles as this, nor should one forget the Wilshire Book Company who has made it available to all who are interested in hypnotism.

André M. Weitzenhoffer, Ph.D.

Los Altos, California
July, 1958

INTRODUCTION

HISTORY OF HYPNOSIS

ANCIENT. Hypnosis is almost as old as civilization itself. It was known to the medicine men of primitive tribes, and to the magicians and priests of ancient countries, such as Egypt, Caldea, Persia, India, Greece, and Rome. In early civilizations it was used for religious and therapeutic purposes. The ability to hypnotize was considered an expression of supernatural power.

MEDIEVAL. During the Middle Ages hypnosis was kept alive by the sorcerers and wizards. It flourished under the cloak of black magic and came to be considered more of an evil power than a beneficent one, for it was believed that the hypnotizer was an agent of the devil and the hypnotized person under his evil spell.

MODERN. It was not until the 18th century that any attempt was made to turn hypnosis into a science. A German physician by the name of Mesmer practicing in Paris presented his theory in 1772. He had found that people went into a trance by touching a magnet and were cured of some diseases. Later he discovered that patients could receive the same effects by touching him. From this he developed a theory of animal magnetism; cures were effected by having a sick man become harmonized with the "universal fluids." The final refinement of his work was the construction of a large oak chest from which protruded iron rods for patients to touch.

Mesmer's explanation of hypnosis was wrong and his hocus pocus was not necessary to produce hypnosis, but the phenomenon he produced was genuine. His work, however, was criticized by a scientific commission in Paris which included Benjamin Franklin. He was declared a charlatan and thoroughly discredited. But he had succeeded in introducing hypnosis to the modern world.

Thereafter the history of hypnosis is made up mostly of the attempts of medical men to induce anesthesia for surgical purposes and to achieve cures for mental disorders.

In the middle of the 19th century a physician by the name of Braid recognized the true nature of hypnosis, namely that the phenomenon was psychological and not due to animal magnetism. He had begun his investigations as a skeptic, but soon recognized its genuineness. At first he was interested in the physiological aspects of hypnosis, but soon turned to the psychological side. He coined the expression "neuro-hypnosis" (nervous sleep), and later condensed it to hypnosis. Mesmer had resorted to astronomy, Braid tried to explain it by physiology, and ended up with psychology.

The students of hypnosis now divided into two schools, and engaged in what is called the Nancy-Paris controversy. The followers of Charcot who constituted the Paris School declared that hypnosis was primarily a physiological or neurological state. The followers of Liebeault (the Nancy School) taught that hypnosis was psychological in nature.

In the 19th century the psychological explanation prevailed and the term suggestion was used to explain hypnosis. This psychological explanation became universally accepted and caused many to believe that hypnosis was merely a matter of suggestion. This explanation may have been one of the reasons why medical men dropped hypnosis at the end of the 19th century.

The main reason, however, why the doctors deserted hypnosis is that narcotic drugs such as ether and chloroform had been found, and their use made the anesthetic power of hypnosis superfluous. Until those drugs had been discovered in the middle of the 19th century, hypnosis had been used by some physicians to alleviate pain in surgical operations. Dr. J. Esdaile, for instance, reported that he had performed nearly 300 major operations and several thousand minor ones under hypnosis.

The other medical function of hypnosis was therapeutic. French and German psychiatrists used it with varying success in the last century. It received a little attention during the first world war, but it was during the second world war that it received extensive recognition.

For the most part hypnosis was left in the 20th century to entertainers on the stage and to psychologists. During the first quarter of the century psychologists gave it only passing attention. The theatrical men exploited this phenomenon for their own purposes and perpetuated the horrifying conception of hypnosis that is found in du Maurier's sentimental novel called *Trilby.*

Freud had seen the value of hypnosis and used it in the beginning of his practice. He abandoned it because he found that only a few of his patients achieved a deep trance. Psychoanalysts, however, have recently resumed its use in their technique called hypnoanalysis.

During the last 25 years laboratory psychologists have quietly experimented and materially added to our knowledge of hypnosis. The experimental findings of these laboratories have cast considerable doubt on many of the old concepts.

With the high incidence of neurosis caused by war, hypnosis has come into its own both as a diagnostic and a therapeutic agent in mental disturbances. Physicians have learned that hypnosis, whether induced by drugs or psychological means, has a place in the treatment of neurosis. Thus hypnosis from the work of Mesmer has finally become of age, and research in hypnosis is sponsored by as reputable an institution as the Menninger Foundation.

THEORIES OF HYPNOSIS

There are a number of different theories of hypnosis. The reason for this lies in the fact that we have not been able to decide what constitutes the hypnotized state. Perhaps when we have been able to agree on what is essential to hypnosis and what is only incidental, we shall be able to formulate a theory acceptable to most scholars. Until then it is advisable to explain briefly the chief theories of hypnosis.

1. ANIMAL MAGNETISM. The earliest theory to receive serious attention was the one used to explain mesmerism. Hypnosis was considered to be due to a magnetic force called animal magnetism. This force emanated from the body of the hypnotizer and affected the subject. It is this theory that has been responsible for the popular belief that hypnosis is due to the influence of one mind over another.

While animal magnetism was thoroughly discredited even in Mesmer's time, it still has some modern exponents. Some of them believe that an imperceptible force or magnetic influence is given off by the human body. There is no objective evidence, however, to show that a human magnetic force is the cause of hypnosis.

2. SLEEP. One of the older theories that has slowly been losing ground is the belief that hypnosis is a form of sleep. This theory was originally based on the apparent resemblance between sleep and hypnosis, but it is explained on the grounds that monotonous stimulation of a sense affects the sleep centers of the brain. Gazing at an object, therefore, is one of the best ways of producing hypnosis because this center in the brain is very close to the sleep center.

Hypnosis and sleep may both be altered states of consciousness and outwardly resemble each other, but their exact relationship has never been established. In fact, hypnosis can be induced without any reference to sleep and without producing any characteristic of the latter. Most of our laboratory results indicate that they are quite distinct. The pulse, respiration, and motor responses are the same during hypnosis and the waking state. Moreover, the knee jerk disappears in sleep but not in hypnosis. On the other hand, the galvanic reflex seems to disappear in hypnosis. Hence the evidence is inconclusive, but stronger on the side that sleep and hypnosis are separate phenomena.

3. SUGGESTION. This theory was first elaborated by Braid. It was an important milestone in the history of hypnosis because it stressed the psychological nature of hypnosis. There is no doubt that suggestion is an ingredient in the hypnotic procedure, but there is some confusion between the belief that hypnosis is caused by suggestion, and that it is a form of suggestibility.

Early in this century it was pointed out that there are two types of suggestion, a direct and an indirect form. The direct type of suggestion is positive and instigates action. The negative or indirect suggestion inhibits action by drugging consciousness or cloaking the communication so that its true nature is not understood. Hypnosis may be the result of either type of suggestion, but more likely the latter. Sometimes by suggestion in hypnosis is meant the response that is made without logical grounds or critical evaluation.

Bernheim, one of the leading champions of this theory, stated that there was no hypnosis, only suggestion. Coue went a step further and stated that there was no suggestion, only autosuggestion. This indicates that hypnosis is really autohypnosis, and that the subject is not an automaton, but an individual who produced the phenomena and acts in the light of his own personality.

Suggestion unquestionably plays a part in hypnosis. Most experimenters agree that hypnosis consists of hypersuggestibility, although there are some reasons to believe that suggestibility may actually decrease in deep hypnosis. Perhaps all that we can say is that suggestibility changes while we are hypnotized. To state suggestion is exaggerated in hypnosis is merely a description and not an explanation.

4. NEUROSIS. Charcot formulated the theory that hypnosis was an artificially induced neurosis and that it could be produced only with hysterical patients. It was a form of hysteria and not

a normal expression of the personality. Charcot arrived at this decision because he had worked with only a limited number of persons, all of whom were mentally ill. Nevertheless this theory is still in vogue.

5. DISSOCIATION. This is really a variation of the same theory. It was first advanced by Janet who believed that hypnosis was a state of artificial hysteria. He thought that parts of the human mind could split off from the main stream of consciousness and work independently. The split or dissociated system might lie dormant or take over and control the individual. Hysterical blindness which causes the patient to think that he cannot see is an example of the former type, and somnambulism in which the sleeping personality controls the individual is an example of the latter. In hypnosis, the part of the personality appealed to by the hypnotist functions separately from the whole personality and may actually dominate it.

This theory is one of the more popular at present, but it fails to explain how hypnosis produced the splitting or dissociation.

6. PSYCHOANALYTIC THEORIES. The Psychoanalysts have given us several related theories of hypnosis. These theories try to explain why the individual wishes to be hypnotized.

Regression. Some of the psychoanalysts believe that hypnosis is a form of regression, that is, the subject reverts back to a childhood state. The regression is partial, since only some parts of the personality regress to childhood.

Oedipus Type. Related to regression is the theory of the Oedipus complex sometimes called "father and mother hypnosis." The former is based on fear and the latter on love. The early childhood wishes of an individual cause him to become hypnotized and thus gain gratification by expressing his Oedipus complex. Thus the individual regresses back to childhood which allows him to express his repressed love for one parent and his fear of the other.

Love. Freud compares hypnosis to being in love. In hypnosis he found the same compliance, subjection, and absence of critical faculty found in lovers. The hypnotizer takes the role of the beloved one and the rapport between the hypnotizer and the hypnotized is an erotic tie. Hence hypnosis is an artificial form of love without any sexual satisfaction included.

Seduction. Some psychoanalysts stress the erotic nature of hypnosis. They believe that they see in the hypnotized woman, for instance, a glance of surrender and trembling which is characteristic of sexual excitement. Unfortunately, only trained psychoanalysts have been able to detect these signs of love and eroticism in hypnotized subjects. Some psychoanalysts have put so much stress on this erotic nature that they have taken hypnosis to be a form of seduction.

7. GOAL-DIRECTION. White has formulated the theory that hypnosis is goal-directed, by which he means that the hypnotized person wants to behave as he understands a hypnotized person should. Most people who have been hypnotized are familiar with the phenomenon and know what is expected of them. In order to behave as he understands he should, the subject may have to exert himself, become helpless, insensitive to stimuli, hallucinated, and forget material he knows. The fact that a hypnotized individual is not an automaton and often does not behave as expected, suggests that his own intentions are an active ingredient in the phenomenon.

Often the subject is asked to alter his personality temporarily, or to expose himself to danger. He may do this in the belief that no harm will come to him since the experiment is controlled by the operator. Helplessness may be expressed because the subject is asked to observe or respond to contradictory sets of impulses. It may be that occasionally they do lose control of themselves or become hysterical and dissociated, thus inducing a mild state of temporary neurosis. The fact that hypnotized subjects improve with experience also indicates that they may be learning to do what is expected of them.

This theory leads to the contention sometimes held that there is no real hypnosis and that it is all a game which the subject agrees to play. Perhaps the subject is sometimes carried away with the game and quite forgets himself as he might in a football game or when swayed by a mob at a lynching, or like one engrossed in a play, so that he is conscious yet oblivious to everything but the drama.

Thus the theories of hypnosis have run the gamut from a magical force that is overpowering to a game that one plays in keeping with one's understanding of the rules or activities of the game. Unfortunately they are all controversial theories, and much experimenting must be done before an adequate one will be developed.

WHO CAN BE HYPNOTIZED?

All normal people are susceptible to hypnosis; perhaps less than 5 percent of the population is incapable of it. Failure to achieve hypnosis may be due to lack of persistence. Operators often try only a few times. There are cases of success after twenty failures. In one instance a man was hypnotized after 700 consecutive failures.

Nationality is not a factor, since all races respond about the same. Sex and social position do not matter. Children appear more prone than adults, and intelligent people are a little better than the dull, who have less imagination. College students have proved to be good subjects, while the feeble-minded and the insane are very difficult to hypnotize.

Belief or faith in hypnosis does not seem to make any difference, for many who claim interest fail to be hypnotized, while frequently skeptics and scoffers are successfully hypnotized. Susceptibility also changes with the environment and mood.

Quiet and proper atmosphere are usually stressed, but theatrical performers appear to be successful under quite different circumstances.

Personality traits are being analyzed in an attempt to determine which characteristics, such as introversion and extroversion, lend themselves to susceptibility. Thus far very little success has been met with. Recently the Rorschach and the Thematic Apperception tests have been employed to determine susceptibility. The latter appears to be a little better than the former, but the evidence at present is still very scant.

In determining susceptibility there are several tests that can be made. They usually consist of determining the subject's ability to relax and follow suggestions. These are some of the more common ones:

The subject is asked to fold his hands as tightly as he can and then is told that he cannot open them. If he fails to open them, or does so with difficulty, he is considered quite suggestible.

He may be seated in a comfortable chair and asked to relax his arms and legs by raising and dropping them. Those who cannot relax are taken to be poor subjects.

The operator may stand behind the subject and ask him to stiffen his body and fall backward into the operator's arms. If he falls willingly without fear he is a good subject.

It might be pointed out that methods like the above are more than tests of susceptibility: they may actually be mild forms of hypnosis.

Many people have apparently succeeded in hypnotizing animals, such as rabbits, frogs, guinea pigs, chickens, birds, etc. Their claim is based upon the animal's display of catalepsy or rigidity of body and apparent lack of will. This reaction very likely is not hypnosis but a simulation of death adopted by some animals from their instinctive knowledge that animals of prey usually do not attack what is dead. The catalepsy is shammed by birds even as it is by beetles when they are turned over on their backs. In some cases there may be a temporary paralysis from fright or stroking. The immobility, however, is not itself a sufficient basis for calling the state one of hypnosis.

The method of "hypnotizing" animals is simple. The animal is held firmly in some position and stroked in a monotonous way for several minutes. After the restraint has gradually been removed, the animal remains motionless for some time. Chickens can be made to display catalepsy by holding their beaks to the ground or by stroking them gently.

METHODS OF INDUCING HYPNOSIS

There are many different ways of hypnotizing. Some of them are closely related, but others are so different in nature that it has not been possible to state what is common to all of them. This implies that the true nature of hypnosis has not yet been thoroughly understood.

The best ones are fully explained here so that the reader can understand the techniques. Competent hypnotists are acquainted with all of them.

1. PASSES. Hypnosis can be induced by passes. This is an old method and has been practically abandoned for more modern techniques. It is now used chiefly for theatrical purposes of attracting attention and to impress the audience. The use of passes takes longer to produce hypnosis and must be accompanied by an explanation of its purpose or it is apt to be futile. The fact that people could be hypnotized whether their eyes were open or closed, in a light or dark room, as well as the fact that blind people could be hypnotized, showed the operators that the use of passes was not essential.

There are detailed accounts of how to use passes, but these are not described here for obvious reasons. The various movements of the hands called passes can be made at a short distance, or the hands can be used to touch the body. Contact or touching the body enhances the value of passes.

2. CONTACT. This consists of placing the hands on the body and the use of pressure. Mesmer, who used both passes and contact, began bringing his hands down the length of the arms and to the very tips of the fingers. After holding the fingers or thumbs firmly, he repeated the process. Sometimes one hand was over the heart while the other was used to stroke the forehead. The method of contact is reminiscent of the method used to hypnotize animals (catalepsy).

3. SENSE STIMULATION. Hypnosis is often produced by stimulating or overstimulating any of the senses. The most common method is to fatigue the sense of sight by having the subject stare at a bright object held above the line of vision. The patient is asked to stare at the object and to try to keep all thoughts out of his mind. Eventually the eyes close from fatigue and the subject is told that he has fallen into a light form of hypnosis.

The object may be anything bright, such as a lancet-case, a small mirror, a coin, spoon, etc. Occasionally a revolving mirror or an illuminated object is used. An illuminated metronome is particularly good because it combines the use of both the sense of sight and the sense of sound. The most common auditory stimulus, however, is the sound of a ticking watch or clock. The sense of smell is less often used. Soft music and monotonous poetry are also effective.

Sense fatigue is usually accompanied by suggestive speech. The gazing or fixation method of sense-fatigue is being abandoned because of the eye strain that may follow, pains, and in some cases a mild eye inflammation called conjunctivitis.

4. SLEEP. The most common method of producing hypnosis is the suggestion of sleep. The subject is made comfortable on

a cot or chair and asked to relax. He is told that he is gradually falling asleep. Monotonous repetition of this suggestion usually produces hypnosis. Suggestion of sleep is usually preceded by relaxation. The patient is asked to think of sleep and rest. He is told that soon he will become weary and sleepy, that his eyes will get tired, and that he will fall into a gentle sleep.

Sleep hypnosis may be used by itself, in the form of suggestion or command, or accompanied by sense fixation or any of the other methods. Below is an account of sleep hypnosis based on relaxation quoted from Dr. Kraines:

"I want you to relax. Relax every part of the body. Now when I pick up your hand I want it to fall as a piece of wood without any help from you. (The examiner then picks up the hand and lets it drop to the couch.) No, you helped raise the hand that time; just let it be so relaxed that you have no power over it. (The test is repeated as often as is necessary for the patient to learn to let it drop.) That's the way. Now relax your legs the same way; just let them be limp. Now take a deep breath and let it out slowly. Now concentrate on your toes. A warm sensation starts in the toe and sweeps up your legs, abdomen, chest, into your neck. Now relax your jaws. Relax them more, still more. Now your cheeks; now your eyes. Your eyes are getting heavier and heavier. You can hardly keep them open. Soon they will close. Now smooth out the wrinkles in your forehead. Good. Now make your mind a blank. Allow no thoughts to enter. Just blank. You see a blackness spreading before you. Now sleep. Sleep. Sleep. Sleep. Your entire body and mind are relaxed,—sleep, sleep. (This phrase is repeated several times in a soft and persuasive voice.) Your sleep is becoming deeper, still deeper. You are in a deep, deep sleep."

Here is another example taken from Dr. Tucker. After explaining the process, the value of relaxation, and the outcome of the experience, he says in a firm, deep voice:

"All right, take this seat. Lean your head back against the

chair. Close your eyes lightly and breathe through your mouth, and think of going to sleep. Soon all will become quiet, you will get drowsy and sleepy. I will talk to you to help you concentrate.

"You are getting sleepy, sleepy, sleepy, so-o-o sleepy.

"Now you feel quiet all over. Your muscles are relaxed. Everything is dark to you. You do not hear anything but my voice. You are drowsy and sleepy. You are going to sleep. Sleep! Sleep! Sleep!

"By the time I count ten you will be fast asleep. One, two, three, four, five, six, seven, eight, nine, ten. Now you are fast asleep, fast asleep.

"By the time I count five you will be sound asleep, sound asleep. Just as sound asleep as when you lie in bed at night. One, two, three, four, five, and you are sound asleep, sound asleep. You will not awake until I tell you to.

"Every second you are going into a deeper and deeper sleep, a deeper and deeper sleep. You will not awaken until I tell you to.

"Now you cannot feel anything or hear anything except what I tell you. Sleep on until I tell you to awake.

"When I count three this arm will be stiff—so stiff you can't raise it. One, two, three; now your arm is stiff and you can't move it. (Subject tried and couldn't move it more than an inch.)

"When I count to three you will be able to move it again. One, two, three, now you can move it. Try it."

In the older literature we find that the induction of hypnosis through sleep was commanded rather than suggested. This is a description from Bernheim:

"I say, 'Look at me and think of nothing but sleep. Your eyelids begin to feel heavy, your eyes tired. They begin to wink, they are getting moist, you cannot see distinctly. They are closed.' Some patients close their eyes and are asleep immediately. With others, I have to repeat, lay more stress on what I say, and even make gestures. It makes little difference what sort of gesture is made. I hold two fingers of my right hand before the patient's eyes and ask him to look at them, or pass both hands several times before his eyes, or persuade him to fix his eyes upon mine, endeavoring at the same time to concentrate his attention upon the idea of sleep. I say, 'your lids are closing, you cannot open them again. Your arms feel heavy, so do your legs. You cannot feel anything. Your hands are motionless. You see nothing, you are going to sleep.' And I add in a commanding tone, 'Sleep.' This word often turns the balance. The eyes close and the patient sleeps or is at least influenced.

"I use the word sleep in order to obtain as far as possible over the patient a suggestive influence which shall bring about sleep or a state closely approaching it; for sleep properly so called does not always occur. If the patients have no inclination to sleep and show no drowsiness, I take care to say that sleep is not essential; that the hypnotic influence, whence comes the benefit, may exist without sleep; that many patients are hypnotized although they do not sleep.

"If the patient does not shut his eyes or keep them shut, I do not require them to be fixed on mine, or on my fingers, for any length of time, for it sometimes happens that they remain wide open indefinitely, and instead of the idea of sleep being conceived, only a rigid fixation of the eyes results. In this case, closure of the eyes by the operator succeeds better. After keeping them fixed one or two minutes, I push the eyelids down, or stretch them slowly over the eyes, gradually closing them more and more and so imitating the process of natural sleep. Finally I keep them closed, repeating the suggestion, 'Your lids are stuck together; you cannot open them. The need of sleep becomes greater and greater, you can no longer resist.' I lower my voice gradually, repeating the command, 'Sleep,' and it is very seldom that more than three minutes pass before sleep or some degree of hypnotic influence is obtained. . . .

". . . . I sometimes succeed by keeping the eyes closed for some time, commanding silence and quiet, talking continuously, and repeating the same formulas, 'You feel a sort of drowsiness, a torpor; your arms and legs are motionless. Your eyelids are warm. Your nervous system is quiet; you have no will. Your eyes remain closed. Sleep is coming, etc.' After keeping up this auditory suggestion for several minutes, I remove my fingers. The eyes remain closed. I raise the patient's arms; they remain uplifted. We have induced cataleptic sleep."

It should be noted that this method is accompanied by the use of other means beside sleep.

Sometimes it is necessary to test the subject to determine whether he is really hypnotized. The subject in that case is told that he cannot unclasp his hands, or open his eyelids. The operator says something to this effect:

"Your eyelids are as heavy as lead. In fact, they are locked together so that you cannot open them. They are locked tight, tight, tight. Your eyelids are locked so tightly together that you cannot open them. Just try and you will see that you cannot open them.

"Your hands are clasped together very tightly. Clasp them tighter, tighter, tighter. They are locked so tightly that you cannot open them no matter how hard you try. You cannot open them. Just try."

If he tries and cannot, he is apparently in some stage of hypnosis.

The quiet, semi-dark atmosphere and relaxing chair are often considered necessary. And yet the stage hypnotist uses a different type of surroundings. He hypnotizes people in bright lights, in front of big crowds, and often in uncomfortable chairs where they are not able to relax.

5. TURNING SLEEP INTO HYPNOSIS. While a subject is asleep an operator sits by his side and talks to him in a soft voice. He asks the sleeping subject to listen to him. He is told that he will continue to sleep, but that he will listen to what is being

said. He will hear voices just as if he were awake. Gradually
the operator raises his voice to its natural tone and volume.

If the subject responds, he is treated like any other hypnotic
subject. He may be asked to open his eyes, walk around the
room, and answer questions. About four-fifths of the people
wake up rather than become hypnotized when approached in this
manner; the other fifth fall into a natural state of hypnosis.

6. WAKING HYPNOSIS. This method of hypnosis avoids all
reference to sleep. Apparently there is no relation between sleep
and hypnosis, since the latter can be induced without the use of
the former. Braid, who coined the word hypnosis, at first thought
it was a form of sleep, but later saw his error and tried to divorce
the two concepts by suggesting the term monoideism. Waking
hypnosis has been known for a long time, but it was first fully
explained by Professor Wells of Syracuse University. He has
found it easier to learn and to take less time to give than the
sleeping method. Moreover it is successful with a greater percentage of people, and can be used for group hypnosis.

The method of waking hypnosis consists of relaxation, and
the concentration of fixation of attention until "dissociation" is
achieved. After a few experiments in the susceptibility of the
patient, he is asked to focus his attention on an object such as a
pencil, a light, fountain pen, etc. The operator then says something like the following: "You must exclude all other thoughts
and keep your gaze riveted on this point, eyeballs turned up as
though you were looking at the middle of your forehead. Watch
it steadily, fixedly, thinking of nothing else. Note every detail
so that if I ask you to close your eyes you will be able to picture
it as though you were still looking at it. You will be able to do
this only if you give it your complete attention and literally feel
that you are memorizing it. Watch it closely, try not to blink.
Don't let your gaze shift to right or left. . . , etc." When his
attention has been fixed for several minutes, he is told: "Now

close your eyes voluntarily as tight as you possibly can. Tight until they tremble. Tight until they tremble. It's all right if you have to make a face in order to do so. Just as tight as you can, eyeballs turned up, remember, just as if you were still looking at my fountain pen. Now I'm going to count to 7 and when I reach 7 you will find that your eyes are stuck tight and that the harder you try to open them, the tighter they stick. Your very effort to open them will have just the opposite effect. They will be stuck tight, just as if they were glued. One . . . two . . . tighter . . . three . . . four . . . five . . . . . . tighter . . . six . . . seven. Now try to open them and you will find that the harder you try, the tighter they stick." If the patient is convinced after trying that he has no ability to open his eyes, he is ready to be put into a deeper form of hypnosis.

In waking hypnosis the patient is brought out of the trance by a pre-established signal, just as in sleeping hypnosis.

7. DRUG HYPNOSIS. This refers to the use of drugs rather than to a physical or psychological means of producing hypnosis. It is used by physicians to save time, and when other methods have failed. Once the drug has been used, subsequent hypnosis can be induced by verbal means. Disadvantages are the dependency upon a drug and the harm of the drug to the human system.

Drugs have been used to produce hypnosis for some fifty years. Their early value was seen in mute or depressed cases that would not cooperate. Toward the close of the 19th century the drugs used were mainly Cannabis Indica and Chloroform. These drugs were quick acting and hypnosis had to be achieved before the patient fell into a deep slumber. Modern drugs used for narcotic hypnosis are chiefly sodium amytal and sodium pentothal.

The drug method has been used more often than the verbal or psychological method in World War II by the armed forces. Some of the leading experimenters claim that there is no relation between the trance produced by drugs and hypnosis, while others feel that normal sleep, hypnosis, and narcotic hypnosis are all forms of the same thing.

After the injection of the drug, the patient is asked to count backward from twenty. He usually loses the power to concentrate before he gets to one. Some physicians merely keep up a conversation with the patient until he is no longer able to do so.

Hypnotherapy by the use of drugs is of two types, called Narcoanalysis and Hypnosynthesis. Narcoanalysis is diagnostic. The patient is asked to remember forgotten material that is causing him trouble. This repressed material is gotten from the patient while he is partly asleep. Patients relive their terrifying experiences; this tends to relieve them and gives the doctor some insight into the cause of their neurosis.

In hypnosynthesis the patient is not asked to utter buried information. The nature of the method is therapeutic, and suggestion is used by the therapist without trying to discover the cause.

8. AUTOHYPNOSIS. Autohypnosis is hypnosis produced by the self. This is the method used by Coue, although he did not employ the word hypnosis in his work. One can produce autohypnosis by staring at objects or talking to himself, but for the most part only the light stages of hypnosis can be achieved. One can produce numbness of limbs, hallucinations, and post-hypnotic suggestions.

METHOD OF TERMINATING HYPNOSIS

There are a number of different ways of arousing a subject from a hypnotic state. Since some subjects respond faster to one method than to another, it is well to be acquainted with all of them.

1. PHYSICAL METHOD. Use of physical means. Hypnosis is often terminated by the use of physical force or stimulation. These are some of the most common means:

a. Blowing on the subject's eyes or forehead.

b. Rubbing the eyelids and eyebrows.

c. Giving the face a sharp slap, often accompanied by the command to wake up.

d. By a loud noise or the causing of a sharp pain.

e. Sprinkling cold water on the face, or exposing the face to cold air. Some people who are not responsive to loud noises or physical injury are sensitive to cold water or air.

f. Forcible opening of the eyes.

2. PSYCHOLOGICAL METHODS. Use of verbal suggestion. This is by far the best and most common form used. The method consists of telling the individual to wake up, usually accompanied by some preparation. During the hypnotic state the operator tells the patient that he is to wake up at a given signal. The choice of signal is incidental. One may be told to awaken at the count of three or five or seven. This is repeated several times. Then the operator begins to count in a clear, loud voice. He may even accompany this counting by clapping his hands. When the numbers have been counted, the subject is asked to wake up. This usually works, though it is sometimes necessary to repeat the whole performance several times. Some operators accompany the counting by suggestive comments, such as *one*, you will soon awaken, *two*, you are beginning to awake, *three*, you are waking, *four*, you are almost awake, *five*, you *are* awake.

3. NATURAL METHOD. Allowing the subject to sleep off the spell. If the operator leaves the subject, the latter is apt to awaken in a short time. This is true of all three stages of hypnosis, the mild, the dream, and the somnambulistic. In the profound stages of hypnosis, and in hypnotic coma, the subject falls into a normal sleep and awakens after the usual length of a night's sleep.

STATES OR DEGREES OF HYPNOSIS

There are various degrees or states of hypnosis. Authorities do not agree on the number, and from three to nine different degrees are claimed. The following four states appear most acceptable.

1. MILD HYPNOSIS. This is the first stage the subject enters when he submits to hypnosis. The individual is awake and aware of what is going on. He knows that he is the willing subject of an experiment, knows who is in the room with him and what is going on. He realizes that he is cooperating and responding.

In this mild form of hypnosis, which is easily induced, the subject obeys verbal commands and finds that he is unable to perform certain actions which he is told he cannot do, such as open his clasped hands, raise a limb, or open his eyes, if they are closed. The fact that he cannot do these things, or, in other words, that he obeys and believes in the suggestions, is proof that he is in a state of hypnosis.

This state is readily terminated. Even a distracting noise may bring the experience to a sudden end. In this state the subject is amenable to some suggestion, and, since he has not lost contact with reality, has no amnesia for the experience, in fact, vividly recalls the incident, although he may be at a loss to explain why he was unable to perform certain movements.

2. DREAM HYPNOSIS. This is a state that follows the mild hypnosis in which the individual feels that he is daydreaming. He is still in contact with reality, but acts as if he were indulging in dreams at the suggestion of the operator. He usually recalls his experiences and knows that they were dreams rather than actual facts in space and time. These dreams have all the color, limitations, and reality of dreams in sleep. Disagreeable suggestions may cause him to terminate the spell and awake.

3. SOMNAMBULISM. This is a profound state of hypnosis.

The individual apparently has lost all contact with his surroundings, and can be hallucinated in any sense, such as visual, auditory, olfactory, etc. He is not critical of his experiences, and believes that they are real. He may display anasthesia, paralysis, analgesia, and the rigidity of limbs called catalepsy.

The somnambulistic person is unusually amenable to therapeutic suggestion, and to post-hypnotic suggestions to be later executed. When the hypnosis is over he is not apt to recall any of his experiences. This amnesia is usually made complete by telling him that he will not recall anything when he has awakened. The ending of this state is more difficult and requires more time than the mild or dream hypnosis. It is a state of hypnosis that should be induced only by competent hands.

Each of these three states, the mild, the intermediate or dream hypnosis, and the profound somnambulistic form, are successive states.

4. HYPNOTIC COMA. There is a fourth form of hypnosis in which the subject falls into a profound sleep and is not responsive to suggestion. In this type the individual usually cannot be awakened by suggestion or forceful means, and will fall into a heap if placed upright. He should be allowed to sleep out this coma, which may be equal to an ordinary night's sleep.

This form is not a part of the successive stages of hypnosis, and since the individual does not respond to suggestion, it has no practical therapeutic value. It is best not to hypnotize these individuals again, although the suggestion that they will awake when commanded at a given signal has in some cases proved practical.

There is a continuous scale that can be used to determine the depth of hypnosis as well as one's susceptibility. The value of the different stages of hypnosis has been questioned because the stages are arbitrary, without any fixed bounds, and the charactersitics of one stage have sometimes been produced in another.

WHAT CAN BE OBSERVED IN HYPNOSIS

There are many physical and mental conditions that can be observed about a hypnotized subject.

One of the first muscular changes observed is a gradual closing of the eyes. The eyelids are not always completely closed and may remain motionless or quiver. Sometimes the eyeballs roll upward or inward. The eyes may be opened during the trance upon the suggestion of the operator.

Catalepsy or rigidity of the limbs is often produced. Stiffening of the arms, legs, and torso is common. The arm, for instance, may be kept in one position for a long time.

Limbs may be temporarily paralyzed by suggestion. Modern experiments have cast some doubt on the genuineness of the paralysis, even though the subject acts as if the paralysis were against his will.

Skin changes such as redness and blistering have been observed. Faces appear to flush from supposed warmth described by the operator and teeth chatter from the supposed cold.

Tears have been made to appear in the eyes and flow during hypnosis. It has been reported that success was achieved in having one eye fill with tears while the other remained dry.

Hallucination of the senses is often reported, but some of the recent experiments have thrown considerable doubt on this point. To the casual observer, at least, hallucinations and illusions and delusion or false belief do appear.

Anesthesia or loss of sensation and analgesia or loss of sense of pain are also common. Since pain is subjective and only an interpretation of sense stimuli, indifference to painful stimuli has been taken at its face value.

Amnesia or loss of memory is a common feature of hypnosis when it is suggested by the operator, otherwise the subject usually has memory for his experiences.

Post-hypnotic suggestions are usually carried out, but there are many instances on record of individuals who failed to do so, or responded inaccurately.

Greater ability to see, recall, and perform are mostly exaggerated and have not withstood close laboratory scrutiny.

DANGERS OF HYPNOSIS

Many objections have been raised to the use of hypnosis. The clergy, medical men, and the laity have objected for different reasons: the clergy because it seemed to impair man's freedom of the will, doctors because it appeared to infringe on their profession, and the laity because it did not understand the nature of hypnosis. Many people have considered it a mysterious, supernatural agency harmful to man.

The objections to hypnosis can be listed under three heads: moral harms, psychological harms, and physical harms.

Moral Harms. Some people fear that hypnosis injures or weakens the will. In hypnosis the subject does not surrender his will, but actually uses it in cooperation with the psychotherapist. The objection in itself is merely theological or metaphysical. It is the moral implication that arouses the opponents of hypnosis.

By surrendering one's will in hypnosis, it is believed that one's morals can be endangered. Thus virtuous women might become the victims of lechers, or moral people be persuaded to do immoral acts, such as committing murder or theft. The fear is unfounded, though often used in fiction.

The hypnotized individual is still the same person and will not do anything that he would not do under ordinary conditions. Hence a modest girl will not strip off her clothes, even though she is told that she is a dancer and should do so, unless she would be inclined to do so without hypnosis. Rather she will demur, resist, refuse, and very likely end the hypnotic state. But a girl who has done as much at a party after having a few highballs is likely to comply. Hypnosis merely removes inhibitions, just as alcohol does. A substantial citizen will likewise not commit theft or murder, although he will indulge in mock crimes. Criminal suggestions are adopted only by criminal minds.

PSYCHOLOGICAL HARM. The psychological evils of hypnosis are not as often urged. Hypnosis does not weaken the mind any more than it weakens the will. It is usually induced with the consent or knowledge of the subject, and cannot be a violation of either his mind or his will. The argument that hypnosis is a detrimental interference with the mental processes as evidenced by the production of hallucination and delusions is also pointless. The delusions and hallucinations are temporary, if genuine, and do no more damage than our distorted dreams, which are subject to all the limitations of hypnotic experiences.

Some psychiatrists have mentioned the danger of hypnotizing psychotic patients and the possibility of crystallizing the delusions of pre-psychotic people. The only caution that should be taken with normal individuals is to insure that hypnotic elements that are harmful are not carried over into the waking state. These are always removed before the subject is brought out of the hypnotic trance.

PHYSICAL HARMS. There are no physical harms intrinsic to hypnosis. One might suffer physical injury if abused while in the hypnotic state, either by physical means or suggestion. This is more a criticism of the personnel who use it, than of hypnosis. Medicine, too, may be injurious if ill used. Even the suspicion that some doctors have prescribed it for their own gain does not invalidate its universal use. The evidence that people have suffered physical harm from hypnosis is very meager, and the result of ill-advised treatment at the hands of incompetent people.

We may conclude, then, that there are no real known dangers in hypnosis. The few mishaps are neither numerous nor serious. The actual cases cited usually are discovered to be innocuous or false when investigated.

VALUE OF HYPNOSIS

1. ACADEMIC. Hypnosis is often used for experimental purposes and class demonstrations in college courses in abnormal psychology. Many of the abnormalities such as amnesia, hallucination, hyperesthesia, and anesthesia can be demonstrated in class under laboratory conditions. It is also used with profit in courses in general psychology. Hypnosis arouses the student's interest in psychology and reveals the psychological value of suggestion and subconscious motivation.

2. SCIENTIFIC. It can also be used for experimental purposes in investigating both conscious and unconscious activities. It may help us not only in learning more about the function of the human mind and personality, but may also be used for specific purposes such as determining the creative ability of an individual. A Harvard-trained psychologist has given numerous students brief plots and asked them to tell a story. This brought out their creative powers as well as revealing the hidden motives in their lives.

3. THERAPEUTIC. The therapeutic value of hypnosis has long been recognized. Its value in this field is of three types:

Hypnosis has been used occasionally as an anesthesia despite the discoveries of drugs. Under its influence teeth have been extracted, tonsils and adenoids removed, and babies delivered apparently without pain.

Hypnosis has been used for a long time to cure or correct psychological and organic disturbances. Formerly subjects were told under hypnosis to rid themselves of their ailments. But we have learned that to make the cure lasting it is usually necessary to reeducate the patient. It is often easier to do this in the hypnotic state. Hypnotherapy today is of two types: either recovering forgotten material that is harmful to the personality, or treating the symptoms as they appear. The former attempts to reach back into the subject's childhood while the latter deals with the subject's recently disturbing material. Hypnotherapy has been particularly useful in treating psychosomatic problems during World War II. These illnesses are usually lumped into a common group and called war neuroses even as they were called shell-shock in the last war. The method most commonly used is called the abreactive method: the patient is hypnotized by drugs or psychological means and asked to relive his war experiences so that their force might be spent.

Some of the common organic or psychosomatic illnesses successfully treated by hypnosis are: neuralgia, constipation, tics, nervous indigestion, asthma, rheumatism, headaches, warts, seasickness, enuresis, sciatica, skin diseases, vomiting, and anorexia. Some of the more common psychological ones include: stage fright, stuttering and stammering, drug habits, insomnia, excessive smoking, hypochondriasis, phobias, manias, morbid sexuality, and amnesia.

AMERICAN CONTRIBUTIONS TO
THE SCIENCE OF HYPNOSIS*

Frank A. Pattie, *The Rice Institute*

EDITOR'S NOTE

This article serves as a good introduction to the subject of hypnosis. It is authoritative, clearly written, and covers a number of the most important problems that confront the student of hypnosis today. It is perhaps the best general account of the modern aspects of hypnosis in the literature of the subject.

Hypnosis is a curious and baffling phenomenon. To put a person into the hypnotic trance we tell him he is going to sleep, yet the hypnotic state is not a form of sleep. We tell him he will be under our control and he is, but only up to a certain point. He appears extremely obedient and eager to give the operator the results desired; but hypnosis is something more than a particular attitude of obedience assumed by the subject, since some of his abilities in the trance are greater than they are in the normal state when he assumes a similar attitude of obedience. We can produce anesthesias of various organs of sense; in some ways these anesthesias appear genuine, in others feigned. The field of hypnosis thus encloses many unresolved paradoxes.

The most recent assaults on these paradoxes have come from psychological laboratories in the United States. This fact itself is remarkable, for until about eighteen years ago American psychologists had made no significant contribution to our knowledge of hypnosis. It is true, of course, that in their treatises some American psychologists — James, Muensterberg, and Titchener among them — gave space to hypnosis, but they observed it only casually. They did not formulate problems and then set to work to solve them by means of experiment.

To some extent the failure to carry on experiments on hypnosis may have been owing to the too perfect theories devised to explain it. For example, Titchener's theory reduced hypnosis to the level of the commonplace; it was, according to him, merely an exaggeration of certain features of normal everyday mental life — concentration of attention was invoked to explain suggestibility. Inability to remember events occurring in the trance was to Titchener no more mysterious than the fact that a man on the golf links forgets his office. To some extent also this neglect by Titchener and other psychologists following the tradition of Wundt grew out of their rather exclusive interest in "the generalized mind of the normal human adult." Hypnosis was not part of the subject matter they proposed to investigate. But the most important cause of the neglect doubtless lay in the unrespectable and unsavory associations — obtaining since the time of Mesmer — of hypnosis with quackery, occultism, and the performances of itinerant showmen. George du Maurier's sentimental novel *Trilby* in the nineties presented a false and terrifying picture of hypnosis. It is significant that Muensterberg never hypnotized anyone "for mere experiment's sake but always for medical purposes only." Associations of hypnosis with the unrespectable were no doubt influential not only in securing the dominance of the clinical over the purely scientific motive; they may also have had something to do with the formulation of those all-too-perfect theories that disposed of the subject by leaving little or nothing to be investigated.

But, in spite of its early handicaps, hypnosis was too interesting a phenomenon to escape the attention of the experimental psychologist forever. It came at last into the laboratory largely through the influence of the late William McDougall of Harvard and of Clark L. Hull of the University of Minnesota and Yale. Under McDougall's direction Paul C. Young in 1923 performed the first hypnotic experiments leading to an American doctorate in psychology. And Hull stimulated research both among his own students and others by an article published in 1930 that listed no fewer than 102 problems deserving investigation in this field. While it was hardly to be expected that the experimental psychologists would revolutionize a branch of science worked over by medical men for 150 years, they have nevertheless made important advances in our knowledge.

The results of the work of experimental psychologists on hypnosis have been to a considerable extent negative in character — they have shown what hypnosis is not, that it will not do certain things claimed for it. It was natural that this should be the outcome of many of the investigations; from the beginning the subject had been almost exclusively in the hands of physicians whose principal interest in it was confined to its therapeutic value, a condition favorable not to the increase of scientific knowledge but to the accretion of mistaken ideas. Then, too, certain American psychologists have oversimplified matters. Some of these oversimplifications have already been corrected. Despite these negative factors the effects of hypnosis are acknowledged to be remarkable even by the most tough-minded scientist; by its aid illusions and hallucinations can be produced, anesthesias for major surgical operations can be induced, old memories not available in the normal state can be recovered and peculiar alterations of personality can be brought about. Hypnosis remains an attractive field of research, for not only do many facts await discovery but there remains the task, hardly lightened at all by recent experimentation, of formulating a comprehensive theory of hypnosis.

One of the oldest problems, the relationship between the hypnotic trance and sleep, was one of the first to be attacked by a student of Hull. Over a long period of years hypnosis has been associated with sleep. In the usual technique for inducing hypnosis the subject reclines in a comfortable chair while the operator tells him that he feels very tired, that he is thinking of nothing but going to sleep, and that his eyes will close, whereupon he will be asleep. The suggestions continue monotonously and without intermission either until the subject's eyes close or until the operator concludes that the experiment is a failure These associations with sleep quite naturally led James Braid, an English physician, in 1843 to name the phenomena of the trance "neuro-hypnotism" or nervous sleep. But Hull's student, M. J. Bass, proved that the physiological signs of sleep are absent in the trance. The tendon reflexes, diminished or entirely absent in sleep, are of normal strength in hypnosis; a tap on the patellar tendon over the knee-cap elicits a normal kick. Subsequently other American workers demonstrated that the respiration, heart action, and brain potentials in the trance are characteristic of the waking state rather than of sleep. Moreover, the essential phenomena of the hypnotic trance can be produced when all references to sleep or eye-closure are omitted in the suggestions made to the subject.

What are the characteristics of a good hypnotic subject? The difference between the responses of good subjects and subjects who prove refractory is so great that one might expect the two classes of persons to be sharply differentiated in their personalities. But the search for distinguishing marks has failed almost completely. The first theory in this field, important principally because its author was a French neurologist of the highest distinction, Charcot, proved to be wrong. In the 1880's Charcot asserted that susceptibility to the deeper stages of hypnosis is a symptom of a mental disorder, hysteria, and that only neurotic persons of hysterical type could be hypnotized. His contemporary, Bernheim, and other medical men opposed his theory. By means of various measurements of personality traits, American psychologists have confirmed Bernheim's opinion. Charcot's only subjects were a few hysterical women; his error was one of too hasty generalization. It is now established that susceptibility carries with it no stigma of neuroticism. To say this, however, is not to deny that there are certain striking similarities between the phenomena of hypnosis and the amnesias, paralysis, and anesthesias of hysteria.

Though a good hypnotic subject is by no means a neurotic, he is suggestible. What is this trait of suggestibility? Is it merely suggestibility in the hypnotic situation or is it a trait pervading the whole personality and making the good subject in his everyday life show more than average credulity, gullibility, proneness to accept the opinions of others? American investigators have found that there is no relation between these latter traits and the ability of the subject to go into the trance. Nor is susceptibility related to extraversion and introversion or to dominance and submissiveness. Intelligence has in some investigations in this country been found to be unrelated to susceptibility, whereas in others a small positive correlation has been discovered — that is, a very slight tendency for the more suggestible subjects to be somewhat above the average in intelligence. These results are enough, in the words of Hull, "to dissipate the somewhat vague but widespread belief that for a person to be susceptible to hypnosis is an indication of feeble intelligence." Recently R. W. White of Harvard has discovered a small positive correlation between a subject's "need for deference" (that is, deference to a person in a position of authority) and susceptibility and a small negative correlation between susceptibility and the "need for autonomy or independence." In other words, the higher the subject's rating on the "need for deference" the higher his susceptibility, and the higher his "need for autonomy" the lower his susceptibility. The coefficients of correlation are so small, however, that if one were to try to predict the susceptibility of a number of persons by referring only to their ratings on one of these needs, the predictions would be only one-tenth less in error than guesses based on no knowledge of the subjects whatever. Susceptibility to hypnosis is either a relatively isolated trait, not strongly linked with other traits, or else a characteristic resulting from a number of different patterns of traits — patterns not revealed by our present techniques of personality measurement. Perhaps, as White suggests, our next step, if we are to determine how hypnotic susceptibility originates in the individual, will consist of the study of very detailed life-histories. We might thus discover certain types of trait-patterns or organizations giving rise to susceptibility.

Any discussion of hypnosis always raises two questions among laymen. One is this: Is hypnosis real? When a teacher demonstrates hypnosis in his class he usually finds that some students are skeptical; they believe that the subject, knowing what is expected of a hypnotized person, is merely faking, playing a role. But the ordinary student does not know enough to enable him to imitate the behavior of a hypnotized subject in all situations. The operator can be sure that a person who is apparently in a deep trance is not simulating if his behavior conforms to certain generally unknown criteria. If, for example, a subject is genuinely in a deep trance and is given a suggestion to be carried out after he comes out of the trance, he spontaneously goes back into the trance (that is, into a state of heightened suggestibility) during the performance of the suggestion and comes out of it after the suggestion is completed. This spontaneous induction of a state of heightened suggestibility while the subject is carrying out a post-hypnotic suggestion occurs no matter whether the suggestion is carried out ten minutes or ten days after the original trance. Since very few persons used as subjects in experiments know anything about this feature of hypnotic behavior, the operator can be practically certain that if they conform to this pattern they have been genuinely in the trance and not simulating it. Americans did not discover this fact, but the psychologist's understanding of this and related phenomena has been made more precise and detailed in a recent paper by Milton Erickson, a psychiatrist of Eloise, Michigan, who has made studies of hypnosis from both the clinical and experimental points of view.

The other question the layman nearly always asks is this: How far does the subject's suggestibility go? Can the operator pass beyond the innocuous suggestions of the usual experiment and induce the subject to harm himself or others? Older and newer authorities alike say no. The subject will do nothing contrary to his moral standards or harmful to himself. In most instances this statement is correct; the subject is by no means an automaton. In fact, we often see a subject offer successful resistance to certain rather trivial commands which he does not like. Yet there is some evidence, both experimental and clinical, which contradicts the usual answer. In a recent experiment, devised by Loyd Rowland of Baylor University, subjects in the trance were directed to pick up a live rattlesnake, apparently in an open box but actually behind an invisible pane of glass. All but one of his four subjects tried to grasp the snake. Two other subjects were given a bottle of strong acid and told to throw it at the experimenter's face, also behind invisible glass. They threw the acid. Normal subjects in the same situation all refused to carry out the orders. (It seems unlikely that the hypnotized subjects were able to detect the invisible glass.) It might be argued that the hypnotized subjects acted as they did because they knew they were participating in a laboratory experiment and were under the care of a responsible person who would not allow them to injure themselves or him. The normal subjects, it would be assumed, did not feel an equal degree of protection. The experiment would therefore not throw much light on what might be done in a situation outside the laboratory.

Following Rowland's work, Erickson reported an extensive series of experiments in which he tried to induce subjects to commit certain objectionable acts in situations designed to appear as little as possible like laboratory experiments and in which the responsibility for the acts was shared to a minimum degree by the experimenter. The subjects were asked to steal small sums of money, to read their roommates' letters, and to do other things of like character. Erickson was uniformly unsuccessful. In a few cases the subjects reluctantly performed the desired act but nullified its effect either then or later. For the rest they stub-

bornly, and with a good deal of resentment toward the experimenter, refused or evaded the instructions. In some cases subjects
in the trance refused to do certain things (such as the playing
of practical jokes on other persons) which later in the waking
state they did very readily of their own volition.

There is another type of experiment, first reported in 1941,
on the production of crime. The subject is shown a coat and
told that he will "falsely perceive" it as his own and that he will
"falsely remember" having put a dollar in its pocket. He is then
directed to remove the dollar from the coat and to spend it at a
later time. In the original experiment, reported by Wesley R.
Wells of Syracuse University, the coat belonged to the experimenter. It is curious that the act of taking the money in these
circumstances should be regarded as criminal from the point of
view of either the subject or the witnesses to the experiment.
How could it be seen as anything more than the receipt of a
peculiarly indirect gift from the experimenter? The experiment
would be more convincing if the ownership of the coat were
unknown to the subject. Margaret Brenman, a research worker
at the Menninger Clinic, reports three experiments in which,
though ownership was unknown, the subjects took the money.
Yet these experiments were performed in the atmosphere of a
laboratory and the subjects were well aware that the situation
was experimental. Further modifications of the procedure should
be made before we can be sure that in a non-experimental situation, when we use a technique that eliminates moral conflict by
implanting false perceptions and memories, subjects can be made
to perform acts contrary to their moral nature.

In the book *Das Verbrechen in Hypnose* (Crime in Hypnosis),
published in 1937, a study that seems to have escaped the attention of recent writers, Ludwig Mayer, a German physician, gives
us clinical evidence on the same problem. This book describes
the case of a woman, pronounced mentally normal by psychiatrists, who came under the influence of a criminal hypnotist. He

represented himself as a physician and pretended to treat her. Over a period of seven years he controlled the woman and compelled her to steal money for him, to make attempts (that were abortive) to kill herself and to shoot her husband, and to submit to other abuses. Ultimately the man, who seems to have been a psychopathic personality, received a prison sentence of ten years. But a case of this kind is very unusual.

It has been said that repeated induction of hypnosis will make that subject highly suggestible in his daily life, will "weaken his will" and make him unduly dependent upon the hypnotizer. Among American investigators, however, fear of such undesirable consequences seems to have vanished completely.

Although as early as the 1840's James Esdaile, the English surgeon, performed hundreds of operations, major and minor, in India with no other anesthetic than hypnosis, the nature of hypnotically-produced anesthesias is not yet clear. Ten years ago R. R. Sears of Yale University, investigating hypnotic anesthesia of the skin, discovered that when an ordinarily painful stimulus was applied to a leg anesthetized by hypnosis, the usual physiological accompaniments of pain appeared but were diminished in amount in comparison with those elicited when the non-anesthetic leg was stimulated in the same way. Those bodily changes most amenable to voluntary control were most diminished and those least amenable were least affected: the respiratory reactions were practically absent when the anesthetized leg was stimulated, the rise in pulse rate was 77 percent less than normal, and the variability of pulse was 50 percent of normal. Least affected of all was the impalpable sweat secretion that accompanies the onset of a painful stimulus. Sears concluded that these effects could not be caused by a mere pretense of anesthesia on the part of his subjects. He asked his subjects to try to simulate an anesthesia while they were in the normal state but their efforts produced almost no effect. Erickson, who has studied hypnotically-induced deafness, has found that some subjects, selected from a large number, appeared to be genuinely deaf when various tests were applied.

It must be remembered, however, that a subject may be made deaf to the voices of all persons in a room except that of the operator or blind to one card in a deck but not to others. These limited anesthesias, corresponding, in the words of White, to no "plausible biological units," are obviously cases of voluntary ignoring of the particular stimuli chosen by the operator. Experiments of this sort consequently raise the question: Are the cases of apparent total deafness or apparent total skin anesthesia due primarily to the subjects' deliberate will to ignore all sensations of sound or touch; or are these anesthesias due to an actual blocking somewhere in the central nervous system of nerve currents originating in the ear or in the skin? In other words, do they behave, except for the fact that they can be terminated by command, like those caused by severing a sensory nerve?

Experiments by the present writer compel him to return a negative answer to the last question. The fingers of the subject's hands were interlaced in such a way that when one finger was touched the subject could not tell whether the finger belonged to the right or the left hand. When one hand was made anesthetic in the trance and the fingers of the two hands were touched a number of times in quick succession by two experimenters, with the subject asked to count the number of times he was touched on his sound hand, it was found that he could do very little if at all better than a normal subject could when his hands were similarly clasped and similarly touched. The supposed anesthesia availed nothing when the subject had his hands in a position preventing him from knowing whether a given touch fell on the right or on the left hand. Another experiment, in which the writer tried to produce blindness of one eye, gave similar results. With all but one of five subjects, simple tests showed that both eyes, the "blind" and the normal, were being used. This one subject, not obeying instructions and cleverly evading detection, was able to pass certain simple tests seeming to indicate that one eye was blind. She was finally given a card on which there was a confused array of lines in several different colors. If she used both eyes the material would be unintelligible; if she used only the eye behind the red glass she could easily read letters and numerals since the red glass made red, yellow, and orange lines in the printed material invisible. This test trapped her and revealed that she was using both eyes.

These results are negative. They do not, of course, logically exclude the possibility that sometime a person may be found whose anesthesias are genuine in the sense of behaving like those caused by the cutting of nerves. The writer's results, which strongly suggest that anesthesias are primarily caused by an effort to ignore some part of the environment, are not necessarily in conflict with the results of Erickson's experiments on deafness. His subjects (selected from a large number of hypnotizable persons) may be regarded as those who were most successful, in a population of some size, in ignoring their auditory environment. Furthermore, his subjects could be made totally deaf to one kind of sound and at the same time not deaf to others. The writer's experiments indicate that, where it is impossible for the subject to localize a sensation on the right or the left side, an attitude of purposeful ignoring cannot operate successfully, and the anesthesia of the single eye or hand breaks down. If we interpret anesthesias as originating from a desire to ignore, the problem still remains: Why is the hypnotized person's effort so very successful when he tries to produce total deafness or insensitivity to the pain of a dental operation? Perhaps the hypnotic subject's strong belief that the organ in question is actually anesthetic has something to do with the matter.

The relationship between memory and hypnosis is a question of some popular interest. Students often ask their teacher of psychology, "If I were to take an examination in the trance would I be able to remember more than I could in the normal state?"

Until recently the instructor replied, "No, hypnosis will not help you to remember recently learned material. We do have evidence, though, that old memories such as memories of poems learned by heart in childhood are more extensively recalled by the average person in the trance than otherwise. Moreover, in some cases memories of events of early childhood, not available in the normal state, can be brought up in the trance." This reply was based upon an experiment, carried on in Hull's laboratory, in which the recently learned material was made up of nonsense words. The result obtained with nonsense was believed to hold for all kinds of memorized material. White and his associates later proved that this conclusion was incorrect and that the recall of recently acquired meaningful material is as much facilitated by the trance as the recall of very old memories of poems. They found that the average subject can remember one and a half times as many items in the trance as in the normal state.

The problem discussed above — anesthesias, the relationships of hypnosis to sleep, to traits of personality, and to memory, the genuineness and the potential dangers of hypnosis — are but a few of the problems attacked by American psychologists in the last two decades. Parallel with these purely scientific developments there has been during the same period a revival of interest in the clinical use of hypnosis for the treatment of the psychoneuroses, not as a means of exorcising the symptoms but as an instrument for exploring the disordered personality and finding the causes of the trouble. Research on the use of hypnosis in psychotherapy and as a means of substantiating some of the newer psychiatric theories is being carried on by individuals and is also being sponsored by the Menninger Foundation.

The simultaneous study of the experimental and the clinical aspects of hypnosis is much to be desired; a purely scientific investigation without application would be useless, as would the merely clinical use of a poorly understood therapeutic instrument.

*From *The American Scholar*, Autumn 1943.

WILL HYPNOTIZED PERSONS TRY TO HARM THEMSELVES OR OTHERS?*

By LOYD W. ROWLAND, *University of Tulsa*

EDITOR'S NOTE

This is perhaps the most dramatic experiment in the history of modern hypnosis. The object of the experiment was to test the old beliefs that a subject would not expose himself and others to great danger.

Hypnotized subjects did seek to reach for a live rattlesnake, and threw acid at the experimenter's face. Thus it must be inferred that some subjects will harm themselves and others. This should caution us against the careless use of hypnosis by incompetent people. The evidence for the commission of anti-social acts, such as stealing and lying, have been variously reported and leave the issue still in doubt.

The purpose of this experiment is to determine the extent to which deeply hypnotized persons (1) will subject themselves to unreasonably dangerous situations and (2) will perform acts unreasonably dangerous to the welfare of others.

It is an old problem about which people have talked a great deal and experimented little. The consensus of opinion in the literature has been that the hypnotized person will not violate his own good judgment with respect to possible harm to self or others.[1] In the experiment to be outlined it was decided to examine this commonly accepted hypothesis by means of a new technique made possible by the development of invisible glass.

There are two parts to the experiment. In Part I the problem was to see if hypnotized subjects would expose themselves to danger; in Part II it was the problem to see if they would try to harm others.

1. Representative statements are as follows: Young, ". . . it is agreed that the subject will not obey the operator in committing an act which is repugnant to the former's moral scruples." Schilder concludes, "If a profoundly hypnotized person is asked to perform an act that is unreasonable, an act in contradiction with his total will, his total personality, the following may happen: In spite of his profound hypnosis, the hypnotized man may refuse to obey . . . or awake from his hypnosis if the demand of the hypnotizer as well as the total situation are no longer in accord with his other ego ideals." Hollander says, "Even a person in the hypnotic state will refuse to perform any act which is contrary to his or her natural disposition. But both normal and hypnotized people will readily accept any notion for which their own nature has already prepared them." Loewenfeld said in 1922 that to date "there is not a single well-authenticated case of severe crime perpetrated through hypnosis."

PART I

Subjects. Four persons participated in Part I.

Subject A, female, a Junior in the University of Tulsa, preparing to teach in high school.

Subject B, male, co-captain of the University football teams, a Senior.

Subject C, female, graduate student, with about twenty years' experience as grade-school teacher.

Subject D, female, about 24 years of age; made frequent visits to the staff of the Department of Psychology for help in the solution of some of her personal problems.

All subjects had been hypnotized at least twice, and there was evidence of deep hypnosis in all cases. There were contractions of muscle groups, amnesias, and hallucinations in all cases.

The subjects were hypnotized in a room across the hall from the large room in which the experiment proper took place.

Apparatus. A large box, open on the front side, was constructed; in the interior was placed a large sheet of glass, bent in such a way that all reflections were cast upward against a black baffle-board roof and there absorbed. In front of this sheet of glass was placed hardware cloth cut in the center and turned back in such a way that the whole box gave the appearance of being an animal cage. The glass in back of the hardware cloth was totally invisible. The experimenter tested this fact by having several of his colleagues come in and reach for a hammer that was placed some distance back of the glass. Not one of them saw the glass, and one woman professor injured her finger when she struck the glass as she reached for the hammer.

A large diamond-back rattlesnake was placed in the box. The animal was allowed to stay in a warm room in the box three days until it became very lively. To add to the activity of the snake during the experiment, holes were bored in the box in many places and the snake poked by means of a wire to incite him to action. The result was a most frightful scene. The snake invariably wound himself into a coil with his head lifted ready to strike, his rattles singing loudly enough that they could be heard within a radius of 100 feet.

Condition I. (*Subjects A and B.*) The subject was placed in the room with the stimulus box and snake thirty feet from it. The following instructions were given:

"Do you see that box?" When the subject said, "Yes," the experimenter went on to say, "There is a piece of coiled rubber rope in that box. Go up to the box, reach through the screen wire, and pick it up."

Subject A went up to the box slowly, without perceptible change of pace until she got to the box. She seemed surprised at first touching the glass. She hesitated a moment and then began to explore the surface of the glass for an opening. Finding no opening, she spread her hand on the glass and began to push. Even though the glass was of heavy plate, some danger was involved if she pushed too hard, and the experimenter asked her to stop exploring the glass.

Asked one week later, while awake, if she could conjecture

why she had been willing to expose herself to such a great danger, subject A said that she did not know why, but that she supposed she was confident that the experimenter would not allow her to be harmed. Actually, subject A remembered nothing about the incident, and was only giving her judgment as to the cause of her behavior.

Subject B went immediately to the box, saw the snake, turned around facing the experimenter and awoke. The experimenter asked if he were awake and he said that he was. (It is only fair to say that the experimenter was skeptical beforehand of the depth of trance of this particular subject.)

Condition II. (*Subjects C and D.*) The hypnotized subjects were taken into the experimental room in full sign of the cage (or box), but thirty feet from it, and asked these questions; the answer, "Yes," was expected and received in every case:

"Have you ever seen a rattlesnake? Is a rattlesnake dangerous? Do you see that box? There is a rattlesnake in that box. Go up to it and reach through the opening in the screen wire and pick up the snake. Go right ahead."

Subject C went directly to the box, stopped briefly when she came in sight of the coiled snake, but when the experimenter urged her by saying, "Go ahead," she thrust her hand through the wire opening and gave evidence of surprise when she touched the glass. She explored the surface area of the glass but showed no tendency to force an opening through the glass as A had done.

Subject D went directly to the apparatus, reached in and touched the glass. She touched the glass in several places until, finding no opening, she stopped and took two steps from the box and stood, apparently uncertain as to what next to do.

PART II

In this part of the experiment the object was to see whether subjects would perform acts unreasonably dangerous to others. The apparatus was modified by removing the snake, and the hardware cloth from in front of the glass. Further, a section 12x14 inches was cut from the back of the box, and against this opening the head of the author appeared during the part of the experiment about to be described. The author's face was well lighted and he read from a book. It must be remembered that the subjects saw nothing intervening between themselves and the author.

The subjects participating in Part II were as follows:

Subject E, female, 16 years of age, a high school student.

Subject F, male, coach of high school athletics, a graduate student.

The procedure was as follows: The subject, hypnotized, was brought into the presence of the stimulus box. Thereupon the experimenter poured sulphuric acid from a bottle into a glass, and in the presence of the subject, dipped a strip of zinc into the acid. The reaction was strong, with fumes steaming from the mouth of the glass. The subject was then asked, "Do you know what sulphuric acid is?" and regardless of the answer the explanation was given that "sulphuric acid is very dangerous. It will scar the skin and put out the eyes." The subject was then told to pick up the glass and throw the acid at the author's face, the author being protected, of course, by the invisible glass.

Subject E picked up the glass and was very reluctant to throw the acid. She hesitated; the experimenter insisted and finally said, "I'm going to count three and when I finish you will throw the acid. One, two, three." The subject threw the acid, set down the glass, shuddered and covered her face with her hands. She seemed very much disturbed.

Subject F was instructed in the same way as Subject E. He picked up the acid, hesitated a moment, and then threw it with such force that the acid spread all over the surface of the invisible glass.

By way of a control, forty-two persons, of every age and degree of sophistication, were asked to come to the laboratory and pick up the snake, as in Part I of the experiment. With one exception all the persons were not only badly frightened at the appearance of the snake, but would not come close to the box; only a few were persuaded finally to pick up a yard stick and try to touch the snake. They all seemed bewildered when they touched the glass which they could not see. The exception referred to was as follows: A young woman was told to reach for the snake and she did so at once, of course striking the glass. When asked why she complied so readily, she said that of course it was an artificial snake and she was not afraid of it. Assured that the snake was real, she made a closer examination of it. She then became frightened, and, even though she now knew she was protected, would not go near the box.

CONCLUSIONS

Within the limits of this experiment it seems possible to conclude that:

1. Persons in deep hypnosis will allow themselves to be exposed to unreasonably dangerous situations.

2. Persons in deep hypnosis will perform acts unreasonably dangerous to others.

A possible explanation, hinted at in two places in the account, is that confidence in the hypnotist causes the subject to forego his better judgment.

If the above conclusions be true, it follows as a very practical application that only professional psychologists and others adequately prepared should be permitted to make use of deep hypnosis.

The author feels that the common acceptation that hypnotized persons will not perform acts that violate their ideals is badly in need of re-examination.

---

*From *Journal of Abnormal and Social Psychology*, 34, 1939.

EXPERIMENTS IN WAKING HYPNOSIS*

WESLEY RAYMOND WELLS

EDITOR'S NOTE

For a long time hypnosis was believed to be a form of sleep and hypnosis was induced by suggesting sleep. Throughout the twentieth century this position has been attacked.

Dr. Wells' article is the first exposition of the theory of waking hypnosis, even though it was known for a long time. He explains his technique of hypnosis, which does not have any reference to sleep. This suggests that sleep is not essential to hypnosis, and that it is only one of the ways of inducing it.

"Waking Hypnosis," written about 20 years ago, is the first in a series of studies by Dr. Wells. His work has been very provocative in the science of hypnosis, and he has challenged not only the sleep theory of hypnosis, but has also demonstrated the fallacy of the old belief that crime could not be produced by hypnosis.

My first practical experience with hypnosis, especially in the effort to illustrate in a course in abnormal psychology points made by Dr. Prince in *The Unconscious,* was with the usual type of sleeping hypnosis. I soon found it possible and expedient, however, to use a completely waking type to illustrate the same points. Now, after having done experiments on several hundred subjects, in groups or individually, by means of the method of waking hypnosis, I have become further convinced of its merits.

The method of waking hypnosis possesses the following advantages, in my opinion, over the various methods of sleeping hypnosis, at least for class demonstration and instructional purposes, and in some cases for therapeutic purposes. First, it is less mysterious in appearance, and the total impression is more desirable. The psychologist who uses hypnosis partly for the purpose of teaching against occultism desires to avoid the appearance of an occult precedure. Second, it usually takes less time.

With an individual subject or with a group, one usually begins to get results in two or three minutes, if not in five or ten seconds; while sleeping hypnosis, when first used with a subject, usually requires a longer time before results are obtained. Third, it is easier, requiring less effort on the part of the experimenter; and it is easier for the beginner to learn. Fourth, it can be employed on a larger percentage of subjects with success at the start than can the usual methods of sleeping hypnosis. Fifth, if for any reason sleeping hypnosis is desired, one can easily change to the methods of producing the sleeping state with greater chance of success if the first suggestions by the method of waking hypnosis have been successful.

The technique of waking hypnosis which I employ may be described in part by contrasting it with the usual methods of sleeping hypnosis. To hypnotize by the most usual sleeping method one begins by explaining to the subject the psychological conditions of normal sleep. One calls attention to the part played by a lessening of external stimuli, especially light and sound, by the concentration of attention on some one simple situation, as in the classic method of putting oneself to sleep by counting sheep, and by the sleep-producing effect of slight monotonous stimuli. One may speak of the way in which the mother puts her child to sleep, and of the sleepiness that often comes upon a man while in the barber's chair, experiencing the manipulations of the barber. The hypnotizer explains that he is about to employ similar methods to induce in the subject first a drowsy condition and finally a condition of deep sleep, like normal sleep except that the subject will always be conscious of what the operator is saying. Then, in terms of the usual immobility of the body during sleep, contractures may be explained. In terms of normal dreams, illusions and hallucinations occurring in the hypnotic sleep are made clear. Amnesia that may follow the hypnotic sleep is compared to the amnesia for one's dreams that ususally follows waking from natural sleep. Somnambulism in the hypnotic sleep is compared with the somnambulism that sometimes occurs in natural sleep. Then the hypnotizer proceeds to suggest drowsiness in various ways. He may have the subject gaze fixedly upon a bright object and at the same time suggest that a feeling of drowsiness will begin to appear. If the eyes soon close so that the subject cannot open them, the operator says this is because of the sleep that is overcoming the subject. Passes may be used, accompanied by suggestions of sleep; and so on, according to old and familiar methods. The subject manifests increasingly the external signs of drowsiness, and actually begins to feel drowsy and sleepy; and finally he may fall into the somnambulistic state, though more frequently stopping short of this.

Now, in all this there have been the following features: first, a preliminary explanation in terms of sleep; second, a continued suggestion of sleep by direct and indirect means; third, an experiencing by the subject of the familiar symptoms of drowsiness and sleep; and fourth, some of the external bodily signs of drowsiness and sleep. Those who, like Muensterberg, Sidis, Coriat, and Prince, as referred to above, explain hypnosis primarily in terms of concentration of the attention and of dissociation, without reference to sleep, would not give a preliminary explanation to the subject such as I have described; but the other three points which I have mentioned would apply in most cases to their practice of hypnotism. In what I call waking hypnosis, however, all four of these features are absent: sleep is not mentioned in the preliminary explanation to the subject; sleep is not suggested, directly or indirectly; the subject experiences neither drowsiness nor sleepiness, if we may trust his introspective account; and there are present none of the objective indications of drowsiness or sleep.

Though Bernheim has recognized and asserted, as has been noted above, that *all* the hypnotic phenomena, including amnesia, can be produced in the waking state, I have not found in the literature any description by him, or by anyone else, of experiments in waking hypnosis involving amnesia and post-hypnotic automatic writing of the forgotten experience, or involving subconscious solution of problems given during the state of waking hypnosis, with amnesia for the problems produced immediately, and the answer given by automatic writing. Such experiments are exceedingly simple; and it is because of their simplicity and ease of performance, and at the same time because of their value for instructional purposes, that I venture to speak of them and to ask if they do not deserve to become a part of the standardized technique of instruction in the fundamentals of abnormal psychology, just as the mirror-drawing experiment, for example, has become universally included among the instruments of instruction in educational psychology.

Waking hypnosis may be used either in group or in individual experiments. The group experiment has two main purposes (aside from its therapeutic uses): first, to teach large numbers easily and quickly, through their own experiences as subjects or through observation of a considerable number of other subjects, the meaning of hypnosis; and second, to select the better subjects for individual experiments. After a preliminary explanation to a group of students regarding the chief principles of dissociation and of suggestion, direct suggestions to the group that their eyes, when closed cannot be opened, or that their hands, if clasped together tightly, cannot be unclasped, will cause such contractures in a considerable proportion, if not in the majority or even all, of the group, if made properly, as a little experience enables anyone to make them. I recently obtained results with 100 per cent of a group of 12, and a few months ago I obtained results with 24 of a group of 28. In no instance have I failed to get results from some members of the group.

In individual experiments the meaning of dissociation and the fact of the independent functioning of dissociated "neurograms" (to use Prince's term) may be illustrated by suggesting to the subject in the waking state amnesia, for example, for his name, and then by causing, through appropriate suggestions, automatic writing of the name while the amnesia still persists. By proper suggestions to a good subject one can cause automatic writing such that the subject is not aware either of what his hand is writing, or even that his hand is writing anything. To do an experiment like this by waking hypnosis takes only a short time, seems very matter of fact, and can be done with subjects who have never been hypnotized before. If one wishes in this connection to illustrate how the planchette works, a planchette may be substituted for pencil and paper. In elementary classes this is worthwhile. It was Gurney, as James relates, who first conceived the idea of using the planchette to "tap" the subconscious processes involved in post-hypnotic suggestions; but Gurney used sleeping hypnosis for this purpose.

Such an experiment as I have described would illustrate what Prince devotes considerable space to, in *The Unconscious*, namely, the conservation of forgotten experiences. An experiment designed to show the independent functioning of dissociated neurograms in a greater degree is Prince's experiment in subconscious calculation. This experiment, however, can be done by means of waking hypnosis, with subjects never before hypnotized. With a subject in whom amnesia can be produced quickly in the waking state, a problem in mental arithmetic may be given, for which amnesia is produced immediately, before there is time for any effort at solution. The suggestion may be made that the answer will be written automatically at the end of five minutes, with complete amnesia for the problem persisting during this time. In the working out of these suggestions we have an illustration of the simultaneous activity of the dissociated cerebral processes involved in solving the arithmetical problem, and of other cerebral processes involved in conscious attention to the class discussion or to some assigned task. Professor Woodworth refers approvingly to one of Prince's experiments of this sort, with a subject, however, who has a double personality; and Professor Woodworth says, "It is weird business, however interpreted, and raises the question whether anything of the same sort . . . occurs in ordinary experience." If the experiment is done with a subject never hypnotized before, selected from the class, and in a completely waking state, there is nothing in the least "weird" about it; and it answers the question which Woodworth asks in the last part of the sentence quoted above, being evidence that "separate [cerebral] fractions of the individual" can and do function independently and intelligently at the same time, in strictly normal and healthy subjects.

An interesting experiment to illustrate the reality of pain in connection with functional diseases, is to cause pain in the subject's hand, or a toothache, or any sort of pain that one may desire, which is to continue for a minute, or any other specified length of time, after the suggestions of the experimenter cease. Amnesia may then be produced regarding the cause of the pain, and the subject, perhaps in embarrassment, will writhe with pain, knowing nothing as to the cause of it, until the suggested time has elapsed. Such an experiment, like the others which I have described, obviously can be performed effectively in waking hypnosis only with subjects in whom amnesia can be produced by direct suggestion in the waking state. And when amnesia can be produced readily in the waking state, post-hypnotic suggestions of all sorts can be illustrated as well as in deep sleeping hypnosis.

The step to effective autosuggestion, or autohypnosis, is shorter from waking than from sleeping hypnosis. My usual routine in giving a first lesson in autosuggestion is first to close the eyes of the subject, then to produce contractures of the hands, and then to produce analgesia in one hand or arm — all by direct suggestion in the waking state. Then I ask the subject to produce the same results by his own suggestion to himself. After he has done this, instruction may be given in the effective use of auto-suggestion in various practical ways. I recently gave an interesting lesson in autosuggestion to one of my students. When he had produced analgesia in his right hand by autosuggestion alone, he was still unconvinced by the test of pinching with his left hand, and he asked for a needle. I gave him one, properly sterilized. He pricked his right hand repeatedly, so that the blood flowed from each needle wound, before he could fully satisfy himself that he had actually learned to produce analgesia by autosuggestion. As a final illustration of the practical applications of the principles of waking hypnosis, I removed by direct suggestion a headache of which the subject had complained at the beginning of the experiments. A further lesson is apparently needed by this subject, however, before he will be able to use autosuggestion effectively in practical ways; for he reported two days later that he had been able to produce contractures by autosuggestion, but not analgesia, when working alone.

The following description of a series of experiments in waking hypnosis carried out during a single class hour, on the first occasion of reference to hypnosis, shows what can be done in a short time. If more time is at one's disposal, variations and elaborations of such experiments are possible. At the end of one class hour I did a group experiment with the whole class, of fifteen students, in order to select the better subjects. Then, at the beginning of the next class period one of these better subjects volunteered for individual experiments. The subject selected was a man of about thirty-five, never before hypnotized (except in the group experiment of the day before), and with a good history of physical and mental health. I first tested him to see if amnesia could be produced in the waking stage. I readily produced amnesia for his name, with the suggestion that his hand would write it, while the amnesia still persisted. Pencil and paper were then provided, and his hand was concealed from his view, behind a screen. His hand immediately began to write his name. When the name was about half written the subject spoke up to say that he was sorry that the experiment did not seem to be working. After the name was completely written, and after amnesia for his name disappeared in five minutes as had been suggested, his writing was shown to him. The genuineness of his surprise and interest may be easily imagined. I next tested his normal ability in mental arithmetic, finding it fair. Then I made preliminary suggestions to him of the waking hypnotic type. I explained that I would give him a problem in multiplication, which he would solve subconsciously and the answer of which he would write automatically, with amnesia all the while both for what the problem was, and for the fact that a problem had been given to him. I then said, "Multiply 175 by 25," and I *immediately* thereafter caused amnesia for the figures and for the fact that a problem had been given. Then, testing his normal conscious attention to the class discussion, which I continued, by asking him miscellaneous questions, I allowed time for the subconscious computation of the problem and for the automatic writing of the answer. His hand wrote 4,325. The correct answer to the problem is 4,375. In tests given to the subject in the solution of similar problems before dissociation had been produced in waking hypnosis, similar errors had occasionally been made. I have in general not found subconscious computation either more or less accurate than the conscious solution of similar problems. I next caused by suggestion a sharp burning pain on the back of one hand, which I touched with a pencil. Amnesia for the cause of the pain was produced, and the pain remained constant for a minute, as had been suggested. I had produced analgesia in his right hand as one of the preliminary experiments. I have found it generally more difficult to cause pain by suggestion than to cause analgesia.

As a final experiment, towards the close of the hour, I illustrated subconscious perception. I tested the subject's memory for details of the clothing of a man on the back seat of the classroom, a man, however, whom the subject had talked with earlier in the day. Finding him unable to recall any details whatever of the man's clothing, I tried the method of automatic writing without the use of hypnosis, and got an imperfect description. Then, through waking hypnosis I obtained a detailed and accurate description of the man's clothes. He persisted in saying that the man wore a white shirt with a dark stripe in it, in spite of suggestions from me that he would gradually come to recall it more accurately. To me the shirt seemed to be pure white; but after the termination of the experiment I discovered that there had originally been a dark stripe, which had faded out to such an extent that it was not visible to me at a distance of ten feet.

In conclusion I might add that I am interested in the employment of the ordinary type of sleeping hypnosis for some purposes, especially in therapeutic work. I am interested in the sort of psychoanalysis by means of hypnosis which Dr. Hadfield, in England, has called hypnoanalysis; and in attempting to remove phobias, for example, through hypnotic exploration of childhood, or later, amnesias, I have thus far preferred the sleeping type of hypnosis. However, I almost invariably begin the induction of sleeping hypnosis by the method of waking hypnosis described above; and I do not begin to suggest sleep until suggestions of contractures in the waking state have been effective. In this paper I have chosen to limit my discussion to waking hypnosis, and to emphasize its possibilities; for if its possibilities were generally recognized, as is very obviously not the case, much of the present disinclination among psychologists to the use of hypnosis for experimental purposes would, I believe, entirely disappear.

*From "Experiments in Waking Hypnosis for Instructional Purposes," *Journal of Abnormal Psychology and Social Psychology*, 1923-24, pp. 389-404.

NOTE TO THE 1924 ARTICLE ON WAKING HYPNOSIS

From the point of view of the author, this 1924 article is largely a museum piece. It was written after less than three years of experimental work in the field of hypnotism. Since its publication the author has experimented with hypnosis continuously, and it would be strange indeed if changes in theory and practice had not occurred.

First, since 1928 I have scrupulously avoided the use of the term "suggestion." Even before 1928 I never employed the art of suggestion as this is understood by physicians and by psychologists doing ordinary laboratory experiments in suggestion. That is, I never tried to induce hypnotic phenomena through attempts to induce expectancy or belief. In this 1924 article the term "suggestion" was used merely as a synonym for "statement" or "verbal stimulation," as is frequently the case in the literature of hypnotism. Most of my researches since 1928 have been directed wholly or partly to an adverse criticism of the suggestion theory of hypnosis; and, unless the term itself is avoided, readers will err frequently in thinking that the real art of suggestion is intended.

Second, after the first few years of my work with hypnotism I have ceased to be much interested in trying to induce slight hypnotic phenomena in large numbers of subjects, but I have become interested almost exclusively in the upper 20 percent, and especially in the upper 10 or even 5 percent of subjects, in whom the most extreme phenomena can be brought about, including criminal acts contrary to the moral natures of non-criminal subjects.

Third, with the passing of the first enthusiasm of hypnotic work I have become more and more impressed with the difficulty of developing subjects for the best hypnotic work. Beginner's luck, the chance finding of some easily developed subjects almost at the start of my work, has been discovered to be just that — luck. It occasionally happens even now. But for many years my two mottoes have been: — "It takes all the patience of Job — and then more"; and "I'll fight it out along this line if it takes all summer." Hypnotizing is work for young men with a great store of physical energy.

Fourth, after the first few years of my work and the passing of the influence of Coue, I have ceased almost wholly to "teach" subjects to practice self-hypnosis, considering it too dangerous for most laymen to try to combine the dual roles of operator and subject, after they have been developed to the somnambulistic stage.   And if they have not been developed to this stage, self-hypnosis is of slight effectiveness.

Fifth, even in the individual development of extreme trance subjects, for many years I have seldom used anything but a waking technique, contrary to my earlier practice as stated in my article on waking hypnosis.   In this one respect my first stress on a waking technique still stands and in a more nearly exclusive form than at the start.

January 21, 1946.   WESLEY R. WELLS.

HYPNOTIC REGRESSION — FACT OR ARTIFACT?*

Paul Campbell Young, *Louisiana State University*

EDITOR'S NOTE

Can hypnosis produce regression, that is, enable a subject to recall childhood memories and relive his earlier experience? If such regression is genuine, then we can rely on hypnotic regression and use it as an extension of the case history method.

Many experimenters have resorted to regression. The method is usually to induce amnesia for the present and then ask the subject to regress to a particular time in childhood. Since we have no way of checking on the authenticity of the experiences reported, Dr. Young devised a clever check by having the subjects regress to a given age and then test them to determine whether they behaved intellectually as a child of that age should. They were told to regress to the age of three, but most of them behaved more like children of six. Since their I.Q.'s were about average, their reactions were not typical of three-year-old children. Moreover, they were not as successful in their attempts as were un-hypnotized subjects. It was concluded, consequently, that the regression was not genuine. This does not prove that the subjects were faking; merely that they were unable to recall their childhood personalities despite their efforts.

Can a subject in the hypnotic trance be "taken back" to a remote age? Realistic as may be the acting out of the hypnotic suggestion to regress, say, to three years of age, it is still doubtful whether, if given an intelligence test, the subject would approximate the mental age of three.

This question has been answered emphatically in the affirmative, however, by Dolin, Hakebush, Platonow, and other Russian reflexologists, who consider verbal suggestion in hypnosis a prime method of psychological experimentation. Dolin has reported two hysterical women's modelling, writing, drawing, and talking in accordance with the age to which ostensibly, they had regressed by means of post-hypnotic suggestion. Dolin, however, has reported no standard test scores for his subjects. Hakebush, judging the mental age by the subject's drawing, word associations, Rorschach Test scores, and responses on the Binet-Simon, has confirmed the ability of one subject to act under post-hypnotic suggestion in keeping with the age suggested, even though that age ranged all the way from the neonate to the eight-year-old. Platonow, using three subjects, has asserted that their post-hypnotically induced regression is a demonstrable fact, as shown by their general behavior, their Binet-Simon scores, and the inability of one of them (or disinclination?) to simulate while awake the ages which he acted out with such verisimilitude under the influence of the suggestion.

In general criticism of these three series of experiments it may be pointed out that there were very few subjects, that the subjects were not tested as to their normal waking intelligence, and that there were no comparable tests of unhypnotizable control subjects trying to simulate the behavior of children of the suggested ages. Use of the post-hypnotically induced regression ("somnambulistic wakefulness" — Dolin) instead of regression acted out in the hypnotic state itself, seems a positive advantage in carrying out this type of experiment, but it is problematical whether the state brought on in fulfillment of a post-hypnotic suggestion is identical with hypnosis.

In working on this problem of regression the writer used a total of 14 somnambulistic subjects and 7 control subjects — all male university undergraduates — in three different sets of experiments. The hypnotic subjects were always hypnotized by the visual fixation and verbal suggestion-of-sleep method. Their ability to go into the somnambulistic trance, showing all or most of the classical phenomena, had been verified previously in several sessions for each subject.

SERIES A: MODIFIED GROUP EXPERIMENT

The testing in the group was not, strictly speaking, a group test. While each of ten well-trained trance subjects was sitting in an ordinary straight-backed chair at an individual table in a large psychological laboratory, the whole group was hypnotized by the writer. Then as a group they were given the suggestion that they would go back to three years of age, in fact to their third birthday, and told that they would be three until they were awakened. After being convinced by inspection of each individual that all ten subjects were carrying out the suggestions, the writer transferred *rapport* to the ten experimenters, each of whom was already sitting beside a subject at a table. Thereupon the experimenters read *verbatim* from mimeographed sheets instructions taken from Terman's *Measurement of Intelligence* (1916) covering 25 items selected from tests for the years 3 to 9 inclusive.

The 25 items, out of a total of 52 items covering the years 3 to 9, were chosen for simplicity both in giving the instructions and also in recording the answers; thus they could be given fairly accurately by the experimenters, who had had only one hour's previous coaching in reading out the instructions and writing down the answers on the mimeographed sheets. On the basis of these records the writer computed a rough mental age for each subject. It should be noted that the items for a given year, say year three, were scattered among the other items in such a way that easy and difficult items were usually in juxtaposition throughout.

Results. Table I shows the individual M.A.'s and I.Q.'s of the ten subjects in the group test, acting under the trance suggestion that were exactly three years old.*

Scrutiny of the table shows that the M.A.'s ranged from 3 years and 9 months to 6 years, with an average of 4 years and 7 2/3 months. If the regression had taken place in accordance with

---

*The tables have been omitted but the results of the tables used.

the hypnotic suggestion, the I.Q.'s of these subjects would have ranged from 125 to 200, with an average I.Q. of 155. When five of these subjects, however, were tested as adults in normal waking consciousness, they proved to have I.Q.'s of 99, 102, 96, 104, and 100 — strictly normal. Judging from their behavior and their quality credits in the university, the other five were not much different in intelligence.

If these tests, which had much in common with the general run of hypnotic demonstrations of regression, produced results which can be trusted at all, these trance subjects were nearer 4½ years old than 3 years old mentally.

Series B: Individual Intelligence Tests

After the conclusion of the experimentation in Series A, in which at best a rough approximation of the mental age of the regressed trance subjects was secured, a better controlled series was planned and carried out. At the time Series A was in progress it was felt that the ten experimenters, being unskilled in giving the tests and awed by the apparent childishness and ignorance of the subjects, may have failed to demand responses which the subjects were capable of giving. Then, too, the arrangement — with easy and difficult questions alternating — may have served as a cue to the subjects to answer correctly the easy questions and to miss the more difficult. In Series B, consequently, the writer, using the standard old Stanford-Binet technique, gave all the tests in his private office with no third person present.

Nine somnambulistic subjects were used while cooperating under the hypnotic suggestion: "You are now three years old; do you understand? You are now three years old. It is your birthday. You are now three years old. You will be three years old until I wake you up. How old are you?" Upon the subject's assertion that he was three, the intelligence test was given. After the test was finished, the subject was dehypnotized, was allowed to rest for ten minutes, and was then tested for his I.Q. in the waking state. It is to be noted that of the nine subjects in this series five had previously taken part in Series A.

Results. Table 2 shows the results of these individual Stanford-Binet tests. As can be seen from the table, when tested under good conditions the trance subjects, who ostensibly had regressed to exactly three years of age, proved to have mental ages ranging from 4 years and 7 months to 6 years and 9 months, an average of 5 years and 11 plus months. If the suggestion brought about the intended regression, all the subjects were thereby proved geniuses, for on the basis of a C.A. of just three years, the I.Q.'s were all the way from 153 to 225, with an average of 198. As seen from the table, however, when these subjects were tested as adults, in full waking consciousness, their I.Q.'s averaged only 102. The simple conclusion to draw from these figures is that the trance subjects when asked to regress to exactly three years of age responded to the test more nearly as they might have responded to it had they been six years of age.

COMPARISON OF RESULTS OF SERIES A AND SERIES B

Did Series A or Series B give a better indication of the stage to which the subjects had regressed? Table 3 shows the contrasting results from five subjects who took part in both series.

With one exception (Subject F did equally well in both) the subjects proved nearer the suggested age in the group test than in the individual test; i.e., they responded on the average as if they were 4 years and 5 1/3 months old in the group test, whereas they answered as if they were 5 years and 9 months old in the individual test. This fact does not mean that there was any noticeable difference in the manner of style of responding — there was not — but that the values of the responses on the Stanford test under the two sets of conditions were as indicated. By referring to averages of Table 1 and Table 2 (omitted here) it will be seen that about the same differences obtained for all the subjects under the two sets of conditions.

It is the writer's opinion that the results of the individual tests, in Series B, more nearly accord with the stage of induced regression that the hypnotic subjects were experiencing, even though the less careful testing under Series A got results nearer what was expected — and, indeed, more consonant with the general behavior, tone of voice, and language of the trance subjects. For the reasons given above it is felt that the group test failed to elicit the maximum responses that the hypnotized subjects were ready to give.

SERIES C: CONTROL EXPERIMENT

Seven unhypnotizable control subjects were given individual Stanford tests under the same conditions as prevailed in Series B except that, instead of receiving hypnotic suggestions to regress, they were given the following instructions: "You are to imagine you are three years old and to respond to the items of the test I am to give you just as you think a three-year-old would respond. Don't forget: you are exactly three years old. Do and say just what a three-year-old would do and say."

Results. Table 4 shows that these 7 unhypnotizable control subjects, when pretending to be just three years old, ranged in M.A. from 4 years and 5 months to 6 years and 9 months, an average of 5 years and 5 months.

The range in I.Q., on the basis of the pretended age of three years, was from 147 to 225, an average of 179. Only three of these subjects were tested as adults, but their I.Q.'s were well within the normal: 110, 105, and 99. The other four, judging by their general behavior and by the quality credits earned in college, were of about the same mentality.

From these results it would seem that the seven normal unhypnotizable subjects, without behaving childishly at all (as all the trance subjects did very realistically) came nearer to staging a three-year-old performance on the Stanford test than did the nine trance subjects tested under similar conditions.

Summary and Conclusions

Contrary to the findings of Dolin, Hakebush, and Platonow, who experimented with from one to three subjects each, the writer, after using 14 trance subjects and 7 unhypnotizable control subjects — all university students — in a series of individual Stanford (1916) intelligence tests, arrives at the following conclusions:

1. When trance subjects were ordered to regress to the third birthday, they tested on the average (in the better controlled of two series of tests) as children about six years old would test. Even in the less well-controlled test they responded to the test as if they were about four and a half years old.

2. These trance subjects felt very young, their speech and grammar as well as their mannerisms were childish, but they could not enter realistically into an intellectual consciousness so circumscribed as that of the three-year-old.

3. Unhypnotizable control subjects had better success on approximating the three-year level of performance when they simulated that age than did the trance subjects who asserted that they were back at that age, attaining M.A.'s of 5 years and 4 months and 5 years and 11 months, respectively.

Certain additional conclusions may also be drawn:

4. There was no correlation between apparent depth of hypnosis and extent of regression.

5. There was great diversity of performance as between individuals in the trance and great spread in the responses by one subject.

6. Whether the inability of the trance subjects to regress beyond the fifth or sixth year when ordered back to their third birthday is due to the fact that the personality takes form about that time, or to the fact that the trance subjects, unlike the control subjects,

were *unwittingly* playing a role, and playing it less skillfully than the controls by virtue of having voluntarily surrendered their critical attitudes during the trance, is a question not solved by this experimentation. On the basis of this and other experimentation, however, the writer would hazard the guess that role-playing will more likely explain the phenomena. Hypnosis is playing a role with all one's heart, but not with all one's mind.

---

*From *Journal of Abnormal and Social Psychology*, 35, 1940.

THE GENUINENESS OF HYPNOTICALLY PRODUCED ANESTHESIA OF THE SKIN*

By Frank A. Pattie, *The Rice Institute*

EDITOR'S NOTE

Hypnotic anesthesia has been known for one hundred and twenty-five years, but only recently has it been subjected to controlled experimentation. These experiments have shown that the anesthesias conform to the layman's conception rather than to the neurological distribution of sensory nerves. Thus the genuineness of hypnotic anesthesia has been questioned.

This account demonstrates that subjects reported anesthesia when they were in a position to know which hand had been touched, but that when the hands were so intertwined that the subject could not know which finger was being stimulated, he failed to report correctly which hand had been touched.

This result agrees with a former experiment made by Dr. Pattie on blindness. Subjects who responded as if they were blind in one eye were found to be capable of seeing when they were tricked by the use of filters. Thus the genuineness of anesthesia is now seriously questioned by the psychologist.

How 'real' or 'genuine' are the anesthesias produced by hypnotic suggestion? Many recent authorities believe that such anesthesias are genuine, i.e., that they show all the characteristics of organic anesthesias except, of course, that they are produced and removed by suggestion.

For example, McDougall explicitly states his opinion that these anesthesias are genuine and involve an actual interruption of functional continuity of neurones. Most other writers simply state that anesthesias of the sense-organs can be produced in the hypnotic trance and leave the matter there without any neurological or other theory and without any questioning of their genuineness. On the other hand, there has been lately expressed a considerable amount of skepticism on this subject. Dorcus and Shaffer recognize the existence of the problem of the nature of anesthesia, saying, "whether pain is felt to any degree when anesthesia is suggested is a question still not satisfactorily answered . . . The arm or hand of a hypnotized subject can be burned or cut without any observable signs. Nevertheless, there is a sensation of pain, since if the subject is re-hypnotized and told to recall his experiences, he will state that pain was experienced." It cannot be said that these authors arrive at any conclusions on this subject. Hull, in his recent work, shows an attitude of healthy skepticism but seems not to go, so far as a general theory is concerned, beyond the conclusions reached by his former student Sears in his study of hypnotic analgesia, which is discussed below.

Indeed, we can hardly blame these authors for not developing any general conception of hypnotic anesthesia, since up to the present not much experimentation has been reported. Bechterew, in a short article, states that, when analgesia of the skin is produced, stimulation by pricking fails to elicit the normal respiratory, cardiac, and pupillary reactions. He gives several Russian references, which presumably contain the data upon which his conclusions are based. It is well established that the galvanic skin reflex occurs when hypnotically anesthetized receptors are stimulated. Sears says that its magnitude is reduced by about 20 percent when painful stimulation is applied; Dynes says that there is a "slight decrease." The others give no quantitative data.

Dynes studied the effect of hypnotic analgesia and deafness on respiratory and cardiac reactions occurring after strong stimulation. He found that suggestions of anesthesia result practically in an abolition of the respiratory and cardiac changes which normally occur after a pistol shot or after a painful sharp stimulus is applied to the skin. Sears performed a similar experiment but restricted his observations to the comparison of the physiological

changes occurring when the two legs of a S are painfully stimulated, when one leg has been made analgesic. The physiological
changes most susceptible to voluntary control were most reduced;
the facial flinch and the increase in respiratory oscillation and
variability were practically eliminated. Pulse oscillation and pulse
variability were reduced 77 percent and 50 percent, respectively.
Hull connects this relative non-modifiability of the cardiac reactions to the fact that these reactions are not under voluntary
control. Dynes states that no changes in the normal cardiac
"rate and rhythm" occur after stimulation of the anesthetized
sense-organs; but, since he did not apply to his records the refined
measurements of "oscillation" and "variability" developed by
Hull and used by Sears, it is possible that there would be no
such great difference between Sears and Dynes on this point if
both sets of data were treated in the same way. Sears concluded
from certain control experiments, in which the Ss were directed
to simulate an anesthesia (in the normal state, however, not while
in the trance), "that hypnotic anesthesia is in any sense a conscious simulation seems doubtful. Voluntary inhibition of reaction
to pain does not present a picture even remotely resembling the
reaction under true hypnotic anesthesia." Dynes likewise found
that his Ss could not inhibit the cardiac and respiratory reactions
to pain and to the sound of the pistol.

The present writer attempted to produce uniocular blindness
by hypnotic suggestion in 5 Ss, but in no case was he successful.
He was deceived by one very clever S, who faked certain visual
tests in such a way as to give the appearance that one eye was
actually blind. For a long time he believed that a genuine blindness had been produced in this S, but finally he contrived a complicated filter-test which showed that the S was not blind. In
the report of this work the methods used by the S in faking the
tests have been discussed, and a considerable amount of evidence
has been presented to show that the conative tendencies which
led the S to simulate blindness were dissociated from her principal

integrate of personality, and that she actually believed that she was blind in one eye, even when she was doing all she could to pass the tests, either by utilizing her knowledge of vision or by furtively disobeying instructions. Another S simulated blindness, but he was easily detected by the tests.

A complete history of this problem should include a reference to the work of Lundholm, although his experiments are not altogether relevant to the work here reported. He produced anesthesias in the post-hypnotic period and for particular impressions; they were not anesthesias involving all impressions from a given sense-organ.

THE EXPERIMENT

The experiment reported here is so simple that it could have been performed just as well a hundred years ago, when the French Academy of Medicine appointed a committee (which reported negatively) to investigate the alleged anesthesias produced by the magnetist Berna. The experiment starts from this fact: If a person clasps his hands in the position of the 'Japanese illusion' and tries to count the number of times he is touched on one hand (the right or the left as specified in advance), while the fingers of both hands receive in the same short period of time several touches, he can seldom report correctly.

To put the hands in the position of the Japanese illusion, extend the arms with the backs of the hands together and the thumbs pointing downward. Now cross the wrists, still keeping thumbs down, interlace the fingers, and clasp the hands. Now bring the hands toward the chin by flexing the elbows, then bring the elbows down until they touch the sides of the body, at the same time rotating the clasped hands through about 270 degrees until the thumbs point upward.

If a functional anesthesia produced in one hand by hypnotic suggestions behaves like an organic anesthesia, it should make no difference whether the S's hands are put into this position of

confusion or not; with the hands clasped in this position he should
be able to count correctly the number of touches received by the
'good' hand, no matter whether or how many times the 'anesthetic' hand is stimulated. If, however, the anesthesia behaves
as if simulated, the S should give a great many erroneous reports
on the number of touches felt on the 'good' hand, just as does
the normal person when put into this situation.

Normal. Before the ability of the hypnotic S can be studied,
it is necessary to investigate the extent of the normal S's ability
to count the touches on one hand when both, in the confusion-
position, are being touched.

Fifteen normal Ss, university students, were tested. All but
D and O were men. The instructions given, after the hands had
been put into position, were:

"Close your eyes. You will be touched on the fingers of both
hands. Count the number of times you are touched on the fingers
of the left hand. No finger will be touched twice in succession.
Do not estimate the number, but count as well as you can."

The S's thumbs were never touched. No report was ever made
to the S as to the nature or the extent of his errors.

The touches were delivered by the E, who touched the fingers
of the left hand, and an assistant, who touched the fingers of
the right hand. The stimulators were pieces of rubber taken
from ordinary large rubber erasers and had dimensions of 1.5
x 0.5 (the surface applied to the skin) x 2 cm. They were
attached to thin strips of brass (11 x 1.5 x 0.03 cm.), which
in turn were fastened to wooden sticks of a size convenient for
the hand. The brass strips projected over the end of the wooden
stick 3.5 cm. A wire fixed above the brass strip marked the
amount of bending of the strip necessary to produce a pressure
of 75 grm. Care was taken to insure that the E's and the assistant's touches were equally intense. The E's touches were applied
at a variable rate, which did not exceed 2 per sec. A stop-watch
was used to time the touches so that the maximum rate might

not be exceeded. The touches on the hand selected for counting should not be delivered faster than the S can count them; a fair check on the rate was afforded by the fact that the E himself had to count the touches as he delivered them. The assistant's rate did not have to be strictly controlled, as the S did not have to count the touches, but it is believed that the rate rarely, if ever, exceeded 2 per sec.

Ten series of touches were applied to each S. Each series consisted of 20 sets of stimulations ranging in number from 11 to 30 applications on the critical hand. The order of these 20 stimulations was determined by chance (numbered cards were used and shuffled before each series was made up). Five series were given in the first hour of experimenting, and 5 in the second hour, which came after two or three days. To be sure that the S knew what he was to do, he was first given 11 or 12 touches on the left hand, while the assistant also was touching him. His report on this first stimulation was not recorded.

Ss were scored thus. The errors made in each of the 20 reports in a series were added without regard to sign (e.g., the error was 4 if the S called 11 touches either 7 or 15).[1]

Hypnotized. Five hypnotic Ss (all men), including 3 university students and 2 graduates (not students), were used. All the Ss were very good somnambulists and had complete amnesia for events of the trance. None had knowledge of the nature of the experiment. Of course it is likely that the Ss could infer its nature while acting as Ss. In order to protect himself from fakers (whom he has sometimes encountered in experimental work) E had each S sign a statement as follows: "I, realizing that the experiment performed on me will probably be published in a scientific journal, solemnly declare that I was not faking or imitating the hypnotic trance but that I was genuinely hypnotized and do not remember the events of the experimental periods."

The procedure used with the hypnotized S was as follows.

---

1. Table I of Explanation omitted.

An anesthesia of the right hand and arm was suggested, and his sensitivity was tested by pinching, pressing, and pricking his hand. If he declared that he sensed nothing, he was then blindfolded by tying a thick newspaper around his head. (After experiences with malingering in the experiment on hypnotic blindness already cited, no chances were taken with the ordinary bandage-blindfold.) The S's hands were then put into the position of the Japanese illusion, and the following instructions were given:

"You can feel nothing with your right hand. You will now receive a number of touches, and since you can feel nothing with your right hand, they will be felt only on the fingers of the left hand. Count the touches received by the fingers of your left hand and report the number as soon as they cease. No finger will be touched twice in succession. Do not estimate, but count as well as you can."

From this point on the procedure was exactly the same as that followed in the case of the normal Ss, except that the sensitivity of the hand was tested once or twice in every series.[2]

Comparison of the normal and hypnotized. A comparison of the data in the two tables shows that there is no reason for claiming that the hypnotic Ss can perform this task better than the normal Ss. The mean total number of errors made in the 20 series by the normal Ss is 394. Three of the hypnotic Ss made fewer errors, three made more than this number. The average numbers of errors in each of the 10 series, placed side by side for comparison, are as follows:

Ss	Series										Totals
	1	2	3	4	5	6	7	8	9	10	
Normal	73	51	44	37	39	32	32	28	30	29	394
Hypnotized	44	36	47	44	52	32	32	25	37	31	359

2. Table II omitted.

The hypnotic Ss are superior to the normal in the first and second series but inferior in the fifth and equal, or nearly equal, in the remaining series. If we neglect the first two series, the degree of improvement in the task is about the same for both kinds of Ss. From this comparison it may be concluded that the suggestion of anesthesia in the right hand does not affect the ability of the hypnotized Ss to count the number of touches received by the left hand when the hands are in the confusion-position. The differences between the two groups in the first and second series, if significant, must be explained as due to greater concentration on the part of the hypnotized Ss or some similar cause. If we attempt to explain this superiority as due to the suggestion of anesthesia, we can find no reason why this superiority should not have persisted through the remaining series.

Qualitative observations. In a large number of cases the hypnotized Ss reported a number which was less, in some cases considerably less, than the number of touches applied to the left hand. In a number of cases, when there was a considerable difference between the numbers of touches applied by the E and the assistant, the S would report the number applied by the assistant on the supposedly anesthetic hand.

Some control experiments were done with each of the hypnotic Ss in the trance after the main experiment was over. The S held his hands in the confusion-position while the E touched him only on the left hand. The S also put his hands, palms down, on the table, with a distance of about 50 cm. between them, and both E and assistant stimulated the hand as usual. The S's ability to report the number of stimulations received by the left hand in these two situations was practically perfect, as one would expect.

After the quantitative experimentation, each S had to answer the following questions in the trance. (1) Did all the touches seem to fall on the left hand? (2) Were you conscious of suppressing some touches that you felt, that is, not counting some of them?

In reply, all Ss said that they had felt nothing on the right hand, that all touches came on the left hand. P's answer was not typical of the rest. When asked, "Did you have the impression that all touches came on the left hand?" he said, "I can't say that I did." "Your right hand has been anesthetic?" "Yes." "Why did you say that you didn't have the impression that they all came on the left hand?" "Because I didn't know where my left hand was." "You're certain that you felt nothing with the right hand?" "I have felt with only one hand, the left." These answers suggest that the S did feel something with the right hand; he reported some confusion, but maintained that his right hand had felt nothing.

The answer given by all to the second question was that they had not been aware of receiving touches which were not counted. The Ss were then asked, after the right hand had been rendered anesthetic by suggestion, to put their hands into the confusion-position again, and they were blindfolded. They were told to say "Now" whenever they felt a touch. Every S except P and R at one time or another reported "Now" when the touch fell on the right hand and failed to report when it fell on the left hand. P's success seemed to depend on the fact that he was rather slow in reporting after being touched. R was rather prompt in reporting. It is signicant that these two Ss made the fewest errors among the hypnotic Ss. They were both touched about 20 times, and in no case made an error.

At the conclusion of these experiments, the nature of the problem was explained to the Ss. It was hoped that they might make some comments of interest, but they made none. This result was probably to be expected, since they were in the trance, a condition usually unfavorable (though not always) to the making of statements indicating independent or spontaneous thinking.

To be complete, this experiment should contain another division, in which various stimuli are applied to the 'anesthetic' hand and the E tries to obtain later from the Ss a description of the stimuli received. This course was not followed, since the nature of the experiment had been explained to the Ss and E thought that this fact would vitiate the evidential value of data so obtained.

CONCLUSIONS AND THEORETICAL CONSIDERATIONS

(1) The suggestion of the anesthesia of one hand is effective only so long as the S's hands are in a position which, in the nontrance state, would not prevent him from knowing, when one hand is stimulated, which one is being stimulated. If, however, the hands are clasped in a position which renders this accurate knowledge impossible, the suggestion of anesthesia has no effect on the S's performance, and he can count the touches received by the supposedly insensitive hand (when both are touched) no better than can a normal person who has no suggestion of anesthesia and who has his hands in the same position of confusion.

(2) The effect that the suggestion of anesthesia produces is an illusion on the part of the S that one of his hands is actually insensitive and that all the touches come to the unaffected hand. The only alternative to this conclusion is that the Ss are consciously lying. There are several reasons for rejecting this latter hypothesis; namely: (a) The number of Ss who, after reflecting on their past experiences, have ever admitted such a deception is either zero or very small. In the writer's experience, none ever has. (b) It seems unreasonable to suppose that a S who can be trusted to carry out instructions faithfully in an experiment in the normal state is so transformed by hypnosis that he knowingly lies to the E and undergoes painful stimulation to carry out the same purpose of deception. (c) It is probably easy to produce the illusion referred to, and the instructions given may act as a determinant of it, just as certain instructions may facilitate the production of a 'normal hallucination' in an unhypnotized person who is a trained introspector. Such an illusion arose spontan-

eously in one of the normal Ss tested and disturbed the testing so much that he had to be discarded. Through one of the first series, this S had the impression that all touches were falling on his right hand, and he could make no report at all on the number received by the left hand, which he had entirely "lost."

(3) Since the Ss report that they are not failing to count some of the touches and we take this statement as truthful, and since at least in some cases there is evidence of an active process of suppression (e.g., 21 touches may be given and only 9 reported), it must be assumed that certain dissociated processes are working at the task of 'sorting out' or discriminating, so far as is possible, the impressions received from the two hands. These dissociated processes are not primarily cognitive — that is, they are not 'dissociated ideas' — but are conative in nature. The suggestion of anesthesia produced an illusion that an anesthesia actually exists and also a dissociation of certain conative tendencies which work, without the knowledge of the principal integrate of personality, in every way possible to make it appear to the E, whom the S wishes to please and to obey, that an anesthesia has actually been produced. This theory owes to Professor McDougall's general theory of hypnosis in terms of submission the idea that the dissociated processes are primarily conative in nature. While this study fails definitely to support McDougall's theory that anesthesias are genuine, nevertheless it offers considerable evidence in support of his general ideas on the subject of hypnosis.

This theoretical formulation is supported strongly, in the writer's opinion, by his study of hypnotically produced blindness, to which he has already referred.

*From *American Journal of Psychology*, 49, 1937.

ABILITY TO RESIST ARTIFICIALLY INDUCED DISSOCIATION*

WESLEY RAYMOND WELLS, *Syracuse University*

EDITOR'S NOTE

Can a person be hypnotized against his will? This question has interested both the psychologist and the layman. The older literature affirmed that it could be done. Some of the modern investigators have concluded that a hypnotized subject can resist the command of a hypnotist. This study supports the thesis that a hypnotized subject cannot resist the commands of the operator, and that if he does, he is not deeply hypnotized.

In a previous paper I called attention to a matter of technique and of interpretation in certain experiments on hypnosis. Some experimenters have failed to produce by means of hypnosis complete and enduring amnesia and post-hypnotic effects. The interpretation made or implied by these experimenters has been that therefore complete and enduring amnesia and post-hypnotic effects cannot be produced. In my own study referred to above I reported an experiment in which complete hypnotic results, permanent for the duration of the experiment (one year), were produced, quite in line with expectation from the older literature. I pointed out that failures in hypnosis, due to an inadequate technique or to the failure to select sufficiently good subjects, should be taken merely at their face value, as hypnotic failures, leaving open the question of the limits of successful hypnosis.

This same problem arises in regard to the experiments reported by P. C. Young in two articles. A study of the older literature on hypnosis, describing especially the work in the 1880's and 1890's — the period which might be called the golden age of hypnotism — would lead one to conclude that *helplessness* on the part of the subject is an essential feature of successful hypnosis.

If a subject is not helpless in a given respect, in this respect he is not hypnotized. A large percentage of persons cannot be hypnotized deeply, according to this older literature. That is to say, only the simpler muscular phenomena, if anything hypnotic at all, can be produced in a considerable proportion of subjects; but to the extent to which they can be hypnotized, to this extent the subjects are helpless and under the control of the hypnotizers. This interpretation seems generally asserted or implied in most of the older literature. Young's studies question the validity of such an interpretation of hypnosis, by reporting experiments in which the hypnotizer was unable to produce hypnotic results if the subjects resisted his efforts.

Professor R. H. Wheeler has included the second of the two articles by Young, referred to above, in his *Readings in Psychology*, introducing it by an editorial note in which he says: "The main theme of the discussion . . . is the fact that cooperation in the trance is limited by purposes which the subject may have had in mind before entering the trance. Heretofore, in the literature on hypnotism, there had been an inclination to overlook the control which the hypnotized person could still exert of his own accord." The fact is that in the older literature the matter of the subject's resistance is taken account of; and when the subject's resistance succeeds, just to this extent hypnosis fails. The older literature tells of subjects being hypnotized "against their wills," even on the first occasion of being subjects, when expecting hypnosis to fail, and when actively struggling against the hypnotizer's commands. But Wheeler's summary of Young's work is correct, namely, that Young failed to get results in cases where the subjects deliberately resisted.

Dorcus and Shaffer, in their *Textbook of Abnormal Psychology*, express an opinion of hypnosis similar to that of Young, to whose experiments they refer. They assert of hypnosis: "Loss of volition is genuine only to a certain extent." "Actions on the part of the hypnotized subject are not involuntary, unconscious, or dissociated." Such statements are surprising in view of the fact that such hypnotic phenomena as hallucinations and amnesia clearly transcend the voluntary capacity of the subject. A normal person cannot voluntarily produce in himself genuine hallucinations or specific amnesias. Young does not assert the contrary, but on the basis of his experiments he does assert that the hypnotized subject can voluntarily prevent the production in him by the hypnotizer of hallucinations, amnesia, and muscular helplessness, through a predetermined effort of resistance.

Is Young's work a real and successful criticism of the traditional view of hypnotism, or is it merely an instance of failure to obtain hypnotic results, due to an inadequate technique or to the selection of subjects not highly hypnotizable? With a view to answering this question, I undertook a repetition of Series Two of Young's experiments. I obtained results directly contrary to Young's, and exactly in line with expectation from the older hypnotic work.

Following, with slight modifications, the general outline of procedure employed by Young in Series Two of his experiments, I conducted a series of experiments with 16 somnambulistic subjects. Each subject, previously selected by group hypnosis and then trained individually to the point of somnambulism, was asked to choose one of the ten hypnotic phenomena of Young's list, and to try to his utmost to prevent the production of this chosen phenomenon in the ensuing hypnotic trance. Young's list is as follows: "(1) Inability to open the eyes. (2) Inability to unclasp the hands. (3) Inability to recall one's own name. (4) Deafness to everything but the E's voice. (5) Inability to raise the feet from the floor. (6) Analgesia. (7) Visual hallucination. (8) Inability to walk. (9) Carrying out of post-hypnotic suggestions. (10) Post-hypnotic amnesia." As in Young's experiments, each subject was asked to write down the item selected, to put the paper in his pocket, and not to show the paper to me or to tell me what item had been selected until the end of the session. I then asked each subject to cooperate in the experiment as a whole, except in regard to the selected item. I gave the subjects no indication in advance as to my own expectation concerning the results, nor, until the end of each session, did I inquire of the subjects regarding their own expectations.

Beginning with the third subject, and thereafter throughout the rest of the experiments, each subject was asked to choose the critical item by lot, by drawing one of ten slips of paper. This procedure was adopted for the purpose of trying to get a better sampling of the items. Beginning with the tenth subject, and continuing throughout the rest of the experiments, I asked for the subject's anticipation of the results in writing before beginning the experiment. This precaution was to make sure that what the subject told me at the end was what he had really expected at the beginning. The subject was asked to put the slip on which his expectation was written into his pocket, along with the paper containing the selected item, and at the close of the experiment I saw both papers for the first time.

All of the subjects were undergraduate students. All but two were students in my classes at the time; these two had been in my classes the previous year. All subjects were in good general health. All were of at least average undergraduate intellectual ability and achievement, and several were superior, later going into graduate or other professional studies. There was a third person present at every session, to assist in observations and in taking notes, as well as to insure my own and the subject's protection, a common precaution in hypnotic work.

Experiment 1. I began the series of experiments with subject Si. He had been hypnotized previously on three occasions in individual work following group hypnosis. He selected item 5, and wrote, "While in a state of hypnosis, I will obey all commands except that of being unable to lift my feet from the floor." This writing, as indicated above, was not shown to me or communicated to me until the end of the experiment. During the experiment

I detected stronger resistance to item 5 than to the other items, but the subject was unable to lift his feet. At the close of the experiment the subject said that he had expected in advance to be able to resist successfully. There was, of course, complete amnesia following the experiment, as this subject, like all the others, was truly somnambulistic. Consequently the subject could not tell whether or not he had been successful in resisting. In order to get an introspective report from the subject, as well as for the hygienic purpose of leaving him free from possible dissociative effects in everyday life as a result of the experiment, I put him into hypnosis again to remove the amnesia. In this second hypnotic state he recalled that item 5 differed from the other items as follows: he was unable even to *try* to resist the other commands; he could try to resist command No. 5, although he found himself helpless actually to resist.

Experiment 2. A few days later I did the experiment on the second subject, Sa., who had previously been a subject in individual hypnosis once. He selected item 4 (deafness). He wrote, "While in a state of hypnosis I will obey all commands except No. 4 (deafness to everything but the operator's voice)." In advance, as he told me later, he had expected to be able to resist. I easily detected the critical item. Though I was able to produce complete deafness for some loud sounds, I could not make the deafness complete for *all* sounds aside from my own voice. Since this circumstance left the result of the experiment a little in question, the experiment was repeated two days later. This time the subject selected item 7 (visual hallucination). During this experiment he seemed to be trying unusually hard to resist *all* commands, but I succeeded in getting complete results with all items. I was not able to detect which was the critical item.

Following the practice of Young in his experiments, I was free to vary my technique and to use whatever hypnotic methods I could think of to secure the desired effects. It is usually easier to get hypnotic results if the subject is cooperative in the sense of not being openly defiant in his resistance. But all subjects resist to some extent, or at least they are asked to do so; and neither the subject nor the operator is (or should be) satisfied that hypnosis has occurred except to the degree to which helplessness has occurred. The art of successful hypnotizing consists of precisely this matter of producing increasing helplessness on the part of the subject. Successful hypnotic methods have to be flexible, and adapted to each individual case. An illustration may be offered from the work in Experiment 2. The second session with subject Sa., unlike that on the first day, produced complete deafness to all sounds except the operator's voice. Having gained experience from my partial failure on the previous occasion, I employed different methods, which were entirely successful. To be sure, item 4 was not the one which the subject was supposed to be trying to resist, as I learned later; but actually the subject was trying to resist the production of all hypnotic phenomena. When the subject was hypnotized again for the removal of amnesia for the two trance states of the experiment, he recalled and admitted in hypnosis that all the hypnotic items had been produced completely in the second session, and all but No. 4 in the first, and this one with partial success.

This subject, always a person of strong convictions and with a somewhat defiant attitude — a person of strong will corresponding to his physical strength (and he was a man six feet tall who weighed 200 pounds) — still asserted that it could not be done again. To prove to him that "once a good hypnotic subject, always a good subject" is the rule in hypnotic work, I proposed that still another test of his helplessness when hypnotized should be given. One of my colleagues, Je., relatively inexperienced at that time in hypnosis but interested in learning, was asked to work the "cigarette test" on Sa. Je. put the subject into a trance state, a lighted cigarette was placed between two fingers, and contractures of the fingers were produced, without analgesia.

Twice the subject was able to remove the cigarette as the burning became intense; but on the third attempt Je. rendered the subject completely helpless until he screamed as a result of the pain and cried out, "I give up. I am helpless. Please release me and stop the burning." This "cigarette test" is well known in hypnotic work as a test of the genuineness of hypnotic helplessness, and it served its purpose well in the present instance.

Experiment 3. I carried out the third experiment with subject Pe., who had been a hypnotic subject on three previous occasions. He drew slip No. 2 with the item, "inability to unclasp the hands." All of my commands were effective, and I was unable to tell correctly which was the critical item. I suspected wrongly that it was item No. 5. The subject had previously expected to be able to resist.

Experiment 4. The subject in this experiment was Pr. He had been previously a somnambulistic subject on four occasions, easily made somnambulistic the first time, but hypnotized afterwards for other purposes. He selected by lot item No. 5. All the hypnotic phenomena occurred, and the critical item was not detected by the operator. This subject had previously expected to be unable to resist.

Experiment 5. The subject, Me., had been previously a hypnotic subject on two occasions. He selected by lot item 2. All hypnotic phenomena in the list occurred completely. From the subject's severe, though unsuccessful, struggle to unclasp his hands, I correctly suspected that this was the critical item. The subject struggled so hard in attempting to resist the hand clasping that he complained of pain in his arms and chest after the experiment. He had expected in advance to be able to resist.

Experiment 6. The subject here was Ed., who had previously been a hypnotic subject on two occasions. The item selected by lot was No. 3 (amnesia for his own name). I detected increased resistance on this point. At first, as is not unusual in hypnotic work under ordinary conditions with the best of subjects, the amnesia was only partial. The subject forgot his last name, but not his first name. Then I succeeded in producing amnesia for all the letters of the alphabet, after which amnesia for his first as well as his last name was complete. Here again is an illustration of how, if one simple hypnotic method does not work, another method may be successful. This subject was the only one of the sixteen to report in advance that he did not have an opinion as to whether or not he would be able to resist.

Experiment 7. The subject, Be., who had previously been a hypnotic subject on one occasion, expected in advance to be unable to resist. Item No. 3 was selected by lot. Hypnosis was successful on all points, and I was unable to detect which was the critical item.

Experiment 8. The subject was Lu., a man who had previously been a hypnotic subject four times, the year before. He expected in advance to be able to resist. He selected by lot item No. 1 (contracture of the eyelids). All points in the hypnotic list worked with complete success, and I could not detect the critical item. Curiously enough, eyelid contractures were so very effective that after the subject came out of the trance, he still could not open his eyes. In order to open them I finally put him back into the trance state. Then I forced him to open his eyes while still in the trance. Imagine my surprise after this incident to learn that the one hypnotic effect so complete that I had experienced difficulty in counteracting it, was the very one which the subject had selected to prevent from occurring at all!

Experiment 9. The subject of this experiment was Wo., previously a hypnotic subject once. The item selected by lot was No. 4 (deafness) and the expectation of the subject was inability to resist. In the result, however, all hypnotic efforts were successful. I was unable to detect the critical item.

Experiment 10. Ap., who had previously been a hypnotic subject twice, was the subject. The item selected by lot was No. 6 (analgesia), and the subject expected to be able to resist. The result was complete hypnotic success of all points, though item No. 6 was detected as the critical one. At first, analgesia was only partial, but additional efforts on the operator's part made the analgesia complete.

Experiment 11. The subject was Su., previously a hypnotic subject three times, and the item selected by lot No. 1 (contracture of eyelids). The expectation of subject was that he would be unable to resist. The result was the inability of subject to resist any of the hypnotic commands; the critical item was not detected by the operator.

Experiment 12. Da. was the subject, previously a hypnotic subject once. No. 5 (inability to raise feet from the floor) was the item selected by lot. The subject expected that he would be able to resist.

Not that I anticipated any special difficulty with this subject but merely to try out a new method which I thought would be a good one to use in case I should sometime find an unusually refractory subject, I varied my procedure this time as follows. At the start, after putting the subject into the trance state, I produced amnesia for the critical item, without asking or finding out what this item was. After this I worked successfully all parts of the experiment without being able to detect the critical item. The amnesia for the critical item lasted even after the subject was brought out of the trance, though I had not intended such to be the case. The subject had to take the slip of paper out of his pocket and read it before he could tell me which had been the critical item, and even then there was no recognition of the item by the subject.

Here is another illustration of a common fallacy in some of the reported experiments on hypnosis where failures to get the best results are due to inadequacies in the operator's art of hypnotizing. For very refractory subjects in such a series of experiments as the one I am reporting, it seems as if the subject could always be rendered helpless to resist the critical command by being rendered amnesic for it at the start. If he could not be made amnesic for it, or for anything desired, then he would not be a sufficiently good subject for the experiment; or at least he would first need to be developed to the point where complete amnesia for anything whatever could be produced. Young reports that his subject H., used in Experiment I of Series Two, had "vague remembrance" after the trance of one incident occurring in the trance. This fact is evidence that subject H. was not a completely somnambulistic subject, and consequently not suitable for such an experiment.

Experiment 13. The subject, Bl., had previously been a hypnotic subject once. The item selected was No. 4 (deafness). Though the anticipation of the subject was that he would be able to resist, the result was complete hypnotic control of the subject on all items. The critical item was not detected, since complete deafness to all by my voice was produced at once, as easily as any of the other hypnotic phenomena.

Experiment 14. The subject, Luk., previously a hypnotic subject three times, selected by lot No. 6 (analgesia). The anticipation of the subject was ability to resist; yet complete hypnotic success was the result with all items. The critical item was not detected. One interesting feature about this case was that subject Luk. had been taught previously to practice effective self-hypnosis; even so, this knowledge did not enable him to resist any better than had the other subjects.

Experiment 15. The subject was Pel., a hypnotic subject once previously, and the item selected No. 4 (deafness). The subject anticipated that he would be able to resist. Complete deafness to all but my voice was produced, along with all the other hypnotic effects. The critical item could not be detected from observation of the experiment.

Experiment 16. Ro., previously a hypnotic subject twice, was the subject, and No. 10 (post-hypnotic phenomena) the item selected. Anticipation of the subject was that he would be unable to resist. There resulted a successful production of all hypnotic and post-hypnotic effects, although I did detect the critical item. The post-hypnotic commission was that the subject, after hypnosis, should take his fountain pen from his pocket when I tapped on the desk shortly after the termination of the trance state. The subject's hand moved slowly and trembled slightly at the signal; nevertheless, the post-hypnotic action was carried out completely.

The results of the whole series of experiments are presented in Table 1 (omitted here).

The main points in the series of experiments may be summarized briefly as follows: In all 16 individual experiments the subjects were unable to resist the critical or any other commands. The second experiment was the only doubtful one, and when this experiment was repeated the results were unambiguously successful. Ten of the subjects expected in advance to be able to resist, contrary to Young's contention that what happens in hypnosis is predetermined by the subject's expectation of what will happen. Five of the subjects expected in advance to be unable to resist. One was uncertain in advance, not venturing a prediction. With five of the subjects I was able to detect during the experiments the critical items, from evidence of greater efforts to resist. With ten of the subjects I was unable to detect the critical items. With the second subject, Sa., on whom I did the experiment twice; I detected the critical item in the first experiment; in the second experiment I did not detect it.

To prove my contention that helplessness of the subject is an essential feature of hypnosis, it was not necessary to get uniform results with all the subjects. To have obtained positive results with only one of the 16 subjects would have been sufficient. Then the other 15 cases would have been set down as failures due to a poor selection of subjects or to inadequate methods. I had, however, selected excellent subjects from group hypnosis; and then I had developed each of these subjects by previous individual work to the point where I might reasonably expect successful results. I tried no other subjects in this series of experiments.

The outcome of these experiments is merely to substantiate what is evident in the work of the older hypnotizers. It is usually easier to get hypnotic results with cooperating rather than with actively resisting subjects, according to the older literature as well as according to the most casual of present-day experience in hypnotizing; but still it has long been reported that some subjects can be deeply hypnotized, even the first time, though they intentionally resist and though they are skeptical of becoming subjects. In my own practice I have refused to attempt to hypnotize subjects unless they will cooperate to the extent of sitting down and of performing a few simple voluntary acts which I ask them to do. But, with this background of general cooperation, I have insisted that they should resist each hypnotic command to the full extent of their ability, since I am not satisfied with the success of hypnosis except as the subject becomes helpless to resist. With the majority of subjects, only a slight degree of helplessness in regard to simple muscular phenomena, or none whatsoever, can be produced, at least in group work or in short individual sessions. This is only another way of saying that the majority of persons cannot be deeply hypnotized, at least without long and persistent effort. This observation, also, is in line with reports in the older literature.

I did not attempt to repeat the third series of experiments reported by Young. These experiments involved two hypnotizers, one of whom trained the subjects in "autosuggestion" before Young tried experiments similar to those of his Series Two (which I repeated). The question here seems largely one of interpretation. One hypnotizer might very well be able to produce effects in subjects which nullify the later work of another hypnotizer, in part or even *in toto*. The implantation during the hypnotic trance of a subconscious inhibition which operates post-hypnotically to protect the subject from being hypnotized at all by other hypnotizers, is a familiar case in point. The usual and most obvious interpretation of this, however, is in terms of the strong effect of hypnosis in rendering the subject helpless to become a subject thereafter at the hands of other hypnotizers, however much he may desire and strive to become a good hypnotic subject.

*From *Journal of Abnormal and Social Psychology*, 35, 261-272, 1940.

HYPNOSIS AS AN AID TO ADJUSTMENT*

FRED G. LIVINGOOD, *Washington College*

EDITOR'S NOTE

The value of hypnosis in helping people to adjust better is demonstrated in Professor Livingood's article. It reports how a case of speech disorder and a case of poor physical coordination were improved by hypnotherapy. This was accomplished without the services of a physician. Of particular interest is the successful use of delayed recall in the first illustration.

The following two described cases are illustrations of the use of hypnosis on a liberal arts college campus in assisting young people whose efficiency was reduced by reason of emotional difficulties. The intimate contacts which exist on a small college campus are no doubt helpful in bringing about the initial contacts and in promoting mutual understandings which make such experiments possible. Both student cases were undergraduate students who came to the instructor in psychology and asked for help with their problems. Having known of the instructor's experiments and demonstrations before classes in abnormal psychology and before selected senior groups, both students were aware of the nature of hypnosis and were willing to cooperate in the experiment. In the instance of the freshman student some additional explanation was necessary. In both instances the students were told that no material improvement could be promised but that the instructor would be glad with their cooperation to give time and make an effort to assist them with their particular problems.

CASE A

Student *A*, a male freshman, was referred to the instructor by an upper classman but came to the instructor on his own volition. Since the age of seven the young man had been a chronic stutterer, stuttering being worse at some times than at other times. While in college he found greatest difficulty in French and Mathematics classes, with which subjects he had the greatest difficulty. The stuttering was not only annoying but also embarrassing. More recently he closed his eyes every time that he stuttered. Much to his chagrin, fellow students began to imitate him in closing their eyes and stuttering.

College instructors in the several classes took the attitude the young man was using his stuttering as a protective device to avoid recitation in classes in which he was unprepared. This may have been true in part since the young man stuttered most in those subjects in which he was not particularly well prepared for daily recitations, although *A* stated that he was making an honest effort to prepare for classes and was not consciously trying to evade reciting in classes.

An offer was made by the psychology instructor to place the student under hypnosis in an effort to relieve the stuttering, to which the young man willingly consented. The first conference was held about the first of March during the second semester, and from that time until the close of the college year the young man was placed under hypnosis three times each week for periods varying between 10 and 25 minutes, the periods becoming shorter as the conferences continued.

Post-hypnotic suggestions made application to confidence in meeting people, to participation in class meetings, and in trying to overcome the habit of closing eyes each time stuttering occurred. Probing to discover the cause of the stuttering yielded no immediate results. The suggestion was then made at each session for the succeeding two months that on a certain day in May the young man would be able to recall the reason for stuttering and would explain in detail the incident or incidents which led to stuttering. Hypnotic conferences continued regularly with post-hypnotic suggestions that the subject would not stutter for certain periods of time, beginning with an an hour at a time and then the periods were gradually extended to 24 hours and for two and three days at a time. Particular emphasis was placed on the specific classes in which the student was having the most difficulty with stuttering. Results from the beginning were manifest but progress was slow.

On a certain day in May, previously suggested to the student, the young man was placed under hypnosis and he was reminded that this was the day when he would be able to recall the occasion which caused him to stutter. Without any persuasion the young man launched on the following account:

When a small boy of seven years his mother had gone on a visit to a distant city, leaving the boy at home in the care of his father. The father had a business which consumed all of his time, with the result that the boy was compelled to look out for himself. The mother, hoping to please her small son, sent him a complete cowboy outfit, including shirt, neckerchief, sombrero, and chaps. Naturally the boy was delighted with the new outfit and arrayed in his newly acquired finery set forth on a neighborhood conquest. The neighborhood boys were engaged in playing in a livery stable yard where there were a great number of wagons and carriages and the games led them to crawl in and out of the vehicles. In his hurry to get out of a wagon the boy jumped from the wagon but did not clear the brake handle on the side of the wagon, with the result that the clothing was badly ripped and torn, including the neckerchief, shirt, and chaps.

The boy was terribly frightened about the consequences of tearing the new cowboy outfit, so he hurried home, took off the outfit, packed it carefully in the box in which he had received it, and hid the box in the attic under the eaves where the box and contents had remained to the time of this recital.

At lunch, following the accident, the boy in a halting manner tried to explain to his father what had happened but the father having had a difficult morning hushed up the boy and showed impatience with the repeated and halting explanation of the day's calamity, with the result that the boy never mentioned the incident again. The mother on her return home had forgotten about the present of the cowboy outfit which she had sent her son, with the result that the entire incident was forgotten by both boy and parents. From that day stuttering became a problem whenever the boy was placed in any difficult situation.

With the cause of the stuttering known, the account was repeated to the boy in a waking state and an explanation was made about the importance of knowing the cause of stuttering. Thereafter post-hypnotic suggestions stressed primarily right habits and confidence in overcoming stuttering. By the end of the semester stuttering had practically ceased. Instructors in the young man's classes were asked to give him sufficient time to recite, and to insure that the young man would make adequate preparations for classes he was told that recitations would be expected in all classes. Today the young man seldom stutters, having learned that if he makes adequate preparation and thinks carefully about what he wants to say, and if he is willing to take time and speak slowly, he can control stuttering.

CASE B

Student *B*, a female senior in a liberal arts college, was led to ask the psychology instructor for assistance due to nervous tension particularly incident to walking. The young lady had an operation performed by an internationally known brain surgeon for the removal of a tumor from the right side of the brain when she was 12 years old. The consequences of the operation were hemiplegia and hemianopsia. The left arm was carried close to the side with a pronounced contracture in the left wrist with a consequent shortening of the wrist tendon. The left leg and the left arm were slightly thinner than the right leg and right arm due to reduced exercise. Steps could be taken one at a time only, and the subject was shy about attempting to go up or to go down steps when others were present. Along with nervous tension came consequent lack of confidence, not only in walking but in other activities as well.

The young lady had been a member of the class in abnormal psychology in which spastic paralysis had been discussed with a comment on the splendid work which Dr. Earl Carlson of the Neurological Institute of New York had been doing in reclaiming the spastics by relieving nervous tension with consequent improvement in coordination. This led the young lady to ask the instructor whether anything might be done for her and whether the instructor would be willing to try to aid her with the use of hypnosis.

Beginning the second semester of the senior year, and continuing for the entire semester three days each week, the young lady was placed under hypnosis and post-hypnotic suggestions were made concerning the importance of relaxation and confidence in walking and related activities. Periods necessary for placing B under hypnosis gradually declined from 25 minutes to a second or two. Each day the young lady under hypnosis walked from one end of a large room to the other end while the instructor gave suggestions affecting relaxation of muscles while walking and stressing the importance of relaxation, physical and mental, for proper physical coordination. Post-hypnotic suggestions were made to overcome fear of steps, stepping in and out of automobiles and street cars, and for confidence in the ability to walk normally with muscles relaxed at all times. Suggestions relative to the subject having a good week-end in walking, confidence and so forth were particularly effective.

Before beginning the periods of hypnosis the young woman walked on the toes of her left foot, swinging her left leg along rather awkwardly and carrying the left arm close to the body at the waist. By the end of the semester B walked in a fairly relaxed manner, placing the heel down before the ball of the foot. So great was the improvement that dormitory residents no longer recognized her step as she walked down the halls of the dormitory. In like manner she learned to carry the left arm at her side in relaxed manner and to make some use of the arm and hand in carrying books, picking up small objects and grasping door knobs. There were days, however, when the subject lost confidence and when she reverted to earlier walking habits and to holding her arm tensed. It was only with repeated suggestion that she continued to improve and would return to the normal improved manner of walking. Any period of emotional stress, disappointment or situation calling for sudden adjustment generally resulted in tension and consequent difficulties in coordination. Interest and solicitation of fellow students was an important factor in stimulating continued improvement.

While post-hypnotic suggestions were instrumental in promoting improvement in B's walking and in the use of her hand and arm, naturally these suggestions could not be expected to restore absolute normal use of limbs. Physicians who examined B before beginning the conferences and at the close of the conferences were surprised at the improvement resulting. Since the young lady graduated from college she has made no further gains in the use of arm and hand; however, she has lost nothing in the improvement in coordination.

The two student cases cited might have made just as great improvement had suggestions been made in the ordinary procedure of a student-advisor conference. Hypnosis cannot be given all the credit. However, under hypnosis it was easier to make the suggestions which led to definite improvement in A and in B. In both students there was pronounced emotional tension, fear, lack of confidence, and the consequent feeling of inability to meet situations. Under hypnosis they responded to suggestions resulting in increased confidence, improved coordination, and in the ability to make adjustments.

*From *The Journal of Psychology*, 1941.

A STUDY OF HYPNOTIC SUSCEPTIBILITY IN RELATION TO PERSONALITY TRAITS*

By Lawrence W. Davis and Richard W. Husband,
University of Wisconsin

EDITOR'S NOTE

Does susceptibility to hypnosis depend upon any particular personality tests, has any direct influence on susceptibility to neurotic traits. This study shows that none of the personality traits, such as introversion and extroversion as measured by personality tests, has any direct influence on susceptibility to hypnosis.

Many fundamental facts about hypnosis are as yet unknown, and very little experimental work of a nature to check the multitude of theories has been undertaken. One rather important topic which has been neglected is that indicated in the title; namely, the relation of one's personality to his success as a hypnotic subject. We know that in some persons deep trances are elicited readily, while others never make even fair subjects. What makes these individual differences? Various theories have been advanced. One is that the operator's will must be stronger than the subject's; another that the subject must be capable of a certain degree of concentration; a third that too high intelligence works adversely because there is so much mental alertness that perfect relaxation is not possible. None of these hypotheses have been subjected to experimental verification.

Therefore, the major topic of this paper is the study of the causative factors of hypnotic susceptibility from the point of view of personality. Various tests of personality traits were used; and hypnotic susceptibility was ascertained from actual trance tests and scored on a specially devised scale.

TESTS

The tests used in this study consist of measures and inventories of personality traits. All are well known and need no detailed description here.

The Personality Schedule, devised by L. L. and T. G. Thurstone, (1) was used as a measure of maladjustment. This actually amounts simply to a neurotic inventory, being compiled largely from several shorter lists, and proposes to determine through a single index the extent of an individual's neurotic tendencies.

In determining the extent of introverted tendency, Laird's C2 and C3 lists were used. Since some persons absolutely refused to allow the operator to hypnotize them, and others had obvious inhibitions, we tried Watson's test of Fairmindedness. The other personality test used was the Pressey X-O affectivity test. Deviations from normal are counted as an "idiosyncrasy" score.

In addition we measured intelligence by means of the Psychological Examination of the American Council on Education.

For the study of hypnotic susceptibility a scale of an entirely new sort was devised by one of the writers, Mr. Davis. This scale was evolved with the particular object in mind of determining trance depth and it came about as the results of research with more than one hundred subjects. This objective method of scoring we feel to be justified by the fact that consistency in trance behavior was observed. For example, if muscular catalepsies could not be induced, anaesthesias were never successful. Other consistencies were likewise noticed.

This scale is reproduced in full in Table I. It will be noticed that we class five main states, with several quantitative subdivisions under each. The first group contained those who were absolutely insusceptible and who consequently were scored 0.

The lightest trance conditions, the hypnoidal, are characterized by a subjective sensation of drowsiness, heaviness of the limbs, and narrowing of attention; objectively there is the failure of the eyes to keep focused, a fluttering of the lids, and a physical relaxation. These symptoms, as the table shows, were scored from 1 to 5, depending upon their persistence.

In the light trance, catalepsy of the eye muscle was used as the criterion of the induction of the trance. It was found that this was one of the first objective symptoms of the trance which could be induced, and unless it appeared no further symptoms of the trance could be brought about. Catalepsies of the limbs, depending upon the success with which they could be induced, were used as the basis for further scoring of this stage of the trance. Additional subjective symptoms occasionally were reported by the subjects; the lethargy which characterized the lighter hypnoidal condition was replaced by lightness, and increasing drowsiness was noticed. Dissociation at this stage was far from complete, however, and no amnesia was observable.

TABLE I

Hypnotic Susceptibility Scoring System

Depth	Score	Objective Symptoms
Insusceptible	0	
Hypnoidal	1	
	2	Relaxation
	3	Fluttering of lids
	4	Closing of eyes
	5	Complete physical relaxation
Light Trance	6	Catalepsy of eyes
	7	Limb catalepsies
	10	Rigid catalepsy
	11	Anaesthesia (glove)
Medium Trance	13	Partial amnesia
	15	Post-hypnotic anaesthesia
	17	Personality changes
	18	Simple post-hypnotic suggestions
	20	Kinaesthetic delusions; complete amnesia

	21	Ability to open eyes without affecting trance
	23	Bizarre post-hypnotic suggestions
	25	Complete somnambulism
	26	Positive visual hallucinations, post-hypnotic
Somnambulistic Trance	27	Positive auditory hallucinations, post-hypnotic
	28	Systematized post-hypnotic amnesia
	29	Negative auditory hallucinations
	30	Negative visual hallucinations; hyperaesthesias

In the medium trance state sensory anaesthesias can be induced in the trance, but ordinarily do not remain post-hypnotically. The anaesthesia is not profound, but is usually reported as a diminution of sensitivity over the area suggested. Post-hypnotic suggestions can be successfully produced in this stage, provided they are of a simple and logical nature. A partial amnesia is characteristic. Ordinarily the subject remembers vaguely what was said to him in the trance.

In the deepest, the somnambulistic, stage of the trance, a complete amnesia was used as the criterion. Post-hypnotic suggestions of the most bizarre order are meticulously carried out; the subject can open his eyes, talk, walk about, and behave naturally without the trance depth being affected in the least. All manner of hallucinations are possible, those of a kinaesthetic nature being the most readily induced, both in the trance and post-hypnotically. Auditory and visual hallucinations may be induced with almost equal facility, although negative visual hallucinations post-hypnotically induced seem to be the most difficult.

It must be admitted that the use of a quantitative index is necessarily arbitrary. However, the symptoms ordinarily occur in a certain sequence, and we have been unable to find any evidence for possible "critical points" which might indicate progress of hypnosis to be qualitative, that is by large steps rather than by gradual increments.

The method of inducing the trance is the most important consideration. In any hypnotic experiment so much of the success depends upon both the personality of the operator and the technique used in inducing the trance that standardization is essential for the results to be at all reliable.

So far as possible external conditions were controlled. All subjects were hypnotized in the same room, under exactly the same conditions of light, warmth, and comfort. No persons other than the operator and the subject were permitted in the room while an experiment was being conducted. In nearly every case the first trials were conducted in the late afternoon. The operator's remarks were, within limits, also standardized.

The subjects were hypnotized after the method of Braid, through the fixed gaze technique. Cooperation was, of course, essential to the successful induction of the trance, and in all but three cases it was obtained. In inducing the trance no suggestions were made until the lids began to flutter and the pulse rate, observed from the throat arteries, slowed to normal. It was noticed that all the subjects, most of whom were quite naive concerning hypnosis, were at first somewhat excited and anxious. Therefore it seemed best to awaken the subject almost immediately after the first trance states had been obtained. The subject's confidence in the operator sometimes wavers if this is not done; occasionally the first venture into a trance frightens a person, and any difficulty which might have been encountered in awakening a subject from a deep trance state is avoided through this careful training.

Th symptoms were suggested separately, usually in the order in which they appear in Table I. If one symptom could not be induced despite repeated suggestion, the next more difficult was attempted; but, as was previously mentioned, it was only very rarely that the more difficult suggestions were successful when the simpler ones had failed. In the trance, training plays such a large part in the success with which the operator can induce successively deeper states that it is absolutely necessary for one to proceed from the simple to the complex; for if a difficult suggestion fails, it is with much greater difficulty that even a simple one may succeed afterward.

In inducing symptoms the same phenomena were always suggested. Catalepsies of the eye were attempted first, then of the arm and leg, and then of total muscular rigidity. Post-hypnotic suggestions ranged from a simple act like crossing the legs or getting up and turning out the light, to such complex behavior as calling the experimenter on the phone the noon following the conclusion of the experiment, or eating dinner only with the left hand. Glove anaesthesias alone were attempted, with sensations of touch, pain, pressure, and kinaesthesis removed. Visual hallucinations ranged from the sound of the class bell in the hall to whole conversations carried on between visually hallucinated fairies who sat upon the edge of the table. Post-hypnotic aphasias and agraphias were attempted in several cases with good results; automatic writing was successfully carried out in three cases; and post-hypnotic intoxication was successful in seven out of ten cases.

The intelligence test was given in groups whenever possible, and some of the personality tests. However, scoring was not done until after the hypnotic tests were run, in order that any possible bias on the part of the operator might not arise.

RESULTS

The experimentation was, on the whole, rather lacking in positive results. Table II gives the correlations between the various personality traits and hypnotic susceptibility. The only trait which shows an appreciable correlation at all for both groups is intelligence, and even here it is so low that the test could not be used with any degree of reliability of prediction, particularly for individual cases. For women the coefficient of +.23 indicates a slight relation between introversion and susceptibility, but it is highly uncertain and may easily have been due to chance.

TABLE II

Correlations Between Hypnotic Susceptibility
and Personality Traits

Trait	Men	Women
Intelligence	.37±.06	.31±.06
Maladjustment	—.05±.12	.14±.11
Introversion	.05±.12	.23±.07
Prejudice	—.01±.12	—.02±.12
Affectivity	.06±.12	—.18±.09

The correlation between intelligence and susceptibility seems reasonably valid. A subject who cannot fix his attention on one thing for any length of time cannot be successful either in a time-performance test or as a hypnotic subject. The difficulty in both cases is probably as much emotional as intellectual, but since the extent of emotionality as measured by the Pressey test correlated only .19 with intelligence, we have no objective evidence for this opinion.

Data given by groups, in the manner of Table III, often show trends more clearly than the correlation coefficient alone.

It is evident from an inspection of this table that a distinct sex difference exists on this test. The affectivity scores are seen to decrease with intelligence for the men, but with women they go with lack of intelligence. Further inquiry into this matter should prove enlightening.

TABLE III

Relation Between Intelligence and Affectivity

Group	Affectivity Score Men	Women
Six most intelligent	194	144
Mean: 30 men, 25 women	188	159
Six least intelligent	177	166

Concerning the claim of Pierre Janet that susceptibility is linked with neurotic tendencies (2) the evidence is entire negative, as shown by the correlation of —.05 between susceptibility and the Thurstone Personal Inventory Schedule. This provided, of course, that we assume both measures to be reasonably valid.

The very slight positive correlations between introversion and hypnotic susceptibility lend no support to the hypothesis of Bernheim and the Nancy School, that an introvert makes a better subject. The correlations are so insignificant that they cannot be construed as even indicative. Suggestibility has been assumed to be dependent upon introversion, and since nearly all writers conclude that the trance is essentially a matter of heightened suggestibility, either the hypothesis is incorrect or the test does not measure introversion.

The lack of correlation (—.01) between fairmindedness as measured by the Watson test and susceptibility shows that either prejudice has nothing to do with success as a hypnotic subject or else that it is so specific that a general test of this nature would not uncover it.

The absence of any significant correlation between affectivity and susceptibility is evidence against the psychoanalytic theory concerning hypnotic predisposition (Freud, 3). In five somnambulistic cases studied, the sexually connotative words in the Pressey test which were crossed out formed only 21 percent of the total. In five other cases, picked at random, the results were practically the same — 23 percent.

A comparative study of the sexes in regard to hypnotic susceptibility and personality traits should prove interesting. Table IV shows the differences among the quartiles for both men and women in regard to susceptibility.

It will be noticed from a comparison of the mean scores for the two groups that the women rank considerably higher than do the men in intelligence. The mean percentile score for the men is 82, while that for the women is 96. This variation can be explained by the fact that most of the women were upper-classmen, while some of the men were freshmen in college.

The fact brought out by the correlation between intelligence and susceptibility is again obvious here; the most intelligent persons are generally the most susceptible to hypnosis. There are a few exceptions to this generalization, of course. For example, the subject who made the highest intelligence score showed susceptibility of only 3; on the other hand, the second most intelligent subject rated 25 on the scale.

In regard to introversion the experimentation brought some interesting results to light. A distinct sex difference is evident; the most susceptible men are unusually introverted, while the most susceptible women are highly extroverted. However, the least susceptible men are also more introverted than the average, and correspondingly the least susceptible women score more toward the extrovert end than their average.

The affectivity distribution for women shows the same bimodal tendency, although the correlation of —.18 shows an inverse trend quite opposed to the Freudian viewpoint. The slight upward trend for men indicated in the table is more or less in line with the Freudian point of view, but is largely offset by the inconclusive correlation of +.06.

It was found that a large percentage of subjects studied were susceptible to at least the lighter stages of the trance. Table V, following, shows the percentages in the various groups formed

TABLE V

Hypnotic Susceptibility Frequencies

Trance State	Scale	Percentages		
		Men	Women	Total
Insusceptible	0	13	4	9%
Hynoidal state only	1- 5	30	28	29
Light trance	6-10	17	20	18
Medium trance	11-20	10	20	15
Somnambulistic trance	21-30	30	28	29

by classing the subjects in accordance with the stage of trance to which they proved susceptible. The figures give us the facts that from an unselected sample of college students, 9 percent were unwilling to permit the operator to hypnotize them, 43 percent were susceptible to trance states deeper than that required to produce anaesthetic phenomena and 29 percent were somnambuls. These percentages, while not as high as those reported by some psychiatrists, indicate that at least two persons out of five are susceptible to the deeper hypnotic states and that one in five will display all possible symptoms.

The susceptibility percentages reported by Bernheim range as high as 90 percent, but his uniformly successful induction of the trance probably depended in large measure upon his remarkable reputation and upon his selective sampling. The results found here are, we believe, more nearly general and probably would vary but little with more extended investigation.

SUMMARY

This paper has been devoted to a study of the relation of various personality traits, as measured by several well known tests, by hypnotic susceptibility as measured upon a specially devised scale.

Fifty-five subjects were used in the experiment, twenty-five women and thirty men. It was found that 43 percent were susceptible to the medium and deep trance states, while 29 percent fell into somnamublistic trances. No significant sex differences in susceptibility were observed.

A correlation of +.34 between susceptibility and intelligence was obtained as a result of the investigation. No other correlation, except possibly one of +.23 between susceptibility and introversion in women, had any significance at all. Tabular results brought out the fact that there was a distinct sex difference in the relation of affectivity to intelligence: it appears to be positively correlated with intelligence with men, but negatively with women.

The results of the study tend to refute the claims of Janet that susceptibility to hypnosis is dependent upon neurotic traits, as neither the correlations nor the tabular data disclosed any significant relations along this line.

The Freudian assumption, the sexuality is related to susceptibility, likewise furnished distinctly negative results. Also the claim of the Nancy School that hypnosis is simply a matter of suggestibility was studied, but with indifferent results.

---

*From *Journal of Abnormal and Social Psychology*, **26, Ap. 1931-** Mr. 1932.

CONCERNING THE NATURE AND CHARACTER OF POST-HYPNOTIC BEHAVIOR*

MILTON H. ERICKSON, M.D. and ELIZABETH MOORE ERICKSON
ELOISE HOSPITAL, ELOISE, MICH.

EDITOR'S NOTE

This is perhaps the only intensive study of the nature of post-hypnotic phenomena. It is an attempt to understand the true nature of the psychological mechanism involved. Since the hypnotic trance is terminated before the post-hypnotic behavior is elicited, its exact relationship to the trance needs investigation. It suggests a temporary dissociation and a return momentarily to the state of trance where it had its origin. It serves incidentally as a check on the validity of the trance.

Despite the general familiarity of post-hypnotic behavior and its extensive role in both experimental and therapeutic work, little recognition has been given to it as a problem complete in itself. Instead, attention had been focused almost exclusively upon the various activities suggested to the subjects as post-hypnotic tasks, with little heed given to the nature of the behavior characterizing, if not constituting, the post-hypnotic state, and which influences and perhaps determines the nature and extent of the suggested post- hypnotic performance. Emphasis has been placed primarily upon the results obtained from post-hypnotic suggestions and not upon the character or nature of the psychological setting in which they were secured. The study of the mental processes and the patterns of behavior upon which those results are based and which must necessarily be in effect in some manner previous to, if not also during, the post-hypnotic performance, has been neglected. Yet, despite a lack of adequate experimental provision, there has been a general recognition of certain significant facts regarding the post-hypnotic performance, which imply directly the existence of a special mental state or condition constituting the background out of which the post-hypnotic act derives.

Foremost among these facts is the occurrence of the post-hypnotic act in response to a suggestion which is remote from the situation in which it has its effect. Next, the immediate stimulus, post-hypnotic signal or cue eliciting the post-hypnotic act serves only to establish the time for the activity and not the kind of behavior, since this is determined by other factors. Also, the post-hypnotic act is not consciously motivated but derives out of a remote situation of which the subject is not consciously aware. Finally, it is not an integrated part of the behavior of the total situation in which it occurs, but is actually disruptive of the conscious stream of activity, with which it may be entirely at variance.

A DEFINITION OF THE POST-HYPNOTIC ACT

We have found the following definition of the post-hypnotic act to be consistently applicable and useful, since it serves to describe adequately a form of behavior we have elicited innumerable times in a great variety of situations and from a large number of subjects, ranging in type from the feeble-minded to the highly intelligent, from the normal to the psychotic, and in age from children to middle-aged adults. For the moment, we shall limit this definition strictly to the act itself, without regard for partial performances resulting from light trances or for certain other important considerations which will be discussed later. A post-hypnotic act has been found to be one performed by the hypnotic subject after awakening from a trance, in response to suggestions given during the trance state, with the execution of the act marked by an absence of any demonstrable conscious awareness in the subject of the underlying cause and motive for his act. We have come to regard as valid this form of the post-hypnotic act since its performance is invariably characterized by definitive and highly significant attributive behavior.

THE BEHAVIOR CHARACTERIZING THE POST-HYPNOTIC
PERFORMANCE

This important attributive behavior belonging to the post-hypnotic response consists of the spontaneous and invariable development, as an integral part of the performance of the suggested post-hypnotic act, of a self-limited, usually brief, hypnotic trance. In other words, we have observed repeatedly, under varying circumstances and in a great variety of situations, that the hypnotized subject, instructed to execute some act post-hypnotically, invariably develops spontaneously a hypnotic trance. This trance is usually of brief duration, occurs in direct relation to the performance of the post-hypnotic act, and apparently constitutes an essential part of the process of response to and execution of the post-hypnotic command. Its development has been found to be an invariable occurrence despite certain apparent exceptions, which will be discussed later, and regardless of the demands of the post-hypnotic suggestion, which may entail a long, complicated form of behavior, the introduction of a single word into a casual conversation, the development of an emotional response or attitude at a given stimulus, an avoidance reaction or even a slight modification of general behavior. Furthermore, the development of a trance state as a part of the post-hypnotic performance requires for its appearance neither suggestion nor instruction. This special trance state occurs as readily in the naive as in the highly trained subject; its manifestations, as we shall show, differ essentially in no way from those of an ordinary induced trance; and it seems to be a function of the process of initiating in the immediate situation a response to the post-hypnotic suggestion given in a previous trance.

THE GENERAL CHARACTER OF THE SPONTANEOUS
POST-HYPNOTIC TRANCE

The spontaneous post-hypnotic trance is usually single in appearance, develops at the moment of initiation of the post-hypnotic act, and persists usually for only a moment or two; hence, it is easily overlooked, despite certain residual effects it has upon the general behavior. Under various circumstances, and with different subjects, however, the trance may be multiple in appearance, constituting actually a succession of brief spontaneous trances related to aspects or phases of the post-hypnotic act. It may appear in a prolonged form and persist throughout the greater part or even the entire duration of the post-hypnotic performance; or there may be an irregular succession of relatively short and long spontaneous trances, apparently in relation to the difficulties, mental and physical, encountered in the course of the execution of the post-hypnotic act. In general, any variation in the form or the time of its appearance or reappearances seems to be a function of individual differences in the subjects and of the difficulties occasioned by the general situation or by the post-hypnotic act itself.

SPECIFIC MANIFESTATIONS OF THE SPONTANEOUS POST-HYPNOTIC TRANCE

The specific hypnotic manifestations which develop in relation to the performance of the post-hypnotic act form an essentially constant pattern, although the duration of the separate items of behavior varies greatly both in accord with the purpose served and with the individual subject. They occur rapidly in direct relation to the giving of the specified cue for the post-hypnotic act, with a tendency toward the following sequence: A slight pause in the subject's immediate activity, a facial expression of distraction and detachment, a peculiar glassiness of the eyes with a dilatation of the pupils and a failure to focus, a condition of catalepsy, a fixity and narrowing of attention, an intentness of purpose, a marked loss of contact with the general environment, and an unresponsiveness to any external stimulus until the post-hypnotic act is either in progress or has been completed, depending upon the actual duration of the trance state itself and the demands of the post-hypnotic task. Even after the trance state has ceased, these manifestations, somewhat modified, continue as residual effects upon the subject, and result in the intent, rigid, and almost compulsive nature of his behavior, and his state of absorption and general unresponsiveness until he has reoriented himself to the immediate situation.

Similarly, to a slight degree, the disappearance of the trance state, or, to a much greater degree, the completion of the post-hypnotic performance, is marked by a brief interval of confusion and disorientation from which the subject quickly recovers by renewed and close attention to the immediate situation. Especially does this confusion and disorientation become marked if, during the state of absorption in the post-hypnotic performance, there occurred any significant change or alteration in the general situation. In addition, there is usually evidence of an amnesia, either partial or complete, for both the post-hypnotic act and the concurrent events arising out of the immediate situation. In those instances in which the subject does have a recollection of the course of events, investigation will disclose his memories to be hazy, faulty, and frequently more deductions than memories, based upon his interpretations and rationalizations of the situation to which he has reoriented himself. Occasionally, however, despite a poor recollection of or a complete amnesia for the attendant circumstances, a subject may recall clearly the entire post-hypnotic performance, but will regard it merely as an isolated, unaccountable, circumscribed impulsion, or, more often, a compulsion having no connection with the immediate or general situation.

An example illustrative of many of these points is the following account given in a hesitating, uncertain fashion by a subject upon the completion of a post-hypnotic act:

"We were talking about something, just what I've forgotten now, when I suddenly saw that book and I simply had to go over and pick it up and look at it—I don't know why—I just felt I had to—a sudden impulse, I suppose. Then I came back to my chair. It just happened that way. But you must have seen me because I must have had to walk around you to get it —I don't see any other way I could have reached it. Then when I laid it down again, I must have put those other books on top of it. At least, I don't think anybody else did, since I don't remember anybody else being on that side of the room—but I wasn't paying much attention to anything, I guess, because, although I know I looked carefully at that book and opened it, I don't even know the author or the title — probably fiction from the looks of it. Anyway, it was a funny thing to do—probably an impulse of the moment and doesn't mean a thing. What was it we were discussing?"

THE DEMONSTRATION AND TESTING OF THE SPONTANEOUS POST-HYPNOTIC TRANCE

Although the various forms of hypnotic behavior spontaneously manifested by the subject in relation to post-hypnotic acts constitute actually a demonstration of a trance state, their brevity and self-limited character necessitate special measures for a satisfactory examination of them and for a testing of their significance.

This may be done readily without distorting or altering significantly the actual hypnotic situation, since the giving of the post-hypnotic cue or signal serves to reestablish that state of rapport existing at the time the post-hypnotic suggestion was given. The task of such a demonstration, however, as experience will show, requires a considerable degree of skill. Usually it is most easily and effectively done by some form of interference, either with the post-hypnotic act itself or with the subject after the post-hypnotic response has been initiated but not yet completed. The demonstration of the trance state may follow one of two courses, depending upon the presence or the absence of hypnotic rapport between the demonstrator and the subject. If there be a state of rapport, the interference may be directed either to the subject or to his performance, and the trance manifestations are of the positive responsive type, characteristic of the relationship between hypnotist and subject. In the absence of rapport, effective interference must be directed primarily to the act itself and the trance manifestations are of the negative, unresponsive type, characteristic of the hypnotized subject's unresponsiveness to and detachment from that which is not included in the hypnotic situation. In both instances, however, the general and specific behavior obtained is wholly in keeping with that which would be obtained under similar circumstances from the same subject in an ordinary induced hypnotic trance.

The interference most effective in demonstrating the trance is that offered by the hypnotist or by some person actually in rapport with the subject when the post-hypnotic suggestion was given in the original trance. It is best accomplished at the exact moment of initiation of the post-hypnotic response by some measure serving to counteract or to alter the original post-hypnotic suggestion, or to compel the subject to give special attention to the hypnotist, as, for example, the deliberate removal of the object which the subject was instructed to examine; the manipulation of the subject in such a fashion as to effect the development of catalepsy in one or both arms, thus rendering the examination difficult or impossible, or the use, even with naive subjects who have had no previous training, of such vague verbal suggestions as, "Wait a moment, just a moment," "Don't let anything change now," "Stay as you are right now, never mind that," "I'd rather talk to you now," or, "I will be waiting as soon as you have done it," and similar remarks implying that an additional assignment may be made.

The effect of such interference is usually a complete arrest of the subject's responses followed by an apparent waiting for further instructions, while his appearance and manner suggest a state identical with that of the deep trance as ordinarily induced, and all the customary phenomena of the deep hypnotic trance, can be elicited from him. Then, if he is allowed to return to the performance of the post-hypnotic task, a spontaneous awakening will ensue in due course, permitting an immediate and direct contrast of waking and hypnotic behavior as well as a demonstration of an amnesia for the post-hypnotic act, the interference, and the events of the trance state. If, however, no use is made of the peculiar state of responsiveness established by the interference with him, the subject tends to return to the problem of the post-hypnotic task. The sequence of his behavior thereafter is essentially as if there had been no interference, but there is then a marked tendency for the spontaneous trance state to persist until the post-hypnotic task has been completed. Especially is this true if the interference has rendered the task more difficult. Occasionally, however, instead of being arrested in his behavior, the subject may proceed uninterruptedly with his post-hypnotic task, and, upon its completion appear to be awaiting further instruction. The phenomena of the deep trance state can then be elicited, but if this is done, it becomes necessary to awaken the subject at the finish.

To illustrate briefly, since other examples will be given later, a subject was told that, shortly after his awakening, a certain topic of conversation would be introduced, whereupon he was to leave his chair immediately, cross the room and, with his left hand, pick up a small statuette and place it on top of a certain bookcase. At the proper time, as the subject stepped in front of the hypnotist to cross the room, his left arm was gently raised above his head, where it remained in a cataleptic state. The subject continued on his way without hesitation but, upon approaching the statuette, he apparently found himself unable to lower his left arm and turned to the hypnotist as if awaiting further instruction. Thereupon, he was used to demonstrate a variety of the usual phenomena of the ordinary induced trance. Upon the completion of this demonstration, he was instructed simply, "All right, you may go ahead now." In response to this vague suggestion, the subject returned to the interrupted post-hypnotic performance, completed it, and resumed his original seat, awakening spontaneously with a complete amnesia for all of the events intervening between the giving of the cue and his awakening and without even an awareness that he had altered his position in the chair.

This same procedure of interference was repeated upon another subject with essentially the same results. When, however, the hypnotist made no response to the subject's expectant attitude, there occurred a fairly rapid disappearance of the catalepsy, a performance of the task, and a return to his seat, followed by a spontaneous waking with a complete amnesia for the entire experience.

SPECIAL TYPES OF SPONTANEOUS POST-HYPNOTIC TRANCE BEHAVIOR

In those instances in which the interference is not given at the proper moment, while it usually has the effect of intensifying and prolonging greatly the duration of the spontaneous trance, the subject may respond to it by bewilderment and confusion succeeded by a laborious compulsive performance of the post-hypnotic act and an overcoming of the interference. Again, he may misinterpret the interruption of his task as a coincidental and meaningless, though obstructive, occurrence which is to be disregarded; or he may behave as if there really had been none.

This last type of behavior is of a remarkable character. It appears in other connections than the situation of mistimed interference, and may serve widely different purposes for the same or different subjects. Thus, it may occur when the inter-ference is limited to the purpose of demonstrating the trance state without affecting the actual performance of the post-hypnotic act. In this case, the subject merely ignores the most persistent efforts on the part of the hypnotist, completes his post-hypnotic task, and awakens spontaneously with a total amnesia for the entire occurrence. Frequently, it develops when the possibility of the post-hypnotic act has been nullified; and it often appears when the post-hypnotic suggestion is rendered objectionable in character to the subject or too difficult as a result of the interference. But of most interest is its tendency to occur almost invariably when, upon the initiation of the post-hypnotic behavior, some person, not in rapport with the subject, intrudes into the situation by means of an interference directed primarily to the post-hypnotic act.

Although these situations differ greatly, the pattern of the subject's behavior is essentially the same for all of them, and the general course of the subject's responses in each type of situation is adequately exemplified in the following accounts: At the previously established post-hypnotic cue, the subject glanced across the room at an easily visible book lying on a table and proceeded to rise from his chair for the purpose of securing the book and placing it in the bookcase in accord with the previously given post-hypnotic instructions. As he shifted his position in his chair, preparatory to rising, an assistant, not in rapport with the subject, quickly removed and concealed the book, this being done at a moment when the subject's gaze was directed elsewhere. Despite this absolute interference with the post-hypnotic act, the subject unhesitatingly performed the task by apparently hallucinating the book, and gave no evidence of any realization that something unusual had occurred. This same procedure, repeated with other subjects, has led in more than one instance to an even more hallucinatory and delusional response, namely, upon actually noting that the book had vanished, glancing at the bookcase in a bewildered fashion, and then apparently hallucinating the book in the place suggested for it and assuming that they have just completed the task. As one subject spontaneously explained:

"It's funny how absent-minded you can get. For a minute there

I intended to put that book in the bookcase, when actually I had just finished doing so. I suppose that's because it annoyed me so much just lying there that the thing before my mind was the doing of it, and that I hadn't got around yet to knowing that I had already done it." Yet, upon resuming her seat, she spontaneously awakened and demonstrated a total amnesia inclusive even of her explanatory remarks.

Repetition of the procedure with these and with other subjects, but with the removal of the book effected while the subject's gaze was directed at it, sometimes led to similar results in that the removal of the book was not detected, thereby indirectly disclosing the defectiveness of the hypnotic subject's contact with the external environment and the tendency to substitute memory images for reality objects, behavior highly characteristic of the hypnotic state. In other instances, the new position of the book was detected and the original position regarded as an illusion. Also, in some instances, plausible misconstructions were placed upon the new position or the detected movement, as, for example: "Why, who left this book lying in this chair? I remember distinctly seeing it on the table," or, "I've been expecting that book to slip off the pile on the table all evening and at last it has. Do you mind if I put it in the bookcase?" And, depending upon the actual experimental situation, the real or an hallucinatory book would be recovered from the chair or the floor, and the post-hypnotic act would be performed, with the customary sequence of events.

Following this general type of post-hypnotic behavior, there develops either an amnesia complete in character and inclusive of both the post-hypnotic act and the attendant circumstances, as well as of the subject's interpolated behavior, or, less frequently, a peculiar admixture of amnesia and fragmentary memories. These partial memories often tend to be remarkably clear, vivid, and distracting in character, and they may relate to the absolute facts or even to the hallucinatory and delusional items of the post-hypnotic trance period. For example, the last subject quoted above, when questioned for her recollections, recalled only that the hypnotist had a habit of piling books, papers, folders, and journals in untidy heaps, but she was unable to give a specific example of this practice. Another subject, in a similar experimental situation, remembered most vividly minute and utterly irrelevant details about the goldfish in the fish globe used only as a part of the environmental setting for the post-hypnotic act, and he was most insistent that these memories constituted a complete account of the entire occurrence. Nevertheless, some weeks later the subject disclaimed any memory of having made such statements.

THE EFFECT OF TIME UPON THE DEVELOPMENT OF THE SPONTANEOUS POST-HYPNOTIC TRANCE

One other general consideration in relation to the development of a spontaneous trance upon the initiation of the post-hypnotic behavior concerns the possible effect of the lapse of time. In this regard, on a considerable number of occasions, subjects have been given specific instructions in the form of a post-hypnotic suggestion to perform some simple act, the nature of which varied from subject to subject. This act was to be "done without fail on the occasion of our next meeting." Among these subjects were some who were not seen after the giving of such post-hypnotic suggestions for varying periods of months. Of this group, all carried out the post-hypnotic act, developing as they did so a spontaneous trance. Two other subjects were actually not seen until three years later and another two were not seen for four and five years respectively, during which periods of time there was no form of contact between the hypnotist and the subjects. Nevertheless, at chance meetings with them, the performance of the post-hypnotic act and the development of a concomitant spontaneous trance state occurred.

APPARENT EXCEPTIONS TO THE RULE OF SPONTANEOUS POST-HYPNOTIC TRANCES

However, before continuing with a discussion of various significances of the spontaneous post-hypnotic trance, it may be well to offer an explanation of the apparently absolute exceptions, mentioned previously, to the development of a spontaneous trance in relation to the execution of post-hypnotic suggestions.

These exceptions, in which there is a performance post-hypnotically of the trance-suggested act without the apparent development of a spontaneous trance, arise usually from certain conditions which will be listed generally and illustrated as follows:

1. Failure of the development of an amnesia for the post-hypnotic suggestions: In this situation there may be actually no post-hypnotic performance as such, since the subject understands from the beginning the underlying motivations and cause of his behavior, and hence, acts at a level of conscious awareness. Consequently, the performance becomes similar in character to one suggested to a person in the ordinary waking state and it is post-hypnotic only in its time relationships.

In such instances, the act is essentially voluntary in character, although frequently another element may enter into the situation, namely, a sense of being compelled to perform the specified task, despite the subject's apparently complete understanding of the situation. Thus, the subject may remember his instructions and be fully aware of what he is to do and why he is to do it, and yet experience an overwhelming compulsion that causes him to perform the act with literally no choice on his part. Occasionally, however, the subject, in responding to this compulsion and executing the post-hypnotic instructions, develops, as he performs the task, a spontaneous trance. This trance often serves to establish for the subject a more or less complete amnesia for the instructions, for the period of waiting with its usually unpleasant compulsive feelings, and for the act itself. The trance is similar in character to that which develops in the ordinary post-hypnotic situation, with the exception that the amnesia it may cause tends to be more limited. Thus, the subject may remember the post-hypnotic suggestions, the period of waiting, and the feeling of compulsion, but have a complete amnesia for his actual performance. Or he may develop an amnesia for the post-hypnotic instructions but remember experiencing a compulsion to perform an apparently irrational act. However, in some instances, the spontaneous trance serves as a defense mechanism against the compulsive feelings rather than as an essential or an integral part of the atypical post-trance performance. Finally, the development of compulsive feelings constitutes a marked alteration of the essential nature of the entire pattern of behavior.

2. Failure to make clear to the subject that the post-hypnotic instructions given concern the act itself and not the process of making provision for such an act: Thus, the subject, instructed to perform a certain task post-hypnotically, may, after awakening, go through a mental process of realizing, sometimes vaguely, sometimes clearly, that a certain act is to be performed and then simply hold himself in readiness for that act. Hence, upon the performance of the task, no spontaneous trance occurs. However, this does not constitute a negation of the statement that a spontaneous trance always accompanies the post-hypnotic performance, since close observation of the subject in this situation will disclose that a spontaneous trance invariably accompanies this process of making ready for the act, provided that this understanding of his task occurs definitely after the subject has awakened from the trance in which the suggestion was given and not while he is going through a slow process of awakening, in which case the situation would become similar to that of the failure to develop amnesia.

3. Unwillingness on the part of the subject to perform the post-hypnotic act, except as a deliberate act of choice on his part:

Thus the subject may, for some reason or whim, object to the purely responsive character of a post-hypnotic performance and react by making his response one of deliberate intention. In this situation, as in the foregoing example, there occurs upon awakening the same process of making ready for the suggested task, and hence, upon the proper signal, the post-hypnotic performance is executed without the development of a spontaneous trance. However, this process of making ready for the act is again accompanied by a spontaneous trance.

4.   The failure of the amnesia for the trance experiences: This is the most common and consists essentially in the spontaneous recovery of the memories of the events and experiences of the trance state. For example, the subject instructed to perform a post-hypnotic act at a given time after awakening, may, before the specified time, more or less slowly begin to recall his various trance experiences, among them the post-hypnotic instructions. This process of recollection is not one of preparation for the post-hypnotic performance, but constitutes rather a recovery of memories, motivated usually by a sense of curiosity, and it is free from any purposeful significance in relation to the actual suggested post-hypnotic task. Literally, it is a breaking through of memories because of an inadequacy of amnesic barriers. With the recovery of the memory of the post-hypnotic suggestions a somewhat similar situation obtains as exists when there is a failure of the development of an amnesia for post-hypnotic suggestion, which has been described above. In general, while this type of behavior is most common, it is exceedingly difficult to understand fully because there is first an amnesia for and then a recollection of post-hypnotic instructions and because the memories, however complete eventually, are recovered in a fragmentary fashion.

Hence, the failure, apparent or absolute, to develop a spontaneous trance upon the initiation of the execution of an act suggested as a post-hypnotic performance does not necessarily constitute a contradiction of our observation. Rather, it implies that there may occur within the subject certain changes in the psychological situation. These, in turn, may serve to alter or to transform the character of the post-hypnotic act itself and thus to render it one for which the subject has a preliminary awareness as well as an understanding of its underlying nature and cause. Hence, the act becomes transformed into one post-hypnotic in time relationships only.

SIGNIFICANCES OF THE SPONTANEOUS POST-HYPNOTIC TRANCE

The significances of the spontaneous trance state as an integral part of the execution of post-hypnotic suggestions are numerous and bear upon many important hypnotic questions. In particular, they relate to such problems as the establishment of objective criteria for trance states and conditions, the training of subjects to develop more profound trances, and the direct elicitation of various hypnotic phenomena without a preliminary process of suggestion for trance induction. In addition, the post-hypnotic trance bears upon the general problem of dissociation, the various problems of individual hypnotic phenomena, such as rapport, amnesia, selective memories, catalepsy and dissociated states, and the general experimental and therapeutic implications of post-hypnotic phenomena. Discussion of some of these considerations will be given in connection with our investigative work, but the reader will note that the experimental findings serve also to illustrate many points not directly mentioned.

THE SPONTANEOUS POST-HYPNOTIC TRANCE AS A CRITERION
OF THE INDUCED HYPNOTIC TRANCE

In relation to the establishment of criteria for trance states, our experience has been that the spontaneous post-hypnotic trance constitutes a reliable indicator of the validity of the original trance, and in this belief we have been confirmed by the experience reported to us by others. Apparently, the post-hypnotic trance is a phenomenon of sequence; it is based upon the original trance and constitutes actually a revivification of the hypnotic elements of that trance. Especially does this inference seem to be warranted since careful observation will often disclose an absolute continuance in the spontaneous post-hypnotic trance of the behavior patterns belonging actually to the original trance state. This may be illustrated by the following experimental findings, made originally by chance and since repeated on other subjects: During a single hypnotic trance, the hypnotist gave a large number of unrelated post-hypnotic suggestions, each of which was to be performed later as a separate task and in response to separate cues. Also, during the course of that trance, the subject's state of rapport with two observers was made to vary from time to time by suggestions independent of the post-hypnotic suggestions. Subsequently, upon the execution of the post-hypnotic suggestions, the spontaneous trance states that developed showed remarkable variations, in that the subject, while always in rapport with the hypnotist, variously manifested rapport with one or the other or both or neither of the two observers. Although this was not understood at the time, subsequent checking of the record disclosed that the state of rapport manifested in each spontaneous post-hypnotic trance state constituted an accurate reflection of the exact state of rapport existing at the time of the giving of the particular post-hypnotic suggestion. Aside from the question of the continuance of patterns of behavior, the bearing of this finding upon the question of rapport is at once apparent.

Since then investigative work has disclosed that proper wording of post-hypnotic suggestions may effect either a continuance or an absence in the spontaneous trance of the general behavior patterns belonging to the trance state in which the post-hypnotic suggestion was given. Thus, the giving of post-hypnotic suggestions so worded as to carry an implication of a change or an alteration of the situation may militate against the evocation of

original trance behavior. Yet, the same suggestion so worded
as to carry immediate as well as remote implications will usually
serve to effect a continuance of the original trance behavior. To
illustrate: During experimental work on this problem, it was
found that this wording of a post-hypnotic suggestion, "As I
jingle my keys, you will invariably——," often served to cause
a continuance in the spontaneous post-hypnotic trance of the
behavior patterns belonging to the original trance, while "To-
morrow, or whenever I jingle my keys, you will invariably——,"
would fail in the same subject to elicit the behavior patterns of
the original trance, since this wording implied possible changes
in the situation. However, extensive work has shown that the
behavior of subjects in carrying over the patterns of response
belonging to the original trance is highly individualistic. Some
almost invariably do so, others seldom or never, some almost
wholly, others only in selected relationships, and the outcome
of any experimental work is highly unpredictable, depending
apparently upon the individuality of the subject as well as his
immediate understandings. Hence, extreme care in wording
suggestions is highly essential and it should never be assumed
that the subject's understanding of instructions is identical with
that of the hypnotist. Neither should there be the assumption
that an identical wording must necessarily convey an identical
meaning to different subjects.

In other words, the "standardized technique," or the giving
of identical suggestions to different subjects, described by Hull,
is not, as he appears to believe, a controlled method for eliciting
the same degree or type of response, but merely a measure of
demonstrating the general limitations of such a technique.

Another type of evidence concerning the validity of the original
trance is the failure to develop a spontaneous trance when apparently executing a post-hypnotic suggestion, by subjects who
were merely complaisantly cooperative or who were over-eager
to believe that they were in a trance, or who, for various reasons,

simulated effectively being hypnotized. In direct contrast to these subjects are those relatively rare persons who actually do go into a deep hypnotic trance but who, because of individual peculiarities, seem unable to realize the fact, or are unable to admit it to themselves and hence refuse to believe that they are or ever have been hypnotized. Yet, invariably this latter class of subjects develops a spontaneous trance upon the execution of post-hypnotic suggestions, an occurrence which, in itself, often constitutes an effective measure in correcting their mental attitudes and misunderstandings.

Furthermore, in studies directed to the detection of the simulation of trance behavior, the failure of a trance state to develop upon the execution of post-hypnotic suggestions discloses any simulations. Nor does sophistication and coaching in this regard serve to enable a satisfactory simulation of the spontaneous trance state, since, on many occasions, trained subjects, purposely kept unaware that the performance they were watching was one of deliberate pretense, have declared the apparent performance of a post-hypnotic act to be "not right," "something wrong," or have stated, "I don't get the right feeling from the way he did that," but without being able to define their reasons, since their own post-hypnotic amnesias precluded full conscious understandings.

In brief, on innumerable occasions and under a variety of circumstances, the spontaneous post-hypnotic trance has been found to be characterized by the individual phenomena of the original trance state in which the post-hypnotic suggestion was given, and to be an excellent measure of differentiating between real and simulated trances, especially so when the subject, by being over-cooperative, deceives himself. Likewise, it has been found to be an effective measure in aiding responsive hypnotic subjects who, for personality reasons, cannot accept the fact of their hypnotization. Also, it can be used to demonstrate effectively the individuality and variety of responses that may be elicited under apparently controlled conditions.

THE UTILIZATION OF THE SPONTANEOUS POST-HYPNOTIC
TRANCE AS A SPECIAL HYPNOTIC TECHNIQUE

Of particular importance is the utilization of the spontaneous post-hypnotic trance as a special experimental and therapeutic technique. Its usefulness is varied in character and relates to the intimately associated problems of avoiding difficulties deriving from waking behavior, securing new trance states, training subjects to develop more profound trances, and eliciting specific hypnotic phenomena without direct or indirect suggestions made to that end.

The method of utilization is illustrated in the following experimental account: A five-year-old child, who had never witnessed a hypnotic trance, was seen alone by the hypnotist. She was placed in a chair and told repeatedly to "go to sleep," and to "sleep very soundly," while holding her favorite doll. No other suggestion of any sort was given her until after she had apparently slept soundly for some time. Then she was told, as a post-hypnotic suggestion, that some other day the hypnotist would ask her about her doll, whereupon she was to (a) place it in a chair, (b) sit down near it, and (c) wait for it to go to sleep. After several repetitions of these instructions, she was told to awaken and to continue her play. This threefold form of post-hypnotic suggestion was employed since obedience to it would lead progressively to an essentially static situation for the subject. Particularly did the last item of behavior require an indefinitely prolonged and passive form of response, which could be best achieved by a continuation of the spontaneous post-hypnotic trance.

Several days later she was seen while at play and a casual inquiry was made about her doll. Securing the doll from its cradle, she exhibited it proudly and then explained that the doll was tired and wanted to go to sleep, placing it as she spoke in the proper chair and sitting down quietly beside it to watch. She soon gave the appearance of being in a trance state, although her eyes were still open. When asked what she was doing she replied, "Waiting," and nodded her head agreeably when told insistently, "Stay just like you are and keep on waiting." Systematic investigation, with an avoidance of any measure that might cause a purely responsive manifestation to a specific but unintentional hypnotic suggestion, led to the discovery of a wide variety of the phenomena typical of the ordinary induced trance. A number of these will be cited in detail in the following paragraphs to illustrate both the procedure employed and the results obtained.

CATALEPSY

The subject was asked if she would like to see a new toy the hypnotist had for her. Contrary to her ordinary behavior of excited response in such a situation, she simply nodded her head and waited passively for the hypnotist to secure the new toy (a large doll) from a place of concealment. She smiled happily when it was held up to her view, but made no effort to reach for it. Upon being asked if she would like to hold it, she nodded her head agreeably, but still made no effort to take it. The doll was placed in her lap and the hypnotist then helped her to nestle it in her right arm, but in such fashion that the arm was in a decidedly awkward position. She made no effort to shift the position of her arm, but merely continued to look happily at the doll.

While she was so engaged, the hypnotist remarked that her shoe string was untied and asked if he might tie it for her. Again she nodded her head and the hypnotist lifted her foot slightly by the shoe strings so that the task might be done more easily. When her foot was released, it remained in the position to which it had been elevated.

Following this, she was asked if she would like to put the doll in its cradle. Her only response was an affirmative nod. After a few moments wait, she was asked if she would not like to do so at once. Again she nodded her head, but still continued to wait for specific instructions. Thereupon the hypnotist told her to "go ahead," meanwhile picking up a book as if to read. The subject responded by repeated futile attempts to rise from the chair, but the catalepsy present, manifested by the continuance of the awkward position in which she was holding the doll and the elevation of her foot, prevented her from making the shift of position necessary for rising. She was asked why she did not put the doll in the cradle, to which she replied, "Can't." When asked if she wanted help, she nodded her head, whereupon the hypnotist leaned forward in such fashion that he pushed her leg down. Taking her by the left hand, he gently pulled her to a standing position with her arm outstretched, in which position it remained upon being released. She immediately walked over to the cradle, but stood there helplessly, apparently unable to move either arm, and it became necessary to tell her to put the doll in the cradle. With this specific instruction, the catalepsy disappeared from her arms and she was able to obey.

RAPPORT AND HALLUCINATORY BEHAVIOR

The subject was then asked to return to her original seat, where she continued to gaze in a passive manner at the first doll in its chair. One of the hypnotist's assistants entered the room, walked over and picked up that doll and removed it to another chair. Despite the fact that the subject had her gaze directed fully at the doll, she made no response to this maneuver, nor did she appear to detect in any way the alteration of the situation. After a few moments, the hypnotist asked her what she was doing. She replied, "I'm watching my dolly." Asked what the doll was doing, she answered simply, "Sleeping." At this point, the assistant called the subject by name and inquired how long the doll had been sleeping, but elicited no response. The question was repeated without results, whereupon the assistant nudged the subject's arm. The subject immediately looked briefly at her arm and scratched it in a casual fashion, but made no other response.

Following this, the assistant secured the two dolls and dropped them into the hypnotist's lap. The subject was then asked if she thought both dolls liked to sleep, thereby causing her to shift her gaze from the empty chair to the hypnotist. She apparently failed to see the dolls in the new position, but when they were picked up and looked at directly by the hypnotist, she immediately became aware of them, glanced hesitatingly at the chair and then at the cradle, and remarked, "You got them now," and seemed to be very much puzzled. Yet, when the assistant quietly took the dolls out of the hypnotist's hands and walked to the other side of the room, the subject apparently continued to see the dolls as if they were still held by the hypnotist. An attempt on the part of the assistant to call the subject's attention to the dolls failed to elicit a response of any sort from the subject.

The subject's mother then entered the room and attempted to attract her attention, but without results. Yet, the subject could walk around, talk to the hypnotist, and see any particular object or person called directly to her attention by the hypnotist, although she was apparently totally unable to respond to anything not belonging strictly to the hypnotic situation.

AMNESIA

The others were dismissed from the room, the dolls were restored to the chair and the cradle respectively, and the subject to her seat, whereupon she was told to awaken. Immediately upon manifesting an appearance of being awake, the subject, returning to the initial situation, remarked in her ordinary manner, "I don't think dolly is going to go to sleep. She's awake." She was asked various casual questions about the doll, following which the hypnotist remarked that maybe the doll did not like to go to sleep in a chair. Immediately the subject jumped up and declared her intention of putting the doll in its cradle, but when she attempted to do so she manifested very marked bewilderment at the presence of the new doll in the cradle. There was no recognition of it, no realization that she had ever seen the doll before, and no knowledge that it had been made a gift to her. She showed the typical excited childish desire for the new toy, asking whose it was and if she might have it. The assistant then re-entered the room and picked up the doll whereupon the subject began addressing remarks to the assistant. The assistant, replying to these, walked over to the chair and picked up the first doll. The subject made full and adequate response to this, disclosing complete contact with her surroundings and a complete amnesia for all trance occurrences.

Repetitions of the procedure upon the subject under varying circumstances led to similar findings. Likewise, similar procedures have been employed with other naive and trained subjects of various ages with comparable results.

This general type of technique we have found especially useful both experimentally and therapeutically since it lessens greatly those difficulties encountered in the ordinary process of inducing a trance, which derive from the need to subordinate and eliminate waking patterns of behavior. Once the initial trance has been induced and limited strictly to passive sleeping behavior with only the additional item of an acceptable post-hypnotic suggestion given in such fashion that its execution can fit into the natural course of ordinary waking events, there is then an opportunity to elicit the post-hypnotic performance with its concomitant spontaneous trance. Proper interference, not necessary in the instance cited above because of the nature of the post-hypnotic performance, can then serve to arrest the subject in that trance state.

However, it must be stated that, to arrest the subject in the spontaneous trance and to have him remain in that state, the entire situation must be conducive to such a purpose, since any unwillingness on the part of the subject will cause him to become unresponsive and to awaken. But under favorable circumstances, the subject submits readily and fully to the new hypnotic situation in a passive responsive fashion. Repeated intensive inquiry of subjects while in such prolonged trance states has disclosed no understanding of how the trance was secured nor any intellectual curiosity about it, and usually little or no spontaneous realiza-responsive behavior so characteristic of the ordinary deep induced tion that they are in a trance. Rather, there seems to be only a passive acceptance of their trance state marked by the automatic trance.

By this general measure, new trance states can be secured free from the limitations deriving from various factors such as the subject's mental set, deliberate conscious intentions regarding trance behavior, misconceptions, and the continuance of waking patterns of behavior. Under ordinary circumstances, the hypnotic subject, obeying a post-hypnotic command, is making a response to a suggestion of which he is unaware at a conscious level of understanding, and which belongs to another situation of which he is similarly unaware. In addition, he becomes so absorbed and so automatic in his performance and so limited in his responses to his general environment, that there is little possibility of and no immediate need for the retention or continuance of conscious attitudes and patterns of behavior. Instead, there is effected a dissociation from the immediate circumstances, more adequate and complete than can be achieved by suggestion in the usual process of trance induction. Hence, the performance becomes exceedingly restricted in character, occurs at a level of awareness distinct from that of ordinary waking consciousness and derives from a remote situation. In brief, it is a phenomenon of sequence, is based upon the revivification of the hypnotic elements of another situation, and thus, is limited to hypnotic behavior.

The applicability of the above discussion to the problem of training subjects to develop more profound trances is apparent. Also, the value of repeated trance inductions to secure more profound hypnotic states is generally recognized, and this same purpose can be served more satisfactorily, readily, and easily by the utilization of the post-hypnotic performance and its concomitant trance. Especially is this so since the post-hypnotic performance provides an opportunity to secure a trance state quickly and unexpectedly without the subject having any opportunity to prepare himself or to make any special and unnecessary adjustments for his behavior. Instead, the subject suddenly finds himself in the hypnotic state and limited to patterns of response and behavior belonging only to that state. Hence, training can be accomplished without a laborious process of effecting by suggestion a dissociation of waking patterns of behavior, provided, of course, that the subject is essentially willing to forego the passive participation constituting a part of the usual training procedure.

The direct evocation of specific hypnotic phenomena without recourse to suggestion has been illustrated in the experimental account above. While the same thing may be done in the ordinary induced trance, there has been frequent and often well-founded criticism to the effect that many times the hypnotic behavior elicited was a direct response to intentional or unintentional suggestions given during the trance induction or to unexpected constructions placed by the subject upon suggestions. Behavior so elicited is expressive only of the hypnotic tendency to automatic obedience and it is not a direct expression of the hypnotic state itself. As shown in the above account, the utilization of the spontaneous post-hypnotic trance permits a direct evocation of specific phenomena without the questionable effects of a long series of suggestions given during the process of induction.

In the therapeutic situation, the utilization of the spontaneous post-hypnotic trance possesses special values for hypnotic psychotherapy, since it precludes the development of resistances and renders the patient particularly susceptible to therapeutic suggestions. Also, the amnesia following this spontaneous trance is less easily broken down by the patient's desire to remember what suggestions have been given, as is so often the case in relation to induced trances. Hence, there is less likelihood of the patient controverting the psychotherapy given. In addition, the spontaneous post-hypnotic trance permits an easy combination of waking and hypnotic therapy, often an absolute essential for successful results. However, this problem of the combination of waking and hypnotic psychotherapy, or, more generally, the integration of hypnotic and post-hypnotic behavior with the conscious stream of activity, does not come within the scope of this paper.

THE SPONTANEOUS POST-HYPNOTIC TRANCE AND DISSOCIATION PHENOMENA

Little that is definitive can be said about the significance of the spontaneous trance in relation to both the original trance and the post-hypnotic performance as dissociation phenomena, since extensive controlled experimental work needs to be done to establish this point as well as the concept itself. However, careful observation discloses consistently that post-hypnotic behavior simply irrupts or "breaks through" into the conscious stream of activity and fails to become an integral part of that activity except as a retrospective addition. Perhaps the best illustration of this dissociated character of the trance and the post-hypnotic act may be found in the following examples: As the subject was conversing casually with others in the room, he was interrupted in the middle of a sentence by the predetermined cue for a post-hypnotic act requiring a brief absence from the room. Immediately upon perceiving the cue, the subject discontinued the remark he was making, manifested the typical post-hypnotic trance behavior, executed the act, returned to his chair, readjusted himself to his original position, seemed to go through a process of awakening, and took up his remark and continued it from the exact point of interruption. Another subject, instructed to respond instantly to a sharp auditory stimulus serving as the cue for a post-hypnotic act, was interrupted in the middle of the pronunciation of a long word while casually conversing with others

present. His performance of the post-hypnotic act was then interfered with and the subject was used for a period of 15 to 20 minutes to demonstrate to the observers present a variety of hypnotic
phenomena, following which the subject was told to "go ahead."
In obedience to this vague suggestion, the subject proceeded to
complete his performance of the post-hypnotic act, returned to
his original position, re-adjusted himself, awakened, and completed the utterance of the interrupted word and continued in
the same line of conversation, apparently totally unaware that
there had been a lengthy interruption.

A subject similarly interrupted in the midst of rapid typing
and used to demonstrate various phenomena, upon returning to
his original position at the typewriter, awakened and unhesitatingly resumed his typing task without any apparent necessity
to reorient himself visually. Apparently he had held his orientation to his task in complete abeyance for ready resumption. This
same type of procedure, with various control measures, has been
repeated many times with similar and consistent results.

Not always, however, do the subjects return after a post-
hypnotic performance with such precision to the original waking
train of thought. Sometimes it is picked up further along in the
natural course of its development, as is shown by an interruption
of the subject by post-hypnotic activity while reciting the first
part of a poem and a continuation by the subject upon awakening
with the recitation of the last part, with a discoverable firm belief
on the part of the subject that the intervening stanzas had been
recited. Some subjects, however, show marked confusion, which
may be illustrated by the subject who declared, "I've forgotten
what I was just talking about," and required aid in renewing
his remarks, but was found to believe that he had said more
on the topic than was the fact. On still other occasions, subjects
have manifested a hazy awareness of the post-hypnotic act and
have digressed briefly to remark about some unusual circumstance apparently just discovered, as if seeking an explanation

of the peculiar change in the situation of which they had just become somewhat aware. But, on the whole, when the subject is left to re-adjust his behavior after an interpolated post-hypnotic performance without interference of any sort from the observers, there tends to be a complete amnesia for the trance and its events and an approximate return to the general situation with seemingly no awareness of any changes in it.

From these examples, typical of numerous instances, the statement is warranted that the post-hypnotic act and its spontaneously developed post-hypnotic trance constitute forms of dissociation phenomena and, hence, that they offer an opportunity to study experimentally the problem of dissociation. Similarly suggestive is the apparent continuance and independence of waking trains of thought during the trance state, despite other interpolated behavior as shown in the examples above.

Another comment that should be made before discussing the direct experimental implications, concerns the usual conditions under which these observations were made, namely, those of a general social gathering in which the topic of hypnosis was discussed with the possibility of demonstrations, but in such fashion that the subjects were unaware of any deliberate specific experimental intentions in relation to them on the part of the authors and their assistants. Maneuvering of the conversation would lead to the recitation of a poem or the giving of some famous quotations by the subject or the carrying on of guessing games, thus permitting a demonstration of the continuance of the original waking trains of thought, despite any interruption that might be occasioned by post-hypnotic acts. Our general purpose in these informal settings was the avoidance of those limitations or restrictions upon patterns of response that obtain when the subject is aware that his behavior is under direct scrutiny. In our experience, the necessity for the avoidance of overt study in hypnotic work cannot be over-emphasized. The natural course of behavior rather than the limited formalized pattern that may be expected in a strictly laboratory setting usually proves the more informative.

APPLICATIONS OF THE SPONTANEOUS POST-HYPNOTIC TRANCE IN EXPERIMENTAL WORK ON DISSOCIATION

The dissociation and independence of post-hypnotic behavior from the conscious stream of activity, and the failure of integration of hypnotically motivated behavior with ordinary behavior constitute significant considerations for which there must be adequate provision in any experimental work involving both waking and post-hypnotic behavior. Hence, in studies directed to the investigation of the capacity to perform simultaneously different tasks, such as reading aloud in the waking state and doing mental addition as a post-hypnotic task, provision must be made to keep the tasks entirely independent and not contingent upon one another. While provision is easily made for the post-hypnotic activity, extreme care must be exercised to insure that the waking behavior derives entirely out of a situation belonging wholly to the waking state and that the development of a spontaneous post-hypnotic trance does not interfere significantly with the waking behavior. In Messerschmidt's experiment, none of these provisions was made, which accounts for her unsatisfactory and inconclusive findings.

One needs only to observe critically a subject in such an experimental situation as Messerschmidt devised to note the constant, rapid fluctuation from one state of awareness to another of a more limited character. The unsatisfactory results obtained under such conditions are not indicative of a lack of capacity on the part of the subject, but, rather, they indicate the obstructive effects of the post-hypnotic trance developments and the interdependence of the two tasks. Accordingly, in experimental approaches to the concept of dissociation, the problem is actually one of devising a technique by which the independence of the tasks is maintained despite any simultaneity of the performances.

In brief, an adequate technique should be one that limits the post-hypnotic act to a single aspect of an entire task, of which the post-hypnotic performance represents only the initiation or culmination of the unconsciously performed activity, while the consciously performed task derives wholly from the ordinary course of events belonging entirely to the waking situation.

To illustrate this type of technique, the following examples may be cited: A farm boy subject was instructed in the trance state that thereafter for a week, every time he pumped water to fill a certain watering trough which was out of sight and hearing from the pump, and which was known by him to require 250 strokes of the pump handle to fill, he was to turn and walk to the trough the instant it was full. Thus, the post-hypnotic act was an extremely limited part of a larger implied task, and any post-hypnotic trance manifestations would necessarily be limited to the specified post-hypnotic act.

A few days later an agreement was made in the ordinary waking state that the subject would be relieved of a certain onerous task much disliked by him if he were able to spell correctly most of the words given him by the hypnotist, the words to be selected from his own school spelling book. To this the subject agreed eagerly, and as the spelling test started, the boy's father appeared, in accord with secret arrangements, and demanded that the watering trough be filled immediately. Accordingly, the spelling test was conducted at the pump, where, as the subject pumped, one word after another was given him as rapidly as he spelled them. Suddenly, the subject interrupted his spelling, ceased pumping, and turned and walked to the trough, his behavior typical of the post-hypnotic trance state. The trough was found to be full. Repetitions of the experiment elicited the same results. Also, independent counting of the pump handle strokes disclosed the subject to be keeping accurate count despite the task of spelling. Yet, repetitions of the experiment in which the subject was instructed to count the strokes silently as the post-hypnotic task itself, while spelling aloud as a conscious task, led to unsatisfactory results, specifically, confusion of the spelling with the counting. This admixture in his performance bewildered him greatly, since, as a consequence of his amnesia for the post-hypnotic suggestions, he could not understand his frequent utterance of a number in place of a letter in his spelling.

When an attempt was made to have this subject count the strokes and spell as simultaneous waking tasks, he was found to be totally unable to do so except by deliberate purposeful pauses and by a definite alternation of tasks. After much effort in this regard, the subject spontaneously suggested, "I can guess the number of strokes better instead of trying to count them while I'm spelling." A test of this disclosed that the subject was able to "guess" accurately, but when he was questioned later in the hypnotic trance, he explained that the "guess" was only a conscious belief or understanding on his part, and that he had actually counted the strokes in the same manner as he had in the original experimental trials.

In a similar experiment, a stenographer was told in the trance state that for the next week, while taking dictation she would change pencils on the 320th word, the 550th word and the 725th word. These instructions limited the post-hypnotic act to a very small aspect of the total task. During that time she took dictation from three psychiatrists, each of whom noted the phrases at which she changed pencils. Despite the fact that she used many combined word phrases (symbols combining two or more words) it was discovered by count later that she approximated the correct number closely, never exceeding an error of 10 and averaging an error of three words.

Another important item is the fact that each time she changed pencils at the specified number of words, the subject became confused, manifested briefly the evidences of a spontaneous post-hypnotic trance and had to have a repetition of some of the dictation. Nevertheless, she could change pencils elsewhere than on the specified words without any interruption of her writing. Furthermore, her general behavior, except for the transient disturbances noted above, disclosed nothing unusual to the three psychiatrists, who, although unacquainted with the experimental situation, had been instructed to observe her behavior carefully, and to give dictation at their customary speed, which ranged between 100 and 120 words a minute. Likewise, when the hypnotist himself gave her carefully timed dictation, no unusual behavior was noted except the transient disturbances in direct relation to the specified words.

Yet, the same subject, instructed as the post-hypnotic task to count the words as they were dictated, failed completely both in her counting and in her writing, as might be predicted if full consideration were given to habituation and learning processes and attention factors, apart from the influence of post-hypnotic trance manifestations.

An attempt was made to have her perform the two tasks as a single waking performance, but she was found unable to divide her attention sufficiently both to count correctly and to attend to the dictation. However, when it was suggested to her that she attend only to the dictation, and merely "guess" when she reached the designated number of words, it was found that she could approximate the correct count. In a subsequent hypnotic trance, she explained that the permission to "guess" permitted her to dismiss the count from her "conscious mind" so that she "could do it subconsciously."

As a control measure for the above experiments, non-hypnotic subjects and hypnotic subjects who had not been used in this type of experimentation were asked to "guess" in similar experimental situations. Their replies in all instances were found to be calculated, inaccurate approximations based upon various general considerations such as time elapsed or the number of pages covered, rather than an attempt to make an actual count.

A slightly different approach to the problem of simultaneous tasks at different levels of awareness is the utilization of post-hypnotic suggestion simply to initiate a form of behavior which then continues as an automatic activity not impinging upon the subject's conscious awareness.

To illustrate: Another stenographer was instructed in the deep trance that the appearance of the hypnotist in her office would constitute a cue for her left hand to begin automatic writing without her conscious awareness of it, and that this writing was to be discontinued immediately upon his departure. Thus, she was given post-hypnotic suggestions serving directly to initiate and to terminate a certain form of behavior. Repeatedly thereafter, whenever the hypnotist entered her office she manifested briefly the development of a post-hypnotic trance with a definite disruption of her activities, particularly so if she were engaged in typing. Under such circumstances, the post-hypnotic trance would persist until she had been excused from one or the other of the two tasks. Care was taken, however, to enter her office frequently when she was sitting at a desk engaged in taking dictation from some one of the hypnotist's colleagues. In this situation, she would manifest a brief spontaneous post-hypnotic trance which would disrupt her immediate activity and this would be followed by a resumption of her normal dictation behavior, accompanied by a continuous automatic writing with her left hand, which would be done on the desk top, the desk blotter, or any handy sheet of paper. If no pencil were available, her hand would still go through writing movements. Upon the departure of the hypnotist from the office, there would again occur a brief spontaneous post-hypnotic trance resulting in a disruption of her normal dictation behavior and a discontinuance of the automatic writing.

On more than one occasion, one of the psychiatrists giving dictation, who had the habit of sitting with his back toward her, responded to the interruption occasioned by the spontaneous trance and her consequent request for repetition, as if it were caused by some unfamiliar medical term or by unclear enunciation on his part, and he did not become aware of the additional post-hypnotic activity. There seemed to be no interference by the automatic writing with the conscious waking performance, although the automatic writing often included phrases from the dictation as well as other sentences and phrases related to other matters.

Conversely, there seemed to be no interference by the waking activity with the automatic writing. Each was done with the same degree of facility and legibility as when either constituted the sole task for the subject.

It was also possible for the hypnotist to give dictation to this subject in the ordinary course of the daily routine, but the spontaneous post-hypnotic trance developing when he entered her office for this purpose tended to be more prolonged than was the case when his entrance merely interrupted the dictation of the other psychiatrists.

When, however, an attempt was made to have this subject take dictation after she had been allowed to become consciously aware of the fact that her left hand was doing automatic writing, it was discovered that she could not take dictation successfully, nor could she do the automatic writing except by a process of alternating the tasks. When ample proof had been given to her that she had performed such tasks simultaneously in the past, she explained that she could probably do it if she were not asked to keep the automatic writing in mind while taking dictation, that she could take dictation adequately if she were permitted to "forget about the automatic writing."

In these three examples, the spontaneous post-hypnotic trance was limited to a minor aspect of the larger implied post-hypnotic task and hence, its interference with the concurrent conscious activity was decidedly brief in character. Also in each instance, neither of the two tasks performed simultaneously was contingent upon the other. The waking one derived entirely out of the routine course of ordinary waking events having no relation, however remote, to the trance state in which the post-hypnotic suggestions were given. In all instances, the subjects were entirely free to engage simultaneously in two wholly independent activities without the burden of a third task of coordinating them.

Apparently, then, the essential technical consideration in the simultaneous performance of two separate and distinct tasks, each at a different level of awareness, which is not ordinarily possible at a single level of awareness, consists in the provision of some form of motivation sufficient to set into action a train of learned activity which will then continue indefinitely at one level of awareness, despite the initiation or continuation of another train of activity at another level.

CONCLUSIONS

1. A survey of the literature discloses that, although there has been frequent recognition of the fact that post-hypnotic suggestions lead to the development of a peculiar mental state in the hypnotic subject, there has been no direct study made of that special mental condition. Neither has there been provision nor allowance made for its existence and its possible significant influences upon results obtained from post-hypnotic suggestions.

2. The significant change in the subject's mental state, in direct relation to the performance of a post-hypnotic act, has been found by extensive observation and experimentation to signify the development of a spontaneous, self-limited post-hypnotic trance, which constitutes an integral part of the process of response to and execution of post-hypnotic commands.

3. The spontaneous post-hypnotic trance may be single or multiple, brief or prolonged, but in general it appears for only a moment or two at the initiation of the post-hypnotic performance, and hence, it is easily overlooked. Its specific manifestations

and residual effects form an essentially constant pattern, despite variations in the duration of the separate items of behavior caused by the purposes served and the individuality of the subjects.

4. Demonstration and testing of the spontaneous post-hypnotic trance are usually best accomplished at the moment of the initiation of the post-hypnotic performance by interference either with subject or with the suggested act. Properly given, such interference ordinarily leads to an immediate arrest in the subject's behavior, and a prolongation of the spontaneous post-hypnotic trance, permitting a direct evocation of hypnotic phenomena typical of the ordinary induced hypnotic trance. Occasionally, however, special types of hypnotic behavior may be elicited by interference improperly given or which causes a significant alteration of the post-hypnotic situation.

5. The lapse of an indefinite period of time between the giving of a post-hypnotic suggestion and the opportunity for its execution does not affect the development of a spontaneous post-hypnotic trance as an integral part of the post-hypnotic performance.

6. Apparent exceptions to the development of the spontaneous post-hypnotic trance as an integral part of the post-hypnotic performance are found to derive from significant changes in the intended post-hypnotic situation which alter or transform it into one of another character.

7. The spontaneous post-hypnotic trance is essentially a phenomenon of sequence, since it constitutes a revivification of the hypnotic elements of the trance situation in which the specific post-hypnotic suggestion was given. Hence, its development is a criterion of the validity of the previous trance.

8. The spontaneous post-hypnotic trance may be used advantageously as a special experimental and therapeutic technique, since it obviates various of the difficulties inherent in the usual method of trance induction.

9. The post-hypnotic performance and its associated spontaneous trance constitute dissociation phenomena since they break into the ordinary stream of conscious activity as interpolations, and since they do not become integrated with the ordinary course of conscious activity.

10. Post-hypnotic suggestion may be utilized effectively to study the capacity to perform simultaneously two separate and distinct tasks, each at a different level of awareness, if adequate provision be made for the nature and character of post-hypnotic behavior.

*From *The Journal of General Psychology*, 1941.

HYPNOSIS IN TREATMENT OF NEUROSES DUE TO WAR AND TO OTHER CAUSES

CHARLES FISHER, M.D.

Past Assistant Surgeon (R), United States Public Health Service
New York

EDITOR'S NOTE

This is a very convincing report on the value of drug hypnosis in the treatment of war neuroses. While the half dozen cases described are all examples of rapid treatment given to men in combat zones, this article reveals the technique used, the type of material elicited, and the result that follows from the use of drug hypnosis. The implication is apparent that treatment by such means extended over a substantial period of time would constitute an effective form of therapy.

Although many authorities on war neuroses recommend the use of hypnosis in the treatment of early traumatic neuroses of war, one gains the impression from a survey of the recent literature on this subject that hypnosis is being little used in World War II. Instead, there appears to be an increasing tendency to use the barbiturate drugs, especially sodium amytal. In discussing the use of pentothal, Hadfield had this to say:

"Does pentothal, then, supplant the use of hypnosis and free association? That has not been our experience. There are as many who object to "the needle" as to hypnosis. Nor is pentothal in every case successful in releasing emotions and amnesias; indeed, free association and hypnosis may succeed where pentothal fails. Furthermore, pentothal cannot be used frequently because of its toxic effects, whereas free association and hypnosis can be used as often as possible. Even when pentothal succeeds the material obtained has usually to be followed up by free association, especially as it is often forgotten again, and needs to be recovered by subsequent free association. Moreover, the cure usually comes about not merely by the mechanical release of repressed emotion but by the readjustment of these experiences and reassociation with the rest of the mind. For these reasons free association and hypnoanalysis are a far more delicate instrument not only for rediscovering the subtle and often very complex changes in the mind which have contributed to the breakdown, but also for adjusting the mind to deal with these morbid moods and emotions. Compared with this, the use of drugs is a crude though sometimes necessary assault upon so sensitive an organism as the mind, and, in spite of its abreactive value, often leaves the more basic moral problems unsolved. Pentothal should therefore be regarded as an adjuvant and not as a substitute for these other types of treatment; it would be a pity if the simplicity of the more mechanical methods should lure the student of psychotherapy from more delicate psychological methods. Both have their specific uses, and both techniques should be mastered."

It is not the purpose of this paper to argue the relative merits of hypnosis and the barbiturate drugs; admittedly each has its uses. Instead, it may be useful, through a series of case reports, to discuss the use of hypnosis in the treatment of war neuroses and others, to analyze some of the barriers which interfere in the use of this "more delicate psychological method" and to indicate the kind of therapeutic result that can be obtained.

Many physicians have a strong, unconscious dread of the use of hypnosis even when they recognize its therapeutic value and are eager to attempt it. This cannot be due to difficulties in mastering the rather mechanical procedures necessary to induce the hypnotic state. It is probable that the resistance stems from two principal sources: first, the necessity of entering into a close personal relationship with the patient, and, second, fear of having to confront the powerful and primitive unconscious forces that may come to light in the hypnotic trance. Any one who can wield a syringe is free to use sodium amytal and is frequently able to produce some kind of therapeutic result, no matter how mechanically he approaches the patient. But hypnosis cannot be applied in any such routine way, and many physicians fail because they are impervious to the needs, wishes and anxieties of the patient.

Altman, Pillersdorf and Ross (1942) have recently ably discussed the therapeutic barriers between patient and physician in the armed services and have pointed out that the problem of transference, necessary for psychotherapeutic success, becomes complicated by a special kind of resistance engendered by military relations. These barriers come prominently into evidence when one attempts to use hypnosis on military personnel. Chief among these is the fact that the military physician is also an officer, and, as Altman has pointed out, the soldier or sailor feels that he is being treated by the same agency that is responsible for his plight. It might be supposed that the authoritarian position conferred on the medical officer by his uniform and rank would be conducive to the induction of the hypnotic state in men of lesser rank. This is certainly frequently the case, especially if one chooses to utilize the awe-inspiring, overpowering technic to induce hypnosis. But the induction of the hypnotic trance in itself does not in the least guarantee a therapeutic result. A patient may be in a deep trance as measured by all the somatic criteria, such as the production of rigidities and anesthesias, but psychologically he may remain rigid and full of resistances and totally unable to recover the lost memories of amnesia or to divulge the unconscious conflict behind a hysterical symptom. It is suggested, therefore, that so far as possible, the hypnotist divest himself of excessive authoritarian trappings (e.g., cover his uniform with a white gown). One's position as a physician will furnish all the prestige that is needed. There is no substitute for sympathy, understanding and the conveyance to the patient by some means that one wishes to help him, not overpower him.

The patients whose cases are to be reported were treated at

the neuropsychiatric service of the United States Marine Hospital, Ellis Island, New York. This is a service with a rapid turnover, to which patients with acute neuroses are sent for disposition, the average length of stay in this hospital being but three or four weeks; hence there is no time for prolonged therapy. Most of the patients treated here are from the United States Coast Guard, the Maritime Service and the Merchant Marine. The hospital is staffed by United States Public Health Service physicians. This has certain advantages when personnel of the Coast Guard are to be treated, because the physicians are not actually part of the hierarchy of officers of the Coast Guard; this tends to weaken the authoritarian barrier. Furthermore, the designation "Public Health" may suggest to the patient that the physician is more concerned with the healing arts than with disciplinary action.

Six cases will be presented briefly and discussed with special reference to the following points: (1) the approach to the patient to get him to consent to hypnosis; (2) certain technical maneuvers useful in the eliciting of unconscious material; (3) the therapeutic results obtained, and (4) the limitations of hypnotic therapy. Two of the patients were merchant seamen who had been torpedoed and had what is usually referred to as "war neurosis." The remaining four were Coast Guardsmen; three of them acquired their symptoms either before or after induction into the service and had not seen combat duty; in the fourth patient a neurosis developed after the bombing of his ship.

It is important to choose the right moment to mention hypnosis; in some cases this may be done immediately, but in others it is best to wait until good rapport is established. To know when this point is reached is a matter largely of intuition. In almost all cases it is advisable to encourage the patient to ventilate freely all his fears, attitudes, illusions and misconceptions about hypnosis. As he does so, one can frequently gain some clews about the technic to be followed and some idea of what to avoid. It is often helpful to explain in as scientific a manner as possible, adjusting the explanation to the patient's intellectual level, what the hypnotic state is. With more intelligent patients one can enter into as objective and theoretic discussions as possible, and such discussions in no way prevent the patient from falling into a trance or detract from the powers of the hypnotist. The hypnotic state is mysterious enough that it can be induced even in the presence of full knowledge on the part of the patient. Such knowledge merely serves to reassure him and does not have the deleterious effect that is engendered by the spreading of misconceptions through the comic strips (Mandrake the Magician and others) and other popular sources of delusion. Most patients have to be reassured about the following frequently encountered ideas: (1) that they may never wake up; (2) that they have a "weak will" if they can be hypnotized; (3) that they will perform criminal acts, and (4) that they will be under the perpetual power of the hypnotist.

As to the actual technic, the usual sleep-inducing suggestions with fixation of the eyes on some such object as a key have been used. One cannot use a rigid, set technic but must vary it to suit the needs of the particular patient. Some patients are anxious about lying down but can be hypnotized in the sitting position; some will struggle against suggestions that their eyes will close but will readily go into a trance if they commence with the eyes already closed; some are apprehensive if the physician stands too close to them. It is necessary to "feel out" the patients's "areas of anxiety," as it were.

Case 1—A 21-year-old Negro merchant seaman entered the hospital with the history that he had had two brief amnestic episodes within a period of three months following the torpedoing and sinking of his ship. During the first session with him it was suggested that hypnosis might help his condition. He readily consented but with considerable satisfaction assured me that he did not think he could be hypnotized. He went on to relate that several weeks previously he had been at a demonstration of hypnosis at one of the servicemen's canteens. He was among fifteen volunteers who participated in a test of mass hypnosis and was the only one who could not be hypnotized, in spite of special efforts made by the hypnotist. He was obviously proud of his resistance and "strong will" and thought that these were in some way related to the fact that he was something of a hypnotist himself. He added that he could hypnotize dogs by stroking "the nerve in the neck that controlled the heart and brain." I agreed that there were such nerves and called them the "vagi." It was then explained to the patient that hypnosis was not "a battle of wills," that he was more concerned in defeating the hypnotist than in getting well and that he could not be helped unless he was willing to cooperate. He appeared to understand this and consented to try.

REPORT OF CASES

He gave the following history: In the early hours of the morning his ship was struck by a torpedo. He was working in the engine room with the engineer, who, according to the patient, became frightened and immediately ran on to the deck, leaving him to shift for himself. In the waking state he related that he ran to the boilers and turned off the two valves which controlled them and then rushed to the deck, in his haste forgetting his life belt. When he got on deck the ship was listing, and he was hit on the forehead by a fragment of steel, sustaining a deep laceration of the left frontal region of the scalp. He immediately jumped overboard and managed to swim to a raft; a few minutes later the captain and the first mate reached the raft and he helped them aboard. When day broke, the mate sewed up the wound in his scalp with a needle and thread and shortly thereafter the patient "fainted from loss of blood" and was unconscious for three days. When he regained consciousness, he was in a hospital. In telling this story he was arrogant and boastful; he expressed a complete lack of fearlessness for all things and persons and boasted of how he had "saved" the mate and captain, although it was clear that he had only helped them to climb on the raft. He manifested intense hostility toward the engineer, who had left him alone, and heaped abuse on his head for his cowardly behavior. It was evident that beneath all this bravado he was badly frightened.

During the first hypnotic session it was possible to reconstruct the two amnestic episodes that the patient had had. One often finds that during the first reconstruction of the events of an amnesia the patient relates the forgotten material in a quite matter-of-fact tone, with the expression of little affect. In subsequent sessions a greater degree of abreaction takes place when the same events are reviewed. After the patient was hypnotized, he was brought back to the time of his last period of amnesia, that is, to the moment when his memory stopped. He was then assured that he would be able to remember what had happened, and it was suggested that he relive the events of this period just as they happened to him. He proceeded to relate how the amnesia had developed while he was traveling in a ferry boat across a river. The point in time when the amnestic episode commenced was related to the visual perception of two valves on a fire hydrant on the ferryboat. The patient experienced a severe headache at this instant and "blacked out." The amnestic episode lasted for about ten hours; he was able to remember all that he had experienced during this period, his experiences culminating in his being picked up by the police. At the time he was in a violent, agitated condition and was expressing much fear of the Nazis and of submarines and was shouting that "they wouldn't get him" and torture him or make him talk. He next reconstructed the second amnestic episode, which lasted for about two hours. Just before entering his hotel room he saw two valves on a radiator; he walked into his room, looked at the clock and two hours later "came to" lying on his bed. He was then brought back to the time of the actual torpedoing and asked to relive this in his imagination just as it happened. He described the scene with some emotion, told about the seawater rushing into the engine room, again expressed much anger toward the engineer and after some encouragement admitted that he was afraid.

It was evident that his emotional conflict centered about the two valves. He was repeatedly praised while under hypnosis for his daring and courage in remaining below after the engineer had deserted him and was told that he had done more than his duty in staying to turn off the valves. By this means it was finally possible to get him to confess that he had become frightened and had run out before he was certain that he had turned the valves all the way off. He felt much shame and guilt over this, and it became evident that he was projecting his own feeling of cowardice on the engineer. It was clear, therefore, that the conflict between his fear and his sense of duty, between his "cowardice" and his need to be brave and fearless, lay behind his amnestic episodes. This conflict was set in motion in both instances by the visual perception of "valves." The patient will permit such a painful conflict to emerge into consciousness only if the hypnotist alines himself with the rejected impulses from which the patient is trying to escape and against the stringent dictates of conscience.

The patient was hypnotized on four occasions. In subsequent sessions it was brought out that he was not "unconscious" for three days on the raft but was in a hysterical stupor. He was able to remember the events of these three days and expressed all his terror at being caught and tortured by the Nazis. After the first session he relived his experiences, with the expression of much emotion and with a great deal of mimetic activity. He carried on conversations as they had occurred, some of them in Spanish, went through the motions of turning off the valves, made swimming movements as he swam to the raft and grimaced with pain as he was having his scalp sutured. Again and again he returned to the subject of the valves, wondered whether he had turned them all the way off and said many times, "I better go back and see. No, I better go overboard."

The patient was seen about five months after he was discharged from the hospital. During this period he had made seven trips to sea, had continued to work in the engine room and had been subjected to the bombardment from the air during the invasion of Sicily, but he had suffered no further amnesic episodes. He continued to have mild headaches but had not had tremors, nightmares or other anxiety symptoms, despite the dangers he had faced. He had purposely gone back to work in the engine room in order to master his fear. He seemed composed and confident and was making preparations to ship out again.

Case 2—A 21 year old white Coast Guardsman was treated in another Marine Hospital for more than six months prior to his admission here. He was hospitalized for treatment of painful palmar and plantar warts and calluses and intense hyperhidrosis of the hands and feet. He gave the following history: He began to exhibit excessive sweating of the feet when he was 4 or 5 years of age, and, along with this, large plantar calluses appeared. As far back as he could remember his feet had been tender. The sweating of the hands was not as profuse as that of the feet. Calluses and warts had formed on the hands only within the past few years, and painful warts had appeared under the plantar calluses some five or six years prior to his admission, when the patient was 16. The hyperhidrosis became progressively worse, and in recent years it had become so bad that at times the tops of a pair of shoes would rot out within a month and he would have to change his socks fifteen times daily. There were times when the sweat literally dripped from his feet. He had noticed that the sweating became worse when he was tense or experienced strong emotion.

During the early weeks of his first hospitalization he received a course of roentgen therapy, which caused the warts on his hands to disappear but did not affect the plantar growths. Later, about three months before his transfer, he was given injections of alcohol to both lumbar sympathetic chains. The sweating of the right foot decreased noticeably immediately after the injections, but that of the left side remained unaffected and the plantar growths were not influenced. Thereafter the patient experienced severe throbbing pain in the lumbar region, with pronounced stiffness and limitation of motion. He was unable to move or walk and had to stay in bed for nine days. He gradually improved so that he could get about slowly, but in about two weeks he had another exacerbation' of lumbar pain and had to remain in bed for a week. During this period he began to exhibit strong resentment toward the physicians who were treating him, because he felt he was getting worse; he became surly and irritable, hypochondriacal and complaining. Accordingly, he was sent to the neuropsychiatric service for observation and treatment.

A physical examination on his admission to the neuropsychiatric service revealed the presence of huge plantar calluses which were rather symmetrically located on both feet, especially on the heels, balls of the feet and large toes. In places they were more than a quarter of an inch (0.5 cm.) thick and more extensive than any I had seen until that time. The left foot was much colder than the right; the skin was flushed, and there was noticeable hyperhidrosis. The sweating on the right foot was minimal, evidently having been influenced by the alcohol block to the lumbar sympathetic chain on that side. Beneath the calluses painful plantar warts were evident. The patient held his back stiffly bent forward slightly and walked in a careful, guarded manner. He complained of severe lancinating pains in the lumbar region which radiated over the abdomen into the testicles. The sweating of the hands was moderate, and the warts and calluses had largely disappeared. There were many deep scars on the skin of the neck, back, shoulders and arms, a result of an old pustular acne, and there were some active pustular areas still present. There was abnormal thickening of the toe nails as a result of a fungous infection.

The patient expressed a great deal of resentment toward the physicians who had treated him, was surly and sarcastic, displayed the attitude of a martyr and felt that he had been medically abused and neglected. He was hopeless and bitter about his condition. For about a week he was encouraged to express his feelings about his condition and his treatment. It was gradually suggested to him that perhaps his excessive sweating had some emotional component. He was given a rather general psychosomatic explanation, to the effect that sweating is a normal accompaniment of strong emotion and that in his case there seemed to be a great deal of anger and resentment that might have become dissociated from the somatic manifestations. It was finally suggested that hypnosis might help his condition, and he consented to the procedure. It is sometimes useful to permit a prospective subject to witness the hypnotizing of another subject, and this was done in this case. The patient rapidly became an excellent subject. He was hypnotized four or five times a week for about a month. The hypnotic sessions were used almost exclusively for the giving of suggestions, and little attempt was made to get at unconscious factors. Suggestions were given in the following manner: The patient's calves were massaged, and he was told that this would improve the circulation of his feet, that all the blood vessels would open up, that this would make his feet warmer and that as they got warmer the sweating would stop. In addition, his back was rubbed and suggestions given that the pain would disappear and the motility increase. These somewhat magical suggestions were given monotonously day after day. Within about a week the patient began to notice a decrease in the amount of sweating of his left foot. The pain in his back began to disappear, and he was able to turn from his back to his stomach while in bed, something he had not been able to do since the lumbar injections. After about a week suggestions were made that the calluses and warts would disappear. Each day the larger ones were rubbed and "talked to" told to soften, become painless and disappear.

In addition to this suggestive therapy, the patient was seen in frequent interviews and a rather superficial kind of psychotherapy was undertaken. His chief difficulty seemed to be in handling his resentment and hostility, which were intimately related to his feelings toward his father, a rigid, strict and unaffectionate man. The patient was able to accept certain interpretations pertaining to his fear of asking for things because he might be rejected; to his compulsion to be overindependent, associated with strong unconscious wishes for dependency; to his reacting with great resentment whenever disappointed and to his unconscious demanding attitude. No attempt was made to analyze deeper unconscious mechanism; only a discussion of certain character traits was attempted.

In the midst of the treatment a severe infection of a pilonidal cyst and an anal fistula developed, with a temporary exacerbation of the patient's vasomotor symptoms. He immediately became resentful, acted as though he were undergoing general bodily dissolution and tended to blame the physicians for his condition. Simultaneously it was discovered that he had an occlusion of a small branch of one of his retinal arteries, and he became apprehensive about this. The pilonidal cyst was treated medically, and the infection cleared up.

Hypnosis was continued, and the patient showed progressive improvement, with a pronounced decrease in the sweating of the left foot, a definite increase in the temperature of the skin and a softening and dissolution of the plantar calluses. His feet became increasingly less painful. He showed a striking transformation of character; he became cheerful and much less resentful. He was finally transferred to another hospital for operation on the pilonidal cyst. By the time he left the hospital the diminution in the degree of sweating and the decrease in the size of the plantar calluses was truly remarkable. However, his condition continued to improve, and about six weeks after his discharge he wrote: "My feet have now completely quit sweating . . . and the plantar callosities have all softened and have almost gone." He reported, further, that the thickening of his toe nails had disappeared, and that the nails had returned to normal. He also felt that his family relationships had improved a great deal. Six months after discharge he reported further improvement and stated that the plantar warts (as distinguished from the calluses) were gradually going away. He stated that the skin of these areas had turned white, was breaking down and in some places had peeled off down to new, firm tissue, and that he rarely had any pain in his feet. He had gained 20 pounds (9Kg.); the rather severe acne which he had had was disappearing, and he had obtained employment.

Case 3—An 18 year old white Coast Guardsman was admitted to the hospital three weeks after he had been kicked in the left temple while wrestling, with the history that since this accident his vision had become impaired. A physician at his station examined him and reported that there were small pinpoint hemorrhages in the left eye; that the vision was 20/40, and that it was said to have been 20/20. At the time of his admission to this hospital, three weeks later, the patient was examined by an ophthalmologist and no evidence of retinal hemorrhages was found. However, there were a serious impairment of vision, the left eye testing 1/200 and the right eye 20/200, and a pronounced ocular nystagmus.

The patient told the following story: Shortly after joining the Coast Guard, he managed to get an assignment to a special group which was taught certain Commando-like activities. This school enrolled mostly big, tough men, who were trained in boxing, wrestling, jiu-jitsu and other defensive and offensive physical maneuvers. He was apparently admitted to this school with reluctance on the part of the authorities and only because he insisted. This was because he was several years younger than most of the men and rather fragile and effeminate in appearance; he weighed only 120 pounds (54.4 Kg.), whereas most of the others weighed from 165 to 230 pounds (75 to 104 Kg.). From the beginning he had an exceedingly difficult time competing with the other men, and in the process took many severe beatings. While boxing he was frequently hit about the head and dazed, and frequently he was "groggy" for days. He was especially apprehensive about wrestling with big men, with whom he was at a great disadvantage because of his weight. He became fearful of being squeezed about the chest. On a number of occasions his testicles were squeezed during wrestling matches, once so hard that he got "sick at the stomach" and felt faint. He gradually became tense and anxious; headaches and dizzy spells developed, and he was unable to sleep. He was constantly worried for fear he would be dropped from the school, and he felt this would be a disgrace and a reflection on his manhood. He wanted to show every one that he was able to "take it" and was afraid that the other men would laugh at him and call him a weakling. A few days before the training period was over, he was accidentally kicked in the left temporal region while he was wrestling; his eyes blurred and he felt dazed, but he did not lose consciousness. A day or two later he noticed that his vision was blurring, and he had severe headaches over the left eye and in the left temporal region.

From the patient's history it seemed probable that his symptoms were on a hysterical basis and that they might be influenced by hypnosis. While obtaining his history I made a few general remarks to the patient to the effect that he seemed to have an unusual need to prove his manhood. To which he replied: "Gee, doc, you know all about me." With the development of this kind of attitude toward the physician, it is not difficult to hypnotize a subject. This patient immediately accepted the proposal that his symptoms might be helped with hypnosis, and he made an excellent subject.

During the first hypnotic session the patient expressed his fear of being squeezed. In the waking state he talked mostly of his fear of having his chest squeezed, but when he was under hypnosis it became clear that his primary fear was of having his testicles squeezed. He was encouraged to express his feelings, and he vented a great deal of anger toward the men who had abused him; he writhed about on the couch and showed much anxiety, at the same time cursing the men who had injured him. He was extremely afraid of and hostile toward big men and wanted to avenge himself on them and to "squeeze them the way he had been squeezed." Every time he saw a big man he would have a severe anxiety attack with marked palpitations, trembling, perspiration and, most striking, a pronounced blurring to his vision. It developed that he had a deep affection for an older brother and was particularly envious of the latter's size and physical strength and of his being in the Air Corps. He was intensely hostile toward a brother-in-law, who was in the Coast Guard and who used to call the patient a weakling and tell him that he was not man enough to get into the service. It was partly because of this man's constant goading that the patient compulsively sought to get into one of the armed services when he was only 17 years of age. He always went out for boxing and wrestling and ran around with "tough boys." He was eager to get married and had bought and stored a whole houseful of furniture in preparation for this event.

During hypnosis certain interpretations were made to the patient. It was suggested to him that he seemed to have an unusual desire to prove his masculinity and in so doing he made fantastic demands on himself and tried to compete physically with men twice his size. It was further suggested that the blurring of his vision might be connected with getting his testicles squeezed and that this had actually happened when they had been squeezed. His phobia for big men was interpreted in the light of these considerations. During each session he was given post-hypnotic suggestions that his vision would return to normal and his headaches disappear; his temples were stroked, and he was told that this would "relax" the muscles in his eyes and improve his vision. His vision was tested before and after each hypnotic session, and by the end of the third session it tested 20/20 in each eye.

He was much relieved after his vision returned to normal, but the improvement did not persist. He continued to have severe anxiety attacks, always in relation to contact with big men, during which his vision would diminish but not to the extent it had. He was discharged from the service after several weeks of hospitalization. About three and a half months later he wrote: "My eyes are better than they were, but at times I get the strangest shaking feeling inside me . . . it makes my hands shake so bad I can't lift a glass of water." In addition, he reported that he had married.

Case 4—The patient was a 28 year old merchant seaman who was admitted to the hospital about six months after his ship had been torpedoed. He had sustained severe burns on his hands and feet. He rapidly acquired a severe traumatic neurosis, which was characterized by nightmares, chiefly of being burned alive, insomnia, violent trembling, hyperacusis and an intense startle reaction. If he was suddenly startled by a loud noise he would throw his arms upward and backward with such force that he frequently broke the back of chairs or violently banged the back of his head against a wall. About a month prior to his admission he noticed an involuntary motion of his left arm which was extremely annoying. The arm would suddenly flex at the elbow and execute a series of spasmodic movements much in the manner of a man shaking his fist. If he attempted to raise his arm above the horizontal position, these spasmodic movements would develop and he would be unable to extend the arm upward.

This patient was not a particularly promising therapeutic prospect because his symptoms had become chronic; he was a rigid, uncommunicative and suspicious man and he had a great deal of resentment against the shipping authorities over a matter of compensation and a feeling that he had not been treated fairly.

With some reluctance he consented to be hypnotized, but it was soon found that he was suspicious of the procedure. Further discussion revealed that he feared the presence of a dictaphone in the room and thought that all that he said while hypnotized would be recorded and turned over to the shipping authorities. Only after he was reassured on this score was an attempt made to hypnotize him. He readily fell into a deep trance. (This case again shows the value of preliminary discussion.)

Under hypnosis the patient told how the torpedo had struck his ship when he was on the deck just above the engine room. The torpedo struck the engine room, and there was a terrific explosion; he was blown high into the air, and he believes that he fell into one of the funnels. As he was falling through the funnel, there was another shattering explosion, and he sailed through the air again, this time losing consciousness. When he regained consciousness, he was scurrying up one of the guy wires that supported the funnel; the burned skin was coming off his hands as he climbed; flames were shooting up around him. In reliving this terrible experience the patient stressed his feeling of helplessness, the indignity of "bouncing up and down like a rubber ball" with the explosions and of climbing up the wire "like a monkey." He expressed his horror at feeling that "he was roasting to death" and described the sickening smell of burned flesh, the sight of a man running about madly with blood running from his penis and one of the mates screaming "like a stuck pig." He finally managed to get to the deck and was seized with the impulse to take some kind of aggressive action against the enemy. He remembered that there was a machine gun on deck and began frantically to run about looking for it but was unable to find it.

In the waking state the patient had remarked that the involuntary motions he made with his left arm were like the movements one made in handling a machine gun. It was thought, therefore, that the inhibition of the impulse to fire the machine gun might have some causal connection with the symptom the patient displayed. Accordingly, as he was living through the episode of searching for the machine gun, I said: "Go ahead. Shoot it." The patient then went through the motion of firing the machine gun and exactly duplicated the movements of the left arm that were present in his symptom. In the midst of this he showed much anxiety, spontaneously came out of the trance and looked bewildered. But he was immediately able to raise his arm above the horizontal, and from that time on this symptom completely disappeared.

The patient was subsequently hypnotized on three or four occasions and during these sessions abreacted a great deal of resentment toward the officers of his ship and the shipping authorities. With the aid of suggestion he gradually made a fairly good symptomatic recovery and after several weeks left the hospital with the advice that he was not ready to return to sea. Several weeks later he returned in an anxious condition, with the recurrence of many of his symptoms but not the spasm of the arm. He had secured a job on a tanker in port, and on the day the ship was to sail he became frightened and rushed back to the hospital. Unfortunately, he had picked the kind of ship best calculated to revive his neurosis, a tanker, on which he might "burn to death," the thing he feared most.

Case 5—An 18 year old white Coast Guardsman was admitted to the hospital complaining of constant headache over the left eye. He gave a history of six episodes of complete loss of vision for periods ranging from fifteen minutes to six hours; all of these had occurred within a period of five months just preceding his admission and dated from a head injury. He had been hit over the left eye with a brick and was knocked "unconscious" for about ten minutes. His glasses were broken, and a piece of glass injured his left eyeball, the laceration just "missing the pupil." The next day he suddenly lost his vision for a period of fifteen minutes. The subsequent periods of blindness became increasingly longer, the last one persisting for six hours. He stated had a headache over this eye for many years. In addition to the periods of complete blindness, he had numerous episodes of blurred vision. He had been rejected by the Army, the Navy and the Marine Corps because of defective vision and had been inducted into the Coast Guard only because he had memorized a chart and so was able to pass the test.

It seemed possible that this patient's visual disturbance was hysterical, and it was thought possible that any visual experiences which he might have had during the periods when he believed himself to be blind might be recovered while he was under hypnosis. This was thought to be feasible since he reported that he always kept his eyes open during the periods when he was "blind." In other words, the patient was treated as if he were suffering from amnesia, but an amnesia limited to the field of visual memory. He readily consented to hypnosis and on the first attempt went into a deep trance. He was then brought back to his last episode of blindness, which had occurred two weeks previously, and asked to relive it in his imagination just as it had happened. At the time this attack occurred he was riding in a bus one night and was engaged in a conversation with the driver about the different types of headlights on cars. Another car approached from the opposite direction; the driver of the bus dimmed his lights, the driver of the oncoming car did not do so. As this was happening, the patient suddenly lost his sight. Under hypnosis he acted all this out and carried on his conversation with the bus driver as if the latter were actually present. At this point the following technical maneuver was carried out: The patient was told that even though he was blind he had his eyes open and it was just possible that images of some of the things around him might have registered on his brain. I told him that I was going to relax the "muscles of his eyes" by pressing firmly on his temples and that as I did this some of these images would develop, just as a photographic plate develops. This was done, and immediately he began to describe what he saw around him during the time when he believed himself to be blind. Whenever he was asked directly what he saw, he responded that he could see nothing. This suggests how important it is not to assault the pride and vanity of such a patient by hinting even in the most remote way that he was not blind. Only by adherence to some pseudophysiologic explanation of the blindness and by constant repetition of the remarks about images of some of the things about him registering on his brain was it possible to overcome his resistances sufficiently that he was able to see. With use of this technic it was possible to restore the visual amnesia of the five remaining episodes of blindness. In addition, it turned out that at the time the patient was hit over the left eye with a brick he was not unconscious but in a hysterical stupor, and it was possible for him to remember under hypnosis what had occurred during this ten-minute period.

The precipitating event for each of the episodes of blindness was also elicited. In five of the six episodes it was discovered that at the instant the patient went blind he was having some sort of fantasy about the smashing of the headlights of an automobile. It was ascertained that he had always been apprehensive when he saw the light headlights of a car and that these reminded him of eyes. He had always been anxious when driving and was a cautious driver. One of his attacks, for instance, occurred while he was driving a truck and he saw some cattle coming along the other side of the road. This was associated with the memory that his father had once run into a cow while driving a car. The headlights of the car had been smashed and his father had been splattered all over with the cow dung, so terrific had been the impact of the collision. Another attack occurred when his grand-parents were discussing the fact that his brother-in-law had had an automobile wreck and at the instant when something was said about the headlights being smashed.

On the day following the first hypnotic session the patient displayed a new symptom, namely, a rather pronounced weakness of the grasp of the left hand. It was found that he had a hypesthesia of the hands and forearms, extending above the elbow, of the glove variety which did not follow any anatomic pattern. He alleged that he had had this condition all his life and had known for many years that he could stick a pin into his skin without experiencing pain. While he was under hypnosis it was possible to restore the strength of the grasp and to increase the pain sensibility of the hands and arms by simple suggestion. Further, by suggestion under hypnosis it was possible to remove the headache over the left brow which he had had for many years. After three or four sessions there was considerable improvement in visual acuity, the right eye testing 20/15 and the left eye 20/20-2. It has been noted that the patient was rejected by the Army, the Navy and the Marine Corps because of defective vision. No evidence of structural damage to the eyes was found.

In spite of the symptomatic improvement, it was considered that the patient had not attained any effective insight into his condition and that he still retained a proclivity for hysterical conversion, and he was given a medical discharge.

Case 6—A 25 year old white Coast Guardsman was admitted to the hospital about thirteen months after the bombing of his ship. He complained of gastrointestinal distress which had appeared immediately after the bombing but had become much worse in the past three or four months. He experienced a feeling of tension in the epigastric region associated with sharp pain radiating into the chest. He felt as if his "stomach were tied in a knot." At times pain seemed to shoot across to his left elbow, and sometimes it radiated down the left forearm into the ring finger. The epigastric pain was associated with much belching. He was treated medically at another Marine Hospital for a month, but nothing abnormal was found on physical examination. He continued to experience intense epigastric pain in spite of medication, and he was therefore transferred to the neuropsychiatric service with a diagnosis of mixed psychoneurosis.

In giving his history the patient dated the onset of his trouble to about a year and a half before the bombing of his ship. During this period he had had a number of threats to his genital integrity which caused him much anxiety. A penile discharge developed which he thought was indicative of gonorrhea but which proved to be non-specific. Shortly thereafter he injured his right testicle, and a swelling developed. He was thrown into a panic by a physician who told him that he had a cancer or a tumor. It turned out that he had an epididymitis which cleared with treatment with a sulfonamide compound. After the bombing of his ship he tore his foreskin during a coitus, and a sore developed; he was told that this might be a chancre of syphilis, again mistakenly.

During the time he was assigned to a ship the patient was under constant apprehension. There were many rumors about submarines or bombers being sighted. His ship finally was bombed in Singapore. He was below deck when the bomb struck and a number of men were killed, among them several of his close friends. He ran on to the deck and saw the burned and broken bodies of his shipmates being carried up from the sick bay. At this time he was extremely frightened and felt sick. He had no nausea nor did he vomit, but he lost his appetite. He remained on ship for over a year, much of the time in a state of anxiety.

After good rapport was established with the patient, hypnosis was suggested and readily accepted. He was given certain psychosomatic explanations of his condition, to the effect that at the time of his bombing experience he was anxious and that possibly this caused his stomach to go into a "spasm." The probable relationships of psychologic states to somatic symptoms were freely discussed in terms that the patient could understand and accept. He was told that perhaps his stomach could be made to "relax" by hypnosis. He made a good subject and was able to abreact a considerable amount of affect associated with his traumatic experiences. He was especially terrified at seeing the burned bodies of his friends. One of them was so badly burned that he kept screaming and begging the physician to shoot him. Someone found the amputated arm of another friend and threw it into the sea, and the patient witnessed this. He kept looking at the arm bobbing up and down in the water and he was horrified when sharks started to poke at it. While reliving this scene under hypnosis, he began to groan and complained of pain in his stomach which, he stated later, was just like the pain he subsequently experienced.

After a number of hypnotic sessions the patient said that he felt much better, and he was able to get through the day without medication. However, he continued to have attacks of epigastric distress, although they were much reduced in intensity and duration. There was also some diminution in the pain which periodically appeared in his elbow. This pain was perhaps etiologically related to the scene of the sharks poking at the arm, for he remembered it was the elbow they centered their attention on.

Although the problem of secondary gain from illness was discussed with this patient, it was not possible to effect more than a moderate alleviation of symptoms. Getting well definitely meant going back to sea, with the possibility of a repetition of his bombing experience, and this prospect he could not face. He was finally given a medical discharge.

COMMENT

In an assessment of the therapeutic results obtained in the cases presented, it must be remembered that a rapid form of therapy was attempted. Most of the men were hypnotized only three or four times for periods ranging up to an hour and a half, and these hypnotic sessions were supplemented with a number of interviews extending over a period of but several weeks. One man, the patient with the hyperhidrosis and calluses, was hypnotized more frequently, four or five times weekly for about a month. The therapeutic results obtained were mostly in the nature of symptomatic cures, and none of the patients were cured in the sense that they had genuine insight into the unconscious mechanisms responsible for their symptoms. With the use of hypnosis it is possible to exert a therapeutic effect in three ways: (1) by the giving of direct suggestions; (2) by the bringing about of the abreaction of repressed affect, and (3) by the bringing into consciousness of dissociated or repressed thoughts after the resistances have been broken through, in the same way as is done in psychoanalysis. The third way is indispensable for genuine cure but is the most difficult to carry out. The whole problem of a short time therapy hinges on the finding of some way to accomplish this quickly. By use of hypnosis one can frequently get a sort of bird's eye view of the essential unconscious conflict or conflicts responsible for a neurosis but is stunned by the problem of effecting an emotional acceptance by the patient of what one sees without resort to a prolonged analysis. Nevertheless, one should not minimize the results that can be obtained through hypnosis with use of pure suggestion and the bringing about of abreaction. These plus even a little interpretation of the unconscious material elicited frequently bring about striking symptomatic relief and perhaps a bit more.

In every case pure suggestion was used to a greater or less degree to remove symptoms. The most remarkable therapeutic result obtained by this means was in case 2, that of the patient with the hyperhidrosis and calluses. How much of this result was due to the effect of suggestion and how much to the effect of the superficial analysis of certain character trends, carried out against the background of a marked positive transference, cannot be estimated. However, one could clearly see that the symptomatic improvement occurred simultaneously with the suggestions while the patient was under hypnosis and progressed with them. It should be remarked, however, that part of the improvement may have been due to a delayed response to either the roentgen treatment or the alcohol block to the sympathetic chains. This seems unlikely because these measures were taken some three or four months prior to the use of hypnosis. The alcohol block decreased the sweating of one foot, but it did not affect the warts and calluses of either foot. It would be difficult to conceive how the block could suddenly take effect on the other side more than three months later. This patient seems to have had a peculiar instability of the vasomotor and trophic functions of his skin. In addition to the hyperhidrosis, warts and calluses, he had extensive acne and a pilonidal cyst. His skin seemed to be a locus minoris resistentiae, and through it he expressed his neurosis. By what means simple hypnotic suggestion can influence such primitive vegetative processes remains obscure. Cure of hyperhidrosis by hypnotic suggestion has been accomplished before; Bramwell (1930) mentioned several cases.

The other patients obtained various degrees of symptomatic relief in the following ways: The patient with amnestic episodes (case 1) recovered his lost memories, and his headache disappeared. In addition, he at least came close to attaining real insight into the essential conflict behind his neurosis. The patient with the episodes of hysterical blindness (case 5) recovered his visual memory for these periods; he also lost his headache and was much relieved to find that there was no structural damage to his eyes. The exposure of the functional nature of a symptom to a patient perhaps has the beneficial effect that he may not be able to utilize the same mechanisms in the future. The patient with the blurred vision and the phobia for big men (case 3) also experienced much relief when he found that he could see normally and that there were no retinal hemorrhages. He lost his headache and showed less anxiety. The torpedoed merchant seaman with the spasm of his left arm (case 4) obtained some symptomatic improvement, as did the patient with the gastro-intestinal symptoms (case 6).

Three of these patients had traumatic neuroses of war, and in two others the neurosis was precipitated by external trauma, in both cases the trauma being an injury to the left eye. In all the cases it was easy to see that there were preexisting neurotic tendencies which intertwined with the unconscious mechanisms set off by the trauma and influenced greatly the form and structure of the neurosis. For example, the patient with the blurred vision (case 3) had a long standing insecurity about his masculinity, and in the face of a real threat of castration acquired a hysterical visual disturbance. The patient with gastrointestinal symptoms (case 6) grew up in a household in which his mother and father did not speak to one another for nearly twenty years and where "oral aggressions" must have taken on an exaggerated signifi-cance. One might speculate on the relationship of this factor to the patient's gastrointestinal disturbance and his anxiety over the attack by the sharks on the amputated arm. In case 5 material was obtained which suggested that the patient's episodes of hysterical blindness were related to hostile, aggressive tendencies toward his brother-in-law and repressed erotic desires for his sister.

As time goes on, more and more men suffering from traumatic neuroses of war will be returning from the combat zones. In the treatment of these men hypnosis can certainly play a valuable role. It is extremely important, however, that treatment be instituted early, preferably within days or a few weeks of the onset of the neurosis. Most of the men whose cases have been discussed in this paper were actually not ideal material for hypnotic therapy because a greater or lesser degree of chronicity had already set in. Nevertheless, even in these late stages hypnosis is of great value. In early stages it is much easier to get at the repressed conflict and to bring about a genuine cure with insight. With no other method can this be done so rapidly, frequently within a few hours, or so effectively as with the use of hypnosis. It has been the chief object of this paper, however, to suggest that these ends can be obtained only if one uses a flexible technic, takes constantly into consideration the play of interpersonal factors and exercises what one might call "psychologic tact."

*From *War Medicine*, December 1943, Vol. 4, pp. 565-576.

EXPERIMENTS IN THE HYPNOTIC PRODUCTION OF CRIME*

WESLEY RAYMOND WELLS, *Syracuse University*

EDITOR'S NOTE

In this article Wells shows that subjects can be made to commit criminal acts. His success in these experiments is due, he asserts, to his technique. He points out that to have a patient commit criminal acts, the use of illusions, hallucinations, and delusions are necessary, so that the patient believes that he is acting with reason and according to moral principles. This removes the possibility of moral conflict and makes the acts laudable in the eyes of the hypnotized subject. The technique described constitutes a real contribution in this field.

Fortunately, the commission of crimes is very unlikely, for it takes an unusually able hypnotist and an exceedingly good subject.

It has been proved in recent experiments that suitable subjects can be rendered completely helpless to prevent the production of hypnotic results, at least such hypnotic results as the control of bodily movements, analgesia, anesthesia, hallucinations, and amnesia. The purposing of the subjects in advance of hypnosis to resist to the best of their ability, and their expectation of being able to resist, were found to be of no avail in preventing hypnotic results in the case of highly hypnotizable subjects. These recent experimental results are confirmatory of what is reported in the literature of the 1880's and 1890's. In the words of Bernheim, "The most striking feature in a hypnotized subject is his automatism."

In the experiments referred to above, however, there was nothing immoral or criminal in the nature of the hypnotic phenomena. Subjects were asked to resist to the best of their ability the production of entirely innocent acts such as amnesia for one's name or the inability to walk. There still remains un-answered in these experiments the question whether the automat-ism and the helplessness of the hypnotized subject can be made to extend to the production of acts which are contrary to the moral principles of the subject. It is possible that a subject who could not prevent the production of amnesia for his name might have his resistance reinforced to such an extent by a moral revul-sion if he were asked to steal money, that the hypnotist would be unable to make him carry out a criminal act like this. The view of the Nancy school was that a small percentage of subjects could actually be made to commit crimes even though the commission of the crimes was completely contrary to their personal wishes and their moral natures. Liebeault did not claim that more than four or five percent of the subjects whom he had encountered were such that "one could with absolute certainty successfully suggest crime." Bramwell says that Bernheim admitted, at the Moscow Congress in 1897, that in many subjects only such hyp-notic phenomena as were "agreeable or indifferent" could be produced. "He still believed, however, that a certain small pro-portion could be induced to commit real crime." In the older literature on hypnotism, e.g., in books by Bernheim and Forel, there are accounts of numerous cases of crime brought before law courts in which it was alleged and sometimes proved to the satisfaction of the courts that the crimes really had been caused by hypnosis.

The decisions of law courts are not necessarily final in a scien-tific question such as this, and there has been a tendency among some psychologists and others interested in hypnotism to deny categorically that real crime ever has been induced by hypnosis, at least in subjects who would not have committed crime willingly without the aid of hypnosis. No one has more strongly opposed the theory that hypnosis can induce helpless obedience which will go to criminal extremes than Bramwell. Bramwell made such statements as the following:

These facts . . . have forced me to abandon all belief in the so-called "automatism," or better termed "helpless obedience," of the subject . . . .

The phenomenon of helpless obedience was invariably absent in my subjects . . . .

Any changes in the moral sense that I have noticed have invariably been in favor of the hypnotized subjects . . . .

The arguments of Bernheim are devoid of value, as they are founded exclusively on cases where, first, a simple and harmless act has been assumed to be thought criminal by the subject, because the operator has stated it to be so; and second, where the subject has permitted something in hypnosis which he would probably have submitted to in the normal state.

Notwithstanding the influence and the general acceptance of the views of the Nancy school, Bramwell was not alone among earlier hypnotists in rejecting the efficacy of hypnosis in bringing about criminal acts. He said, "The views which I have long held regarding the hypnotized subject's power of rejecting disagreeable or criminal suggestions are now shared more or less completely by a good many other observers." Bramwell mentioned no less than nine hypnotists who shared his own views.

Among more recent experimenters and writers on hypnotism there has been a tendency to agree more with Bramwell than with Bernheim. Schilder and Kauders assert, "We are therefore of the opinion that the hypnotized can only be brought to perform such crimes as correspond with a previously existing inclination on his part." Hollander says, "Criminal suggestions would be accepted only by criminal minds." P. C. Young's experiments were in line with Bramwell's position. In his book *Hypnosis and Suggestibility* Hull does not cite any experiments on this subject; but such a statement as the following, "It is usually difficult to secure the successful execution of post-hypnotic suggestions which are at all in serious conflict with the natural inclination of the subject," would seem to make Hull's position more in line with Bramwell's than with Bernheim's. Erickson's recently reported study of the possible anti-social use of hypnosis, based on numerous experiments, ends with this statement, "The conclusion warranted by these experimental findings is that hypnosis cannot be misused to induce hypnotized persons to commit actual wrongful acts either against themselves or others." On the other hand, Rowland's recently reported experiment is squarely in line with Bernheim's position.

This problem is of much greater theoretical than practical interest. If hypnotically induced crime has occurred in the past, and if it is occurring at the present time, it is certainly a rare occurrence; and this should be among the least of the worries of the agencies working to eliminate crime. But it is of theoretic interest, especially in connection with the study of the nature of the hypnotic process, to submit to crucial experiments the question whether such helpless obedience as was found to occur in experiments referred to above for hypnotic phenomena which were a matter of moral indifference would also occur when the action was morally repugnant to the subject.

In this connection, something should be said about the art of hypnosis. Rowland has shown, in the second part of his experiment, that two of his subjects could be forced to do acts which were unquestionably repugnant to the moral principles of the subjects. In this experiment the subjects were made to throw sulphuric acid into the experimenter's face (supposedly, but not actually, since the experimenter's face was really protected by invisible glass). The subjects did this, believing that the sulphuric acid would "scar the skin and put out the eyes" of the experimenter, as indeed it would have done except for the protection of the invisible glass. His results are all the more noteworthy inasmuch as he went at it in the hardest way, not the easiest way. It should have been much easier to have brought about the same results if there had been a more subtle use of the art of hypnosis. Here is an illustration of what is meant. Let us suppose that we wish to see if Subject *A* can be forced to shoot Mr. *B*'s dog. Let us suppose that Mr. *B*'s dog is valuable, much prized by its owner. Let us suppose that the dog possesses only canine virtues, with no canine vices which could in any way be used as a basis for rationalization on the part of anyone wishing to justify the killing of the dog. Let us suppose that our subject, *A,* is a friend of Mr. *B,* is fond of Mr. *B*'s dog, is fond of dogs in general, and has a genuine horror of inflicting suffering on any man or beast. Now one way to go about trying to make *A* shoot *B*'s dog would be simply and bluntly to tell *A* when in hypnosis that after he came out of hypnosis, though his moral sense would remain unimpaired, and though his friendship for *B* and his liking for *B*'s dog would remain as before, he would be overcome by an utterly irresistible compulsion to get his shot-gun, sneak up on the dog after dark, and shoot it. The question would be whether *A,* his friendship for *B* and his horror of inflicting pain and bloodshed being still present as before, would be overcome by the hypnotically induced compulsion to shoot the dog with full knowledge of just how mean and despicable his act really was. It is perhaps this sort of helpless obedience of the subject, in the case of morally repugnant acts, which Liebeault and Bernheim found it possible to produce on an estimated four or five percent of subjects. It is this sort of helpless obedience which Rowland actually brought about, proving to the present generation of psychologists that the thing can be done.

But a more subtle and effective way in which to employ the art of hypnosis, and one likely to succeed with a larger percentage of subjects, would be somewhat as follows. It is to be assumed, of course, that the experiment would be attempted only with a subject who was deeply somnambulistic. This would mean that complete amnesia, vivid hallucinations, and strong delusions could be produced under ordinary hypnotic conditions. The experimenter might say to the hypnotized subject that after he came out of hypnosis, with complete amnesia for all that had been said to him in the hypnotic state (but with complete subconscious retention), the following post-hypnotic phenomena would occur. At some specified time A would take his gun and would ask Mr. B to take his dog and accompany him on a hunting expedition. Then the first time that the dog barked within gun-shot range, the subject, A, would experience an illusion. He would see the dog not as a dog but as a fox. Then, with no moral compunctions such as would be involved if he were in the grip of a compulsion to shoot the dog seen as a dog and recognized as his friend's dog, he would shoot what he saw as a fox without any hesitation. Better yet, he might be made post-hypnotically to see the dog not as a dog or as a fox but as a savage beast, e.g., an enraged bear coming to attack him, which he would shoot in what he considered to be self-defense. If five percent of subjects can be made to commit immoral acts by the first method, it would seem that a larger percentage might be made to commit immoral acts if illusions, hallucinations, delusions, and amnesias were produced post-hypnotically so that the acts would appear to the subject to be praiseworthy instead of immoral.

If a criminal hypnotist were actually trying to force a subject to commit a real crime, e.g., a murder, the hypnotist, if he wished to use the art of hypnosis to the full, would certainly try to prevent any moral conflict in the subject by producing hallucinations, illusions, and delusions, as indicated above. The hypnotist would try to produce amnesia in the subject, not only for everything said to him in the hypnotic trance in which the crime had been elaborated, but also for the fact that he had ever been a hypnotic subject. The hypnotist would then try to implant a post-hypnotic inhibition which would prevent anyone else from ever being able to hypnotize him. If this post-hypnotic inhibition was completely effective, the criminal hypnotist would feel protected from the possibility that the subject, if apprehended and brought into court, could be hypnotized again by someone else and made to recall the actual events, thus incriminating the hypnotist.

This subject had been developed to the somnambulistic stage

at one session in my office, in an hour. He had been hypnotized individually a second time for the purpose of a class-room demonstration, and again he gave evidence of being an unusually good subject, with a percentile rank of 95 or better in hypnotizability. I then told him of my experiments the previous semester, and asked him if he would care to take part in a similar experiment. To this he acquiesced. He had from the first been a skeptic regarding the success of any hypnotic experiments attempted on him. That is, before the group hypnosis in which he had taken part, he had stated in writing that he expected to be below the average in hypnotizability; and he had not expected that I could put him into the somnambulistic state when I worked on him individually in my office. When I told him of my failure with all three subjects in my research experiment the previous semester, he became all the more skeptical about the possibility of my getting results with him. I gave him a sort of "pep talk" when he came to my office for the crime experiment, urging him to do his utmost to resist me in every way, first as regards going into the hypnotic state at the outset, and then as regards the doing of criminal acts if I should succeed, in spite of his resistance, in putting him into the somnambulistic state. I said that if I failed to put him into the hypnotic trance against his resistance, I should then ask him to "turn off his will-power" exerted in opposition to my attempt to hypnotize him, and to assume his former attitude of cooperation for the purpose of inducing hypnosis, after which I would attempt to get him to do a criminal act against his forewarned opposition.

It was not necessary, of course, to have tried the crime experiment in this way. I might have hypnotized him as on the two former occasions, with his willing cooperation, and then I might have proceeded to attempt to produce criminal behavior without having given him any warning in advance as to my purpose. This, it seemed to me, would have been to take advantage of him in an undesirable way, as a really criminal hypnotist would have done; and I desired to prove, if possible, that a fully forewarned subject, urged not to cooperate, except to the extent of sitting down in the Morris chair instead of immediately walking out of the office, might be hypnotized against his conscious resistance, and then might be made to do a criminal act.

When he announced that he was ready to resist to his utmost the induction of hypnosis, I put my hand on his chest and counted seven, whereupon I found that he had apparently fallen into as deep a trance as on either of the two earlier occasions. Tests of muscular control, amnesia, and hallucinations confirmed this observation. The first part of the experiment had been accomplished, of showing that, in the case of a sufficiently good subject worked on by adequate methods and unprotected by a subconscious inhibition requiring the writing of a statement of willingness, conscious resistance to hypnosis "made no difference."

I then proceeded to the second part of the experiment. I said to the hypnotized subject that, immediately after I brought him out of hypnosis, he would get up from the chair, go to my overcoat which was hanging on the south wall of the office, and take from the right-hand pocket a dollar bill which he would find there. I said that he would see the overcoat as *his own* coat. This would be a post-hypnotic illusion. I said that he would remember (falsely) that he had left a dollar bill in the pocket of this coat. I said that he would put this dollar into the breast pocket of the coat which he was wearing, and that he would then return to the chair. I said that, as soon as he had sat down, amnesia would immediately occur for the fact that he had left the chair and for all the circumstances of getting the dollar. I said that when he discovered the dollar in his breast pocket, he would remember (falsely) that he had had this extra dollar when he came to the office. I said that he would go out and spend the money just as if it were his own. I said that when he came out of hypnosis he would be normally adjusted to the environment in every respect except as regards the illusion of his own overcoat on the wall, the false memory about the dollar, and the compulsion to get up from the chair and to secure the dollar immediately.

In order to throw light on a further question regarding hypnotically induced crime, the question, namely, as to whether the hypnotist might protect himself by producing in the subject amnesia for the fact that he had ever been a hypnotic subject, I said to *Yo* that when he came out of hypnosis he would have amnesia, not only for everything which had occurred during the hypnotic session on that day, but also for the fact that he had *ever* been worked on successfully. I said that he would recall taking part in the group hypnosis participated in by practically all the members of the class, but I said that he would recall (falsely) that he had been one of the poorest subjects in the group. I said that he would have amnesia for having come to my office on a previous occasion to be hypnotized individually and for having served on a later occasion as the subject in a class-room demonstration of individual hypnotic phenomena. I said that he would have amnesia for the fact that it was for the purpose of a hypnotic experiment that he had come to my office on the present occasion. I said that he would have amnesia for all of our conversation previous to the present hypnotic session regarding the production of crime by means of hypnosis.

In all this no tricks and no indirect suggestion were used, but only a straightforward hypnotic technique. I did not lie to *Yo* in any respect. I make it a point *never* to lie to any hypnotized subject. I did not say that the overcoat on the wall was his own: I said that he would see it as his own (a post-hypnotic illusion). I did not say that the dollar was his own: I said that he would remember (falsely) that it was his own. If the experiment had not worked, one might say that I had lied to him; but this would have been interpreted by the subject and by most observers rather as merely a case of hypnosis not working. To prevent the possibility of such a criticism in case hypnosis should not work, I added to my statements to *Yo* when in the hypnotic state that the post-hypnotic phenomena would occur as I had outlined them *to the extent that hypnosis worked* in his case. This is a routine sort of statement that I make to all my hypnotized subjects. Then, if hypnosis does not work, no one can say that any untruthful statements have been made to the subjects.

In Part I of Rowland's experiment, the instructions to Subjects *A* and *B* were as follows:

> "Do you see that box?" When the subject said, "Yes," the experimenter went on to say, "There is a piece of coiled rubber rope in that box. Go up to the box, reach through the screen wire, and pick it up."

There was really a rattlesnake in the box, and Rowland lied to the subjects in saying that it was "a piece of coiled rubber rope." He might just as well have produced the illusion of a piece of rubber hose by saying truthfully, "So far as hypnosis works in your case, you will see a piece of coiled rubber rope in that box." With Subjects *C* and *D* Rowland did not attempt to produce in the subjects the illusion of a piece of rope, but bluntly told the subjects that a dangerous rattlesnake was in the box, and that they were to pick it up. He was truthful in this, but he might have been equally truthful in producing an illusion by the art of straight hypnosis.

This is an important point regarding the technique of hypnosis. One should resolve to avoid everything of the nature of the so-called art of suggestion and one should use only a straightforward art of hypnosis if one hopes to get the best hypnotic results. This I have discussed in another article. Any hypnotist who is misled by the frequent association of the words "hypnosis" and "suggestion" throughout most of the literature, and who fails to keep in mind what Sidis pointed out in 1898 regarding the distinction between indirect and direct suggestion, is apt to mar his technique by the use of methods of indirect suggestion. If he does this, he should not expect to get the best hypnotic results. Since the term "suggestion" means indirection both by etymology and by usage, and since Sidis' distinction between direct and indirect suggestion is so often forgotten, it is best to avoid even the appearance of evil by avoiding the use of the term "suggestion" entirely in connection with hypnosis, and by avoiding entirely the use of what is called the art of suggestion, which by usage as much as by etymology means the art of indirect suggestion, involving evasion, concealment, and usually explicit lying.

Now what were the results of this experiment on *Yo,* in which there was the hypnotic attempt to make him steal money? Briefly it may be stated that *the experiment was successful on every point.* When *Yo* was brought out of hypnosis he appeared normal in every respect, except in regard to the details of the forthcoming criminal behavior. There were several of his fellow-students in the office, who had come to observe the experiment. As *Yo* got up and went towards my overcoat to get the dollar, the student, *Ca,* challenged him loudly and abruptly, saying, *"What are you doing with that overcoat? Yo* replied calmly, *"It's my coat,"* in a tone which showed that he was at ease and free from any embarrassment, and which seemed to imply that he felt that he had a perfect right to do whatever he wanted to do with what he obviously saw as his own coat. *Yo* got the dollar and put it into the breast pocket of the coat which he was wearing. Then he walked back to the Morris chair and sat down. To test whether post-hypnotic amnesia for the incident of the dollar and the overcoat had occurred as soon as he sat down, as had been specified in the hypnotic instructions, the other students and I questioned him until we were all satisfied that the amnesia was complete for the fact that he had left the chair and had taken the money. Apologizing for my unmannerly curiosity, I asked him where he carried his money. He said that he carried it in a bill-fold in his pocket. I asked him if he carried all his paper money in this bill-fold. He said that he did. I asked him to search his pockets. He did so in an incredulous manner. When he found the dollar in his breast pocket, his surprise was only momentary. He at once explained (apparently a case of spontaneous paramnesia) that he had forgotten for the moment about this dollar which he had left loose in a pocket outside his bill-fold on this day so that he might be able to get at it easily when paying his fare on the street car. At this point he put the bill into his bill-fold, and I asked him how much money he had (again apologizing for my curiosity and my seemingly bad manners). He counted his money and gave no indication of being aware that there was an extra dollar—a very easy sort of paramnesia to have occurred post-hypnotically.

We then investigated his recall of his own experiences as a hypnotic subject. It was found that everything had worked according to the instructions in hypnosis. He recalled (falsely) that he had been a poor subject when the class participated in group hypnosis. He had amnesia for the fact that he had been hypnotized individually on three separate occasions. When asked why he had come to my office on this particular afternoon, he said that he had come merely to ask some questions about the work of the course and the approaching examination, along with some of the other students.

This was, of course, only the clinical sort of test of amnesia. Whether his amnesia would have withstood "third-degree" methods of the police or the lie-detector methods of the psychological laboratory is another question. On the basis of my previous experimental study of post-hypnotic amnesia I would state it as my opinion that hypnotically induced amnesia in the case of so good a subject as *Yo* would have withstood any possible tests, or at least it might have been made to withstand any possible tests if added precautions had been taken in the hypnotic production of the amnesia. This, however, is a further question which I do not claim to have settled in this instance.

Yo left the office before the others. Then I asked the other students to observe *Yo*'s behavior and to try by argument to get him to accept the fact that he had stolen a dollar of my money. They were asked to accuse him of the crime to which they had been witnesses. They agreed to do so.

The next day when I went to class, *Yo* said to me before class-time that the student, *Ta,* a good friend of his, who had been present at the experiment the day before, had been telling him that he stole a dollar from my overcoat pocket the day before; and he said he thought this was a pretty ridiculous attempt at a joke. I said, *"Well, didn't you do it?"* He said, *"No."* I then argued with him, reminding him of what the students in the course had been taught about hypnosis. I asked him if he could not concede the possibility that through hypnosis he had been made to steal, with hypnotically induced amnesia following. He accepted the theoretical possibility, but said that he frankly could not believe it. He said that even if such things could be brought to pass by means of hypnosis, it would be possible only with good hypnotic subjects; and he said he knew that he was a poor subject, having been found to be such in the group experiment. He could not be made to believe that he had ever been worked on individually. These efforts by the student, *Ta,* and by me were along the line of police accusations, and they made no impression on *Yo.* He showed no tendency to return the stolen dollar. If we had tried to force him to do so on threat of spreading broadcast the report that there were witnesses to the fact of his theft, it seemed certain that he would have persisted in his refusal to be a victim of what would have seemed to him like blackmail. His general reputation for honesty was so good that he felt sure that we could not make people believe our story. It was clear that he thought we had made up this story just to see how he would react, and he was inclined to take it as no more than a practical joke attempted on him. He was a young man of strong convictions, not suggestible in everyday life, not credulous or gullible, an ideal subject for such an experiment in hypnosis.

Criticism is often made in the literature on hypnotism that the usual laboratory experiments in hypnotically induced crime do not prove anything since, it is asserted, only imaginary crimes are attempted, such as having the subject stab another person with a cardboard dagger. Such would be only an imitation crime, and it would not prove that the subject would stab a fellow-man with a real dagger. Since a real murder obviously cannot be attempted in the laboratory, it remains possible for one to say, as James said, "The subject surrenders himself good-naturedly to the performance, stabs with the pasteboard dagger you give him because he knows what it is, and fires off the pistol because he knows it has no ball; but for a real murder he would not be your man." In criticism of James' statement I would like to say that by the art of hypnosis it would be easy with sufficiently good subjects to make them see real daggers as pasteboard daggers, to see cartridges with bullets as blank cartridges, just as Yo was made to see my overcoat as his own, and then what would prevent the occurrence of real murder? But, inasmuch as murder cannot be brought to an experimental test, I devised the simpler crime, of theft, which could easily be brought into the laboratory. This was no imaginary crime which Yo committed. It was a real crime, of picking somebody's pocket, of stealing money and spending it (as events later showed). If he had not eventually returned the money, I should feel a real grievance towards him differing not qualitatively but only quantitatively from my attitude towards some unknown pickpocket in Chicago who once stole my pocket-book containing over $100.00.

Yo's crime was brought about in an easy way, purely by means of the art of hypnosis. In attempting crime through hypnosis, why not really use the art of hypnosis to the limit? Whether Yo could have been made to steal the dollar if he had been without paramnesia and illusions, that is, if he had seen the coat as my own and if he had believed that the money was my own, is another question. Rowland has confirmed the experiments of Bernheim and others proving that this sort of thing can be done; but a subtler art of hypnosis makes possible the elimination of all moral conflict in the carrying out of crime.

Another way to avoid moral conflict in crime experiments would be to produce complete amnesia in the subject for all his ethical knowledge and his moral scruples. If a subject is not a good enough subject for the hypnotic production of amnesia for all that he has ever learned about right and wrong, then he is not a good enough subject for such experiments. There are all sorts of ways in which difficult hypnotic experiments might be made to work. The methods which I used were hit upon as a good example of the sort of procedure which I thought ought to be successful. If one hypnotic method fails, then try another method. Above all things, if one hypnotic method fails, don't conclude that no hypnotic methods will succeed. A thousand failures due to poor technique or poor subjects do not disprove the efficacy of adequate methods on suitable subjects.

It would have been interesting to have let the amnesia in *Yo's* case remain for a few months, or even for a year, as I did in my amnesia experiments referred to above. *Yo's* friends in the class, however, thought that the matter was too serious, with possibilities of moral injury to the subject. They told me that, if they were in *Yo's* place, they would prefer that the theft should not be left to stand through the summer without removal of amnesia resulting in a probable urge to make restitution. Consequently I hypnotized *Yo* once more, the following week. Because of his amnesia for the fact that he had ever been hypnotized, he was incredulous when I mentioned trying to hypnotize him; but he said that he would let me attempt it. He immediately went into deep hypnosis, and I then made him recall, or rather let him recall spontaneously in the hypnotic state, all the details of the theft. Then, with special care to repair by hypnotherapeutic methods any possible moral damage which he might have suffered, I brought him out of hypnosis with all the hypnotically induced amnesias removed, amnesias both for the experiment in crime production, and for the other hypnotic sessions. He did not return the dollar to me on that day, for the obvious reason, as I learned later, that he did not have that much money. In fact, he made no mention of restitution on that day, from embarrassment, I think, at the fact that he was without money. Two days later, at the next meeting of the class, however, he greeted me before class with a dollar bill in his hand. He said:

Here's your dollar. It isn't the same dollar which I stole from your pocket, for I spent that one. This dollar is just as good, however.

If he had not paid back the money after his amnesia was removed, this might have been taken as evidence that he was not at heart strictly honest. His repayment after memory of his theft had been restored by means of hypnosis was simply in line with his strictly honest and honorable type of character, for which I can vouch strongly on the basis of enquiries and a fairly good acquaintance with him in the teacher-student relationship.

Though theft is a real crime, it is not claimed that Yo was responsible, but quite the contrary. If such a case were to come before a court, a just decision would be, "guilty, but not responsible." We have this kind of verdict sometimes in cases of kleptomania or in cases of mental disease characterized by hallucinations, delusions, and amnesias. In such cases the full verdict usually is, "guilty, but not responsible by virtue of mental disease." By means of hypnosis hallucinations (and illusions), delusions, compulsions, and amnesias may be produced, exactly matching their clinical appearance as symptoms of disease. The question was whether Yo could be made to commit a criminal act which was contrary to his usual moral principles. The answer was that he actually stole the money, and that stealing was decidedly contrary to his usual character. Even if the latter assertion were not true, even if he had been dishonest by nature, he would not voluntarily have incriminated himself by stealing when witnesses were present who might later be called on to testify against him.

It is desirable to perform control experiments wherever this is feasible. In the case of some hypnotic experiments, control experiments are not only feasible but highly valuable. For example, in my study of post-hypnotic amnesia, each subject learned a series of non-sense syllables in the hypnotic state with hypnotically induced amnesia following, or else learned the same syllables in the normal state, with amnesia produced by means of hypnosis immediately afterwards. As a control experiment, the same subjects learned in the normal state another list of syllables of equivalent difficulty, and for this list no hypnotic amnesia was produced. For this list only normal forgetting occurred. Then there were later tests, at varying intervals up to a year, of the amounts of amnesia by means of recall tests, recognition tests, and relearning tests of both the hypnotic and the control series of syllables. In such an experiment it seemed obvious that the control experiment should be included, and the inclusion of it added to the value of the whole experiment.

In many hypnotic experiments, on the other hand, control experiments are either impossible or absurd. E.g., to have proved the completeness of hypnotic anesthesia in cases, reported in the earlier literature, of surgical operations in which large abdominal tumors were removed under hypnotic anesthesia, would it have been necessary to have waited for other abdominal tumors to grow in the same persons, and then to have removed these later tumors surgically without any sort of anesthesia, to prove that in these cases the persons were normally sensitive to pain? Or if a patient's left leg had been amputated painlessly under hypnotic anesthesia, would it be necessary to amputate the right leg of the same patient without the use of any kind of anesthetic, to make certain that in this case the patient was not chronically anesthetic?

In experiments on hypnotic anesthesia for surgical purposes, no precise control experiments are possible, even if they were necessary. I have twice administered hypnotic anesthesia for purposes of dental surgery. In the first case, a large and what the dentist considered to be a normally very painful cavity in a molar was filled. The hypnotized subject, with whom I was in conversation during the dental operation, reported not the slightest pain. The dentist could not detect the slightest evidence of pain from the movements of the subject. It was not feasible to have the dentist grind out an equally large cavity in another tooth, without hypnotic anesthesia being applied, to satisfy the subject, the dentist, and the hypnotist that the hypnotic anesthesia had been complete. It was not feasible since the subject had no more cavities, and it seemed inhumane to produce one just for experimental purposes. In another case I produced complete hypnotic anesthesia in a subject for purposes of extraction by a dentist of a badly decayed wisdom tooth. The subject experienced no pain during the extraction, as determined by introspective report at the time of the extraction, and gave not the slightest indication by muscular quiverings that he experienced any pain. The results were quite different, it might be said in passing, from those in an unsuccessful attempt by Erickson to produce hypnotic anesthesia for a tooth extraction. In this case of Erickson's, as described by Hull, "the patient . . . whimpered and flinched decidedly while the tooth was being extracted." It would not have been feasible to have had the dentist extract another wisdom tooth from my subject's jaw just in order to make the demonstration of the efficacy of hypnotic anesthesia conclusive by means of a control experiment, simply for the reason that the subject had no other wisdom tooth which needed to be extracted. The subject's own experience with previous extractions with novocaine, which in his recall were not entirely without pain, the common experience of mankind with dental extractions, and the dentist's experience with all sorts and conditions of mankind in the dentist's chair, were sufficient for comparative purposes to render the demonstration of hypnotic anesthesia for purposes of dental surgery highly conclusive.

In the same way, though a control experiment in the case of Yo and the theft of money would have been possible, it would have been ridiculous. To have tried to make Yo steal money without using hypnosis for the purpose, with Yo fully warned in advance and challenged to do his utmost to resist doing anything of a criminal nature, simply by repeating to him in the normal state what I stated to him in hypnosis regarding the occurrence of illusions, compulsions, and amnesias, was too preposterous to contemplate. Any control experiment could only have been a farce.

The results of the successful experiment with *Yo* is in line with what one would expect from reading the literature of the Nancy school of the '80's. "There were giants in the earth in those days," men like Liebeault and Bernheim who had hypnotized many thousands in the space of a few years, and who knew well the art of hypnosis. To be sure, both Liebeault and Bernheim, being physicians primarily interested in curing their patients by whatever methods would succeed, failed to distinguish ordinary suggestion, which is indirect suggestion, from straight hypnosis, which involves only direct suggestion if it involves suggestion at all (i.e., if direct suggestion, so called, should really be called suggestion at all). But they did know how to get hypnotic results which the present generation of psychologists is largely unfamiliar with. Many of the published results of present-day hypnosis manifest amateurish work by inexperienced psychologists and graduate students, who simply have not learned how to get extreme results. Hull's book on *Hypnosis and Suggestibility* is to a large extent a record of experiments by just such inexperienced operators, who failed to get maximum results from lack of skill in the hypnotic technique and from lack of opportunity to select a few of the best subjects from large numbers by means of hypnotizing groups wholesale. When such experimenters try to repeat classical experiments of the '80's and when they fail (as they often do), they sometimes publish their failures with the implication that, since they do not get the results which Bernheim reported, such results cannot be obtained by anyone and were not really obtained by Bernheim. The fact is, failures are only failures; and numerous failures do not invalidate one single success when the latter comes. Rather than publish results of hypnotic experiments that failed, many experimenters would do better to study more deeply the theory and the technique of successful hypnosis, or else simply admit that they have not yet learned adequately the art of hypnosis.

One of the most glaring examples that has come to my attention of the tendency which I am describing is Erickson's recent article on the possible anti-social use of hypnosis. Erickson writes on the basis of experiments on 50 subjects, in all of which experiments he failed to produce real anti-social behavior on the part of any hypnotized subjects. His conclusion, quoted above in the introduction to this article, is to the effect that therefore anti-social behavior cannot be produced hypnotically by anyone.

Dr. Donald Laird, formerly professor of psychology at Colgate University, has written as follows regarding hypnotic crime and Erickson's work:

> The general public seems to believe that hypnotized persons will do unlawful things directly as a result of being hypnotized. The careful and conclusive work of Dr. Milton H. Erickson, at the Eloise, Michigan, Hospital and Infirmary, shows that this notion is untrue. Neither while hypnotized, nor later as a result of ideas planted while hypnotized, could he get people to do unlawful or wicked deeds, not even tiny ones. Dr. Erickson is an outstanding hypnotist of the present time, and should be able to accomplish this if it were possible.

I would say that Erickson should be able to do this if he understands and can practice well the art of hypnosis. Since he admits that he cannot achieve such results, he is admitting that he has not learned an adequate hypnotic technique. Erickson's failures, contrary to what Laird says, do not invalidate successful hypnotic results by others.

In one important study of hypnotically induced deafness Erickson reported success with six subjects out of the original 100 that he started with, as judged by clinical tests, and with two of these subjects he was able to produce deafness as good as organic deafness as tested by a conditioned-response technique. What if he had reported only the failures with the 94 (or the 98) out of the original 100 subjects, having for some reason failed to find the six or the two sufficiently good subjects, or having failed to develop a sufficiently good technique for achieving success with even these potentially good subjects? Would he have been justified in concluding that successful results in the hypnotic deafness experiment are impossible? If I had stopped my own experiments after my failure with three subjects even to induce hypnosis when attempting the crime experiment, without successfully carrying out the experiment with the fourth subject, would I have been justified in concluding that successful results could not be produced on any subjects by any hypnotists? And yet Erickson does precisely this in his article, which reports failures on 50 subjects, with no successes, when he writes, "The conclusion warranted by these experimental findings is that hypnosis cannot be misused to induce hypnotized persons to commit actual wrongful acts either against themselves or others."

The older literature contains descriptions of hypnotic crime experiments which failed as well as descriptions of experiments which succeeded. Janet has described one classic experiment:

A number of persons of importance, magistrates and professors, had assembled in the main hall of the Salpetriere museum to witness a great seance of criminal . . . [hypnosis]. Witt., the principal subject, thrown into the somnambulist state, had under the influence of . . . [hypnosis] displayed the most sanguinary instincts. At a word or sign, she had stabbed, shot, and poisoned; the room was littered with corpses . . . The notables had withdrawn, greatly impressed, leaving only a few students with the subject, who was still in the somnambulist state. The students, having a fancy to bring the seance to a close by a less blood-curdling experiment, made a very simple . . . [command] to Witt. They told her that she was now quite alone in the hall. She was to strip and take a bath. Witt., who had murdered all the magistrates without

turning a hair, was seized with shame at the thought of un-
dressing. Rather than accede to the . . . [command], she had
a violent fit of hysterics.

Even Janet appears to have accepted this experiment uncritically as
casting doubt on the possibility of producing by means of hypnosis
real anti-social behavior as distinguished from fictitious crimes.

A more obvious interpretation of this incident would seem to be
that the students, being amateurs inexperienced in successful hypnotizing, simply did not know the art of hypnosis well enough
to make their attempted experiment succeed. Casual readers who
come upon this account at the present time are apt to be misled,
interpreting this failure, due most likely to a clumsy technique,
as establishing an essential truth regarding the limits of successful hypnosis. How unfortunate that Janet did not mention, along
with his account of this failure, a similar experiment which did
succeed when performed by the experienced hypnotist Forel!
Moll mentions this successful experiment by Forel, and agrees
with Forel that this experiment forces us to "admit that in excep-
tional cases it is possible for a person to be induced [by means of
hypnosis] to commit acts which are contrary to his disposition."

Bramwell tells of an attempt of his own to make a hypnotized
subject steal a watch. The attempt failed. As has been mentioned
above, Bramwell did not believe that real criminal acts could be
produced by means of hypnosis, basing his conclusions on his own
failures in experiments. Most experienced hypnotists on reading
Bramwell's account of his attempt to make the subject steal a
watch, will be impressed with Bramwell's failure to use a good
technique. Bramwell's technique was so poor that in only one
case did he ever succeed in making a subject carry out even an
imaginary crime, yet the literature on hypnotism is full of accounts
of successful experiments in the production of imaginary crimes.
As Munsterberg expressed it, "All that has been demonstrated by
experiments a hundred times." One can only wonder at Bramwell's reputation in hypnotism when, by his own admission, he

was so unsuccessful in non-therapeutic experiments. A major factor in Bramwell's failures, perhaps, is his confusion of hypnosis with ordinary suggestion. Compared with Bernheim, Bramwell, by his own admission of failures, showed himself a very poor operator in attempting to get results against the subject's will.

Bernheim had his failures, too, some of which he records, but he records them *as failures*. For example, he once tried to induce by means of hypnosis the theft of a spoon. The attempt failed. Bernheim attributed his failure to his own inadequate methods in this particular experiment. At a later date he had occasion to repeat the experiment with the same subject, and this time got successful results.

Erickson describes an attempt to get a hypnotized subject to examine the contents of a friend's purse, though not to steal anything from it. The attempt failed. Careful reading of Erickson's account of the experiment leaves the impression that the subject was a poor subject, and also that the technique was poor. Erickson says that he tried to instill in the subject the "impression" that the friend's purse was her own purse. This did not work. If the subject had been deeply somnambulistic and a good enough subject for such an experiment, it should have been possible to induce, not merely an "impression" of the friend's purse being her own, but a definite delusion based upon an actual illusion. Erickson says, "Upon being rehypnotized, the subject explained that she simply could not do what had been asked, but added that she had 'tried hard'." The last two words quoted reveal a serious flaw in Erickson's technique, and presumably in his theory, of hypnosis. A subject in successful hypnotic experiments should experience just the opposite of what this subject reported, so that an introspective report would be, "I simply could not help doing what was asked, though I tried hard *to resist*."

The "Law of Reversed Effort" as formulated by Coue and by Baudouin is based on a true insight resulting from Coue's extensive experience with hypnosis. Hypnosis is a method of producing dissociation: it is a method of controlling the experiences and the behavior of the subject through controlling dissociated, i.e., subconscious processes. Hypnosis succeeds only when the subconscious factors are more potent than the conscious factors. One of Coue's usual statements to the subject when trying to produce contractures of the eyelids in waking hypnosis was, "Think, I want to open my eyelids, but I cannot do so. They are shut tight—tight—tight—tight," and so on. "I want to, but I can't," or "I wish not to, but I can't prevent it," is the characteristic introspective report of successfully hypnotized subjects. Baudouin has expressed it in these words: "Whenever anyone is in the state of mind, 'I should like to, but I cannot,' he may wish as much as he pleases; but the harder he tries the less he is able."

The point that I am trying to make clear here is that the hypnotic phenomenon of eyelid contractures will not be regarded as having been successfully produced unless the subject is really helpless to open his eyes. Nothing could be worse from the point of view of adequate hypnotic theory and practice than for the operator to say to the subject, "Try to keep your eyes closed" (unless, indeed, the operator was trying to bring about the opposite condition, in which the eyelids remain open against the subject's efforts to close them). Eyelid contractures are a very elementary hypnotic phenomenon. There are many long steps between it and the somnambulistic stage, but no new principles are involved even in the deepest trance states. That Erickson's subject reported that she had "tried hard" to carry out the hypnotic instructions is evidence of something very seriously amiss in Erickson's technique.

Erickson attempted with some of his subjects to induce stealing, but without success. In all the cases described, there is nothing to indicate that the subjects were sufficiently good hypnotic subjects for such an experiment, or that anything but a most casual technique was employed. Erickson says that he worked with "approximately 50 subjects selected from a total of more than 75." In other words, Erickson was attempting with approximately

67 percent of the original 75 subjects, what even Liebeault and Bernheim did not claim to be able to do successfully with more than four or five percent. According to the Nancy school, which has achieved the greatest successes in hypnosis, although over 90 percent of persons are hypnotizable to some degree, only 15 or 20 percent are somnambulistic, and not all somnambules are good enough subjects for difficult experiments. If Erickson had sorted out the best 15 percent of the original 75 subjects, or at most the best 25 or 30 percent, by means of group hypnosis (a time- and labor-saving method without which I personally would have given up hypnosis many years ago on account of the time-consuming difficulty of individual hypnosis used alone), and then if he had refused to waste time on any but the very best subjects, he might have found four or five percent who would have repaid the time and effort of intensive individual experiments by an improved technique.

Erickson reports that his efforts to produce anti-social behavior on the part of his subjects led in most instances to an attitude of ill-will of the subjects towards the experimenter. He says:

> Despite their well-established trust and confidence in the experimenter, almost invariably the experimentation reported here caused them to develop intense resentments and antagonisms towards him . . . Certain of the subjects actually inflicted punishment and humiliation upon the experimenter in retaliation for his objectionable commands.

Such a confession implies something very seriously wrong with Erickson's hypnotic methods. If one were to use methods of ordinary suggestion, with indirection and even lying, an attitude of ill-will on the part of subjects is understandable and indeed commendable. But with a technique of straight hypnosis, involving no tricks and no lying suggestions, ill-will should not be engendered on the part of subjects. I am at a loss to explain the ill-will of Erickson's subjects unless methods of ordinary suggestion were used. I myself would resent the deliberate use of indirect suggestion on myself, by any psychologist or physician; and I have always done my utmost to avoid it in hypnotizing others. I have never had any indication of resentment or ill-will of my subjects as a result of any hypnotic experiments. Even extreme skeptics to whom I have applied the above-mentioned cigarette test have not blamed me. Their attitude has been rather that they would not believe such an extreme degree of helplessness could be produced unless they experienced it themselves. The pain from the burning was taken as an essential part of the test, for which they blamed only themselves for their inability to release their hands.

It is easy to fail to get results in hypnosis. If one wishes not to get results, results will seldom thrust themselves upon the experimenter. If one's theory in advance of hypnosis is that hypnosis is only like ordinary suggestion, e.g., then one should not expect to produce worthwhile results. If one's technique is borrowed in any respect from the methods of ordinary medical suggestion or of ordinary laboratory experiments with what the manuals of experimental psychology call suggestion, one will not get very far with hypnosis. The fact that Erickson did get good results, even extreme results, in his experiment on deafness, with six or at least with two percent of his subjects, would indicate that he could, if he wanted to, get extreme results in other hypnotic experiments. Perhaps he did not wish (consciously or subconsciously) to produce anti-social behavior, lest this should prejudice some people against hypnosis. Such a wish would not be reasonable, but it might exist all the same. Unless hypnosis were powerful for harm if misused, it could not be powerful for good in therapeutic ways when properly used. Physicians might commit crimes by means of drugs and surgery, and hence there is a reason for the oath of Hippocrates which physicians take. Hypnotizing ought to be limited to instructional, research, and therapeutic uses in the hands of psychologists or physicians who are properly qualified both intellectually and morally. People should be taught not to submit to hypnosis except for serious purposes and at the hands of competent and honorable hypnotists. A reliable third person should be present as a witness at every occasion of hypnotizing, as a protection both for the subject and for the hypnotist. But the fact that crime might be produced by means of hypnosis is no more serious an objection than that crime might be produced by means of medicines which physicians prescribe. If persons had it in their power to inhibit at will the effect of drugs, the efficacy of pharmacotherapy would be nullified. If people had it in their power to prevent hypnotic effects, then hypnosis would have lost much of its significance. The majority of people cannot be hypnotized deeply; but so far as they are hypnotizable at all, their memories, their perceptual processes, and their behavior are to some degree under the control of the hypnotist.

Even if, for the sake of argument, it should be admitted that there is something more sinister about the matter of hypnotically induced crime than about the matter of crimes caused by drugs prescribed by physicians, still the truth should be known. A scientist should not indulge in wishful thinking, nor should he let his presuppositions limit his efforts to get at the facts by laboratory methods. Bernheim has written a passage which deserves to be inscribed on the walls of every laboratory in which hypnotic experiments are attempted. It is as follows:

> Certain minds have a horror of the marvelous. They are right: but they are wrong when they consider as marvelous and systematically deny, facts which they have not verified, just because these facts do not agree with the a priori conceptions in their minds. The facts are undeniable: the interpretation of them follows; if that is faulty, do not blame the facts, but the insufficiency of our knowledge of psychology and nervous physiology.

Schilder and Kauders, like Erickson, deny the possibility of hypnotically induced crime. They assert, "There is not a single well accredited case of a real crime having been performed by a hypnotized person on the command of the hypnotizer and against the will of the hypnotized person." Then, in support of this assertion, they take as a lone example of attempted crime experiments the case of an imaginary crime, shooting with blank cartridges in a pretended murder, with failure to get the subject even to shoot with the blank cartridges. They seem to draw their very sweeping general conclusion from this one case of failure. As has been pointed out above, the literature teems with *successful* experiments in the production of *imaginary* crimes, and with occasional experiments in which *real* crime against the will of the hypnotized subject has been caused by hypnosis. The one single case cited above, in which Bernheim succeeded, in the second attempt, in getting a hypnotized subject to steal a spoon, is enough to refute Schilder and Kauders' sweeping negative generalization.

Thinking that they have proved that crime never has been produced hypnotically, and that it never can thus be produced (by citing one lone case of failure!), Schilder and Kauders proceed to make two erroneous statements intended as an explanation of why the asserted impossibility exists. They say, "We must not forget that the hypnotized person is always aware of the general situation, that he is conscious of the fact that an experiment is being made on him." These two assertions would hold only of non-somnambulistic subjects, on whom no experienced hypnotist would attempt any sort of crime experiment. In the case of somnambulistic subjects, at least in the case of those most profoundly somnambulistic, complete amnesia can be caused for the "general situation" and for the "fact that an experiment is being made on him," thus nullifying *in toto* Schilder and Kauders' two assertions. E.g., in the experiment with *Yo,* reported above, *Yo* came out of hypnosis with complete amnesia for the general situation. He not only had amnesia for the fact that an experiment was being done on him, but even for the fact that he had ever been hypnotized. It was in this post-hypnotic situation that *Yo* stole the dollar. Illusions and hallucinations, also, can be produced both hypnotically and post-hypnotically, in the case of sufficiently good subjects, rendering the subjects still further from being "aware of the general situation," as in the case of *Yo*. The false statement by Schilder and Kauders that "the hypnotized person is always aware of the general situation" is flatly contradicted by Schilder and Kauders themselves when they correctly assert in another context, "The fact that conceptions during hypnosis may rise to the stage of actual perceptions (i.e., of hallucinations) has already been repeatedly mentioned by us."

Schilder and Kauders' book is written from the point of view of psychoanalysis. One might as readily look for a satisfactory history of Great Britain from the pen of Adolph Hitler, as for a satisfactory account of hypnosis from the pen of psychoanalysts. Freud stated, "Psychoanalysis itself only began with my rejection of the hypnotic technique." Having rejected hypnosis at the start, it is only natural that psychoanalysis should attempt to minimize the significance and value of what has been rejected, as an excuse for rejecting it.

During the year following my successful experiment with *Yo*, Miss Margaret Brenman was a graduate student in some of my classes, and she desired to learn the practice of hypnosis. She had never done any hypnotizing before, nor had she seen any really successful work in this field. She observed one demonstration of my group hypnosis. She observed my work of developing several individual subjects, and three of my class-room demonstrations of individual hypnosis. She took notes on some of my individual work, and did some special reading in the field of hypnosis, including the rough draft of the first part of this article, with its discussion of hypnotic technique. With this limited background she began hypnotizing towards the end of the year, working on six of the seven best subjects selected from 30 women students who had taken part in group hypnosis which I had carried out during the year. I allow women students to take part in group hypnosis, but I never hypnotize women subjects in individual experimental work because of popular prejudice against hypnosis, campus gossip, and possible parental objection. These six women subjects had received from me only the minimal amount of hypnotic training as subjects which is involved in group hypnosis lasting only part of a class hour. Beyond this point Miss Brenman developed all six to the somnambulistic stage. On three of the six she attempted a repetition, with some variations, of the sort of crime experiment which I did on *Yo*. She achieved success with all three, producing actual theft in all cases. Only one of the subjects was potentially as hypnotizable as *Yo*. With this subject Miss Brenman duplicated in all essential respects my results with *Yo*. With the two other subjects real crime was produced, but in a manner which, though conclusive, was not so spectacular as in the case of *Yo* or as in the case of Miss Brenman's best subject.

Her success with her best subject, however, must be qualified by the discovery, *after* the experiment, that stealing was most definitely *not* contrary to the normal character of the subject. After the experiment she was proved to be a "moral scatter-brain" if not a "moral imbecile" so far as possessing a conscience in financial matters is concerned. The most that Miss Brenman's experiment with her third subject proves is that in the case of this subject an act which was really criminal was brought about by means of hypnosis; and it was brought about against the subject's will in the sense that the subject had declared her expectation and her determination to prevent whatever was attempted in hypnosis: but the act would not have seemed criminal to her in her normal state of mind because of her lack of conscience in such matters. However, she was so good a hypnotic subject that only the mischance of the belated discovery of her lack of honesty, after and not before the experiment, prevented Miss Brenman from devising an experiment which would have involved the doing of something which the subject herself would have considered immoral.

Miss Brenman's successes in the crime experiment with three, or at least with two, of the subjects on whom she tried the experiment, make the failures of experienced hypnotists like Bramwell or Erickson all the more striking. If a beginner in the art of hypnosis, a graduate student in her first year of practical experience in hypnotizing, can successfully carry out experiments in which her subjects are forced to perform anti-social acts against their wills, then psychologists or physicians with more experience with hypnosis who fail in all such experiments should be put to shame, or encouraged to improve their technique until they, too, can get equally successful results. Miss Brenman's account of her own successful production of anti-social behavior in hypnotized subjects will be ready for publication soon.

There are obvious reasons why hypnotic experiments in crime are carried out only under special difficulties. The purpose of such experiments might easily be misunderstood, and unfavorable criticisms might arise locally. On the day following commencement of the year in which I had done the experiments on *Sk, Ba, Th,* and *Yo,* I read in the local newspaper an item to the effect that the father of one of the seniors had had his pocket picked on the campus on commencement day. It was stated that he had lost a sum of about forty dollars, and that he had reported the alleged theft to the University and to the local police department. An incident like this might easily have become associated in campus gossip with experiments in pocket-picking carried out a short time previously in the department of psychology.

This investigation has been devoted to the problem of whether a hypnotized subject who is of non-criminal character can be made to commit real crime. The answer, on the basis of the actual experimental achievement of this result, is most emphatically in the affirmative.

The hypnotic literature has been surveyed in some detail so far as it bears on this problem. The claim of the Nancy school that real criminal behavior can be brought about in a small percentage of hypnotized subjects is supported in the older literature by a small amount of experimental evidence. The claim of hypnotists like Bramwell in the past and like Schilder and Kauders and Erickson in the present, that real crime cannot be produced by means of hypnosis, is supported only by reports of failures on the part of certain experimenters to duplicate the results of the Nancy school. In this article some of these experimental failures have been described, and there has been an exposition of the fallacy involved in interpreting failures as if such failures marked the limits beyond which successful hypnosis could not go. I have traced the failures of some of these experimenters to shortcomings in the hypnotic technique employed or to a failure to select for such experiments only the most highly hypnotizable subjects. I have described experiments conducted by myself on four subjects selected from a total of 36 men students by means of group hypnosis, in the attempt to cause subjects to steal money post-hypnotically. The first series of experiments, on three subjects, failed: the cause of the failure was discovered, and success was achieved with the fourth subject. Reference has been made to the work the following year of Miss Margaret Brenman, a graduate student whom I had been instructing in the art of hypnosis during one college year. She has succeeded in repeating with some degree of success the crime experiment (of theft) on three women students.

The problem is more important theoretically than practically. Hypnosis is so difficult, and the opportunities for criminals to learn the art and to use it in criminal ways are so slight, that little is to be feared in a practical way, especially if hypnosis is reserved for its proper uses, of instruction, research, and therapy, in the hands of properly qualified psychologists or physicians. But the whole point as to the essential nature of hypnosis is missed unless the fact is recognized that even so extreme a phenomenon as real crime against the will of the fully forewarned subject can be produced by means of it. In this connection I have devoted considerable space to a discussion of the art of hypnosis as distinguished from the art of suggestion. The dissociation theory of hypnosis, which is stated or implied throughout my discussion of the theory of hypnosis, lends itself most adequately to the interpretation of extreme results such as the actual production of crime or the production of permanently successful therapeutic results.

---

*From *The Journal of Psychology*, 1941, 11, 63-102.

A FOOTNOTE TO "EXPERIMENTS IN THE HYPNOTIC PRODUCTION OF CRIME"

Miss Brenman continued independently her experiments on crime production through hypnotic methods, begun under my supervision in 1940; and her experiments, published in 1943, are the most extensive of present-day repetitions of classical experiments on hypnotic crime production.

Several times, as opportunities have arisen through the availability of highly hypnotizable subjects, and as provocation has arisen from expressions of skepticism, I have repeated the sort of experiment that I reported in 1941 on the subject *Yo*, sometimes with even more striking success. The last time that I did this was no longer ago than last week. I have not attempted the experiment on any subjects except those truly somnambulistic by the amnesia test; but I have succeeded in the production of criminal acts, such as stealing, in cases where I was unable to produce either hallucinations or anesthesia sufficient for surgical purposes. In other words, I have found it less difficult to bring about criminal acts in unwilling subjects through hypnotic methods than to bring about hallucinations and anesthesia sufficient for surgical purposes in willing subjects through similar methods.

Any hypnotist who cannot succeed in such experiments is simply admitting that he has not yet learned an adequate hypnotic technique. That crime can be brought about through hypnosis is no argument against the use of hypnosis any more than the possibility of criminal uses of drugs and surgery is an argument against the use of drugs and surgery. Hypnotizing is serious business, and it should be restricted to responsible and adequately trained psychologists and physicians, for instructional, research, and therapeutic purposes; it should never be used for entertainment purposes by showmen on the stage or over the radio.

January 18, 1947.   WESLEY R. WELLS.

AN ANALYSIS OF MOTIVATION IN HYPNOSIS*

ROBERT W. WHITE
Psychological Clinic, Harvard University

EDITOR'S NOTE

The susceptibility to hypnosis seems to depend upon motivation as well as aptitude. The motivation consists mostly of the needs that are aroused and satisfied by the prospect of hypnosis. They are intrinsic factors that hinder or facilitate hypnosis, and take precedence over aptitude, since they are encountered before one's aptitudes. The need for deference and autonomy are common; need for love and aggression may also be factors.

It has long been recognized that successful hypnosis depends to some extent on the subject's willingness to be hypnotized. The operator must allay the ordinary anxieties, induce confidence, and evoke favorable attitudes toward the whole proceeding, for it is at least approximately true that no one can be hypnotized against his will. The factors which contribute to this willingness have been called "finalistic" and "dynamic," but since there are objections to both terms it will be more satisfactory to designate them simply *motivational*. It is the purpose of the present paper to scrutinize these motivational factors and to estimate their part in the production of hypnosis. Stated in another way, the problem is to discover what needs are awakened in a person by the attempt to hypnotize him, and in what manner these needs affect the outcome.

It is unlikely that motivational factors alone determine susceptibility to hypnosis. Most workers agree that in addition to willingness there must be a suitable *aptitude*, perhaps a constitutional capacity, if the hypnotic trance is to take place. The best somnambulists do not always give evidence of being the most strongly motivated, and there is convincing genuineness in the disappointment not infrequently shown by eager subjects who cannot advance beyond a light stage. As in most human activities there no doubt must be a confluence of aptitude and motive to bring about a successful result. In the case of hypnosis, moreover, the aptitude is by no means a matter of secondary interest, for there is at least some reason to believe that it stands in a special relation to hysteria. But the analysis of motivational factors necessarily comes first, because in the hypnotic experiment they are the first to be evoked. The aptitude, whatever its nature, cannot begin to be effective until the procedure for inducing hypnosis is well under way. Motivational factors, on the other hand, become active the moment the subject knows that hypnosis is to be attempted, which may be some time beforehand, and they receive an additional impetus when he enters the room and confronts the operator. Being thus first in possession of the field, the subject's needs are in a strategic position to prevent the aptitude from exerting any influence whatsoever. Previous investigators have rarely made a satisfactory allowance for this circumstance; they have tried to examine hypnotic aptitude without first rescuing it from a snarled traffic of motives. If aptitude is to be brought into even an approximate isolation, it is essential first to consider seriously the part played by motivation in hypnosis.

A. THE HYPNOTIC SITUATION

The first goal of the inquiry is to discover what needs are aroused in subjects when they are confronted with a test for hypnotic susceptibility. But before the needs can be properly apprehended it will be necessary to analyze the situation or press. It is often convenient to think of the hypnotic session as a test yielding numerical scores, but this should not be allowed to obscure its peculiarities. In most tests there is at least a fairly clear indication of what constitutes a good performance, and reason to suppose that nearly all the subjects have tried their best to achieve it. With hypnosis there is no such standard; complete resistance to every suggestion may be thought a triumph rather than a failure. Furthermore, entrance into the hypnotic sleep is less a question of trying than of letting something happen, and the attainment of the requisite relaxation is not, like active striving, a readily recognized virtue. Hypnosis, in contrast to the ordinary experimental situation wherein the subject's attention is centered on some specified task before him, must be regarded as fundamentally a special kind of relationship between two persons. More than this, it must be viewed as an emotionally toned relationship. Janet, after a lifetime of experience, expresses himself strongly on this point: "I am confident," he writes, "that we shall always arouse intense emotion when we try to hypnotize." In this relationship the hypnotist takes the lead, making requests and giving orders which seem designed to take away from the subject, at least for the time being, control over his actions and thoughts. However earnestly the operator disclaims such formidable intentions and strives to put the experiment in its most innocent light, it is impossible to banish from a subject's mind these inevitable features of hypnosis.

In a social relationship the attitude of the leading participant is a matter of fundamental importance. Yet it is distinctly uncommon to find this attitude specified in the literature on hypnotic susceptibility. Even when the technique is given in some detail, it is not always clear whether the operator was friendly or impersonal, eager or indifferent, domineering or unpretentious. McDougall classified the available attitudes under two general heads which he called "domination" and "co-operation." The former "consists essentially in adopting a domineering, commanding tone," designed to throw the subject into an attitude of submissive awe toward the operator. The other method "consists in explaining as clearly as possible to the patient the nature of the operation, and of the results to be expected; taking him into one's confidence and eliciting his voluntary co-operation." One must agree with McDougall's further comment that many of the surprising discrepancies among reports on hypnotic susceptibility may be due to unstated differences of attitude on the part of the operators.

The task of defining the situation is made no easier by the somewhat startling conceptions of hypnotism which prevail in popular fancy, in literature, and in the theater. Unlimited and malign dominance, whereby the hypnotist moves to some criminal end such as rape or robbery, lends itself to dramatic treatment more readily than the restricted and qualified powers which the scientific operator claims for himself. Impressions of this sort are often firmly lodged in a subject's mind, and the experimenter is badly deceived who fancies that he can pry them loose by reciting a fixed set of instructions or even by energetic persuasion. For the average person without special training, the word "hypnotism," far from being a simple stimulus, is caught in a web of far-reaching ethical implications which contribute sometimes momentously to his attitude.

The hypnotic situation thus constitutes a press of somewhat complex and variable character. Its most invariant feature is the press of dominance: the subject is to behave in certain ways not of his own free will but in automatic response to assertions proceeding from the operator. This is, of course, a special form of dominance, demanding rather more complete, even though provisional, surrender and suspension of judgment than are implied in ordinary attempts to lead or persuade. But although dominance is always the central press, it is usually modified, as we have seen, in two important respects, by the purpose and attitude of the operator, and by the subject's natural misconceptions. Thus when the operator is a physician and the subject a suffering patient, hypnosis becomes a press of benign dominance from which benefit is expected. If the hypnotist adopts a co-operative attitude, the dominance inherent in the situation is modified in the direction of friendly mutual enterprise. On the other hand, if the subject has been impressed by moving-picture plots he may sincerely believe that hypnosis offers a crucial test of his strength of character and ability to withstand malign influences. In a given case it is often difficult to determine just what factors are effective unless the subject is able and willing to tell.

B. MANIFEST NEEDS

Having considered the nature of the hypnotic situation, we are in a position to ask what needs are aroused in the subject. We shall divide the inquiry between manifest and latent needs, meaning by the former such needs as are freely manifested in overt behavior, by the latter such needs as express themselves only in indirect ways like dreams and fantasy.

The older literature on hypnosis is full of statements concerning the influence on susceptibility of age, sex, race, nationality, occupation and the like. The statements do not always agree, and in many cases the categories, while socially important, possess little psychological significance, so that even the most certain statements would add nothing to useful knowledge. The factor of age, however, might conceivably yield important insights, and it must therefore be regretted that no conclusive studies have been made. Bramwell examined a good deal of evidence and pronounced it the consensus of opinion that children even as young as two and a half years can be hypnotized more easily than adults. Quite a different conclusion was reached by Moll who declared, "Infants under three years of age can hardly be hypnotized at all, and even up to six years of age children can only be hypnotized with difficulty." An experiment of Messerschmidt reported by Hull shows that responsiveness to suggestion of postural sway increases from five to eight years and decreases from eight to sixteen. Unfortunately the correlation between postural sway tests and hypnosis is not high enough to make this finding the basis for a final conclusion, and the relation between hypnotic susceptibility and age remains insufficiently understood.

1. *Sex*

Concerning the sex factor, on the other hand, the evidence seems to be clearer. Hull combines three sets of data, representing several hundred subjects, to show that women do not significantly exceed men in hypnotic responsiveness, and this conclusion has recently received additional support from an investigation by Friedlander and Sarbin. If the overt or manifest sex need played an important part in hypnosis one would expect, since the operators in every case were men, that women would make higher average scores. The evidence makes it safe to dismiss the hypothesis.

2. *Extraversion*

Various writers, especially McDougall, have argued that extraversion ought to be positively correlated with hypnotic susceptibility; a few, on the contrary, have believed introverts to be the best subjects, especially for the deeper stages. The supposed relationships have been attributed sometimes to an underlying peculiarity of nervous organization, sometimes to the rapport between hypnotist and subject. It is useless to discuss these theories, for the facts themselves have been tested in no less than five investigations, with such results as to discourage further speculation. M. M. White, to be sure, using the Neymann-Kohlstedt Test, found extraversion correlated with hypnotizability +.70 +.11, but Barry, MacKinnon and Murray, who used the same test together with combined estimates by three experimenters, obtained no significant correlation, while Davis and Husband, employing Laird's *Personal Inventory* C2 and C3, found themselves with slight negative correlations, —.05 +.12 for men and —.23 +.07 for women. Two further investigations, using similar methods, confirm the conclusion that extraversion, as defined and measured by self-rating tests, bears no more than the slightest relation to hypnotic susceptibility.

3. *Submission*

McDougall attributed differences in hypnotic susceptibility in part to "the native strength in the individual of the submissive tendency," further defined as the propensity "to defer, to obey, to follow, to submit in the presence of others who display superior powers." This means a reasonable proposal which says little more than that people who frequently behave in the fashion described are more likely to do so in the hypnotic test. Various experiments have been arranged to test McDougall's proposition, but the results have been uniformly negative. Barry, MacKinnon, and Murray used the Allport *A-S Reaction Study* to provide an index of submissiveness, but found an absence of correlation with hypnotizability. W. R. Wells, using a technique of "waking hypnosis," reported a tendency toward positive correlation not with submissiveness but with ascendance, and he showed further that the most susceptible subjects in "sleeping" hypnotic tests scored above average on ascendance. Friedlander and Sarbin found a correlation of $+.15 +.09$ between hypnotic tests and the "dominance" index of the Bernreuter *Personality Inventory*. As was true in the case of extraversion, submissiveness, as defined and measured by self-rating tests, appears to be unrelated to hypnotic susceptibility.

4. *Deference*

The preceding negative findings seem little less than an affront to common sense. It is important to realize, therefore, that the investigations suffered from two very grievous defects: they relied almost entirely on questionnaires despite the known limitations of this procedure, and they used personality variables which stand badly in need of more refined analysis. It is unnecessary to amplify this second remark in respect to extraversion, which has been dissected independently by the Guilfords and by Murray, but it is well worth while to consider the factors involved in the concept of a submissive propensity, especially in their relation to hypnosis. The hypnotic situation, as reported in scientific papers, calls for submission to a person of superior status, a physician, a teacher, or at the very least an older and more experienced student. To defer in such a situation is by no means inconsistent with a prevailingly dominant attitude toward equals and inferiors. Some very dominant subjects are favorably disposed toward hypnosis because they wish to practice it afterwards on their friends. Thus the motivational trait which is directly relevant to hypnotic susceptibility is not general submissiveness but specifically *deference,* the tendency to yield willingly, not to say eagerly, to the wishes of a superior person. McDougall's definition of the submissive propensity explicitly mentions "the presence of others who display superior powers," but the makers of questionnaires, wedded to the shot-gun technique, have indiscriminately included situations involving equals and inferiors. It is thus impossible to feel satisfied with any of the foregoing results. The problem calls for more precisely limited personality variables and for a method of measurement more dependable than self-rating. The writer has reported an investigation in which it was fortunately possible to realize these conditions, the ratings being derived from an intensive study of the subjects by a staff of workers. Under these circumstances hypnotic susceptibility was found to correlate with the need for deference $+.43 \pm.11$, a small but probably significant relationship.

5. *Autonomy*

On closer scrutiny, the expectation that dominance or ascendance would correlate negatively with hypnotic susceptibility proves somewhat ill-founded. Hypnosis offers the subject little opportunity to dominate the operator; the most he can achieve is a kind of passive resistance. It is persons who are sensitive in regard to freedom and self-direction who will most forcibly experience hypnosis as a threat and feel outraged by the operator's presumptuous position. Thus it is essentially a need for *autonomy* rather than a desire to dominate which throws a subject into an attitude of resistance. In the last mentioned investigation, the writer found a correlation of —.43 +.11 between hypnotizability and the need for autonomy, while the coefficient for the need of dominance was only —.12.

6. *Passivity*

In a paper on two types of trance the writer discussed in some detail another motive which sometimes contributes to the success of hypnosis. Certain subjects perceive in the hypnotic situation a welcome opportunity to rest and to relinquish responsibility. The trance which follows is of the passive type, characterized by extreme drowsiness, inertia, and signs of an unwillingness to awaken. In these subjects the press of hypnotic dominance evokes a kind of willing surrender, a glad abasement to anyone who will relieve them of the necessity to put forth energy and guide action. In everyday life such subjects display rather marked passivity, meeting difficulties by avoidance and retreat or waiting for the assistance of others to overcome them. There is more than one pattern of motives which leads to successful hypnosis, a circumstance which seriously complicates the use of correlation methods.

7. *Other Manifest Needs*

It would simplify matters if we could believe that the motivational problem involved no more than the deferent, autonomous, and passive tendencies. But the moment we seriously undertake the task of observing our subjects and listening to what they tell us we are obliged to agree with Morton Prince that almost any motive may occasionally play the decisive part. Prince described the case of a woman patient who could be hypnotized only after the challenge that she was afraid. Schilder gives examples of obvious unrepressed sexual tendencies contributing to successful hypnosis. If there is an audience witnessing the experiment, tendencies toward exhibition and self-dramatization probably influence the result. The writer remembers a subject upon whom suggestion of eyelid and limb catalepsy succeeded while amnesia failed; he explained afterwards that he resisted the latter suggestion because he wanted to use his experiences for conversation at a forthcoming party. The poignant desire to be cured probably accounts for the high degree of success reported in the writings of medical hypnotists. The motives for opposing the operator are perhaps no less varied. Some subjects are frankly afraid. "It made me feel acutely nervous," such an one afterwards reported, "as I often feel in dramatics and debates, and it didn't pass away, so that as soon as I realized I was feeling perfectly calm I'd get nervous again." Others believe that to yield would be a sign of weakness with rather grave implications. A far-reaching concern of this kind can be detected in the following statement made after two unsuccessful trials of hypnosis:

> I had some feeling of resentment, my mind was working all the time the other way; I should think if you did it very often it might have a weakening, detrimental effect on your character, weakening your self-respect and so on. I don't suppose there are many malicious hypnotists walking the streets, but still . . .

A few subjects imagine, despite reassurance, that they will be made to perform humiliating stunts or to reveal personal secrets. "I did have a certain feeling that I might be made ridiculous, as people sometimes are," one young man declared, and another felt, "that hypnosis was sort of like talking in your sleep, giving yourself away." Finally, there are those who seize the opportunity offered for an indirect release of aggression; they deflate the seemingly exalted pretensions of the hypnotist by proving through action that each of his statements is incorrect. "In the back of your mind," one such subject observed, "there may be always a feeling of wanting to double-cross the experimenter and prevent him from doing what he wants. When he said I couldn't raise my hand, I said to myself, *'Well, watch me!'* " It seems to be generally agreed that compulsion neurotics, in whom aggression is strong, are highly refractory to hypnosis.

C. Latent Needs

The development of an individual amid the discipline and ideals of society involves an inevitable sacrifice of certain needs. Infantile sexual impulses, unlimited aggression, omnipotence, and excessive dependence have to be outgrown if the individual is to become an acceptable member of his culture. The Freudian school is neither the first nor the last, but certainly the most vehement and convincing, to argue that such needs are not regularly exterminated in the process of growth, but held in a condition of partial latency in which they continue to affect behavior indirectly, coloring the content of dream and fantasy, influencing sentiment and judgment, even at times controlling the course of overt behavior in ways of which the person himself remains unaware. These latent needs are given a certain opportunity for expression by the rather unusual press of hypnotic dominance. We can more easily understand their action by considering a borderline case in which a motive unsuspected at the outset became conscious to the subject during the course of the hypnotic experiment. A graduate student in psychology was eager to serve as a subject for hypnosis, believing it to be an enjoyable and at the same time instructive experience. During the trial he appeared deeply relaxed and evinced no anxiety, but the suggestions all failed. Afterwards he explained that much to his surprise his mind was invaded by antagonistic thoughts, especially when the hypnotist declared that he could not do certain things such as unclasping his hands. Although he knew beforehand that such suggestions were a regular part of the procedure, they seemed to awaken a wave of pride, so that he found himself thinking, "He can't put anything over on me, I possess a strong will," and being irritated by images of the operator boasting at his expense. From this and many similar experiences it is but a short step to latent needs which remain unconscious while continuing to influence the hypnotic experiment.

The psychoanalytic theory of hypnosis is based upon the analysis of persons who at some time submitted to hypnotic trials, and could recover by free association the thoughts and fantasies, conscious or unconscious, which occupied their minds on such occasions. This evidence is not altogether satisfactory because of the small number of subjects examined and also because of the uncertainty which attends any results obtained by analytic technique. Nevertheless, it is better than no evidence at all, and in the absence of more accurate methods it is entitled to serious consideration. Psychoanalytic writers have laid special emphasis on unconscious infantile needs, arguing that it is particularly these which function during hypnosis and contribute to the impression of forced or imposed behavior. Considerable attention was given to this question by Ferenczi, who pointed out that "the situation during hypnosis tends to favor a conscious and unconscious imaginary return to childhood, and to awaken reminiscences, hidden away in everyone, that date from the time of childlike obedience." In hypnosis, exactly as in psychoanalytic treatment, there is a transference of the loving, hating and fearing attitudes which were first aroused by the parents. If the operator adopts an authoritative stern attitude, he calls out the image of the father and sets in motion appropriate need integrates dating from the early years. If on the other hand he is gentle and soothing, he invites a projection of needs originally centered around the mother. The techniques which McDougall called "domination" and "cooperation" thus became in the hands of Ferenczi "paternal and maternal hypnosis."

"The capacity to be hypnotized," he concluded, "depends on the positive, although unconscious, sexual attitude which the person being hypnotized adopts in regard to the hypnotist; the transference, however, has its deepest roots in the repressed parental complexes. The medium is really in love with the hypnotist, and has brought this tendency from the nursery."

Freud is impressed by numerous similarities between hypnosis and being in love; in particular he calls attention to "the same humble subjection, the same compliance, the same absence of criticism, . . . the same absorption of one's own initiative." But he explicitly mentions a somewhat different factor, an "additional element of paralysis derived from the relation between someone with superior powers and someone who is without power and helpless . . . What is thus awakened is the idea of a paramount and dangerous personality, towards whom only a passive-masochistic attitude is possible, to whom one's will has to be surrendered." Such an idea Freud considers to be an "archaic inheritance" which undergoes an "individual re-animation" in the childhood relation to the father.

If we divest from these theories the language of the libido hypothesis, we may restate them substantially as follows. The hypnotic situation, with its general atmosphere of strangeness, its special press of dominance, and its peculiar relation between subject and operator, tends to arouse latent needs which were more active in childhood than they can be at the subject's present age. One of these motives is the need for *love* such as might have been gratified by adoring parents when their child behaved well. The subject momentarily loves the hypnotist as he once loved one or both of his parents, and he wants the hypnotist, as he wanted the parents, to return this love. Another motive is the need for *abasement* or *compliance,* the echo of a relation with parents of a more stern, forbidding disposition. The subject momentarily stands in awe of the hypnotist, and yields to his demands rather than risk his displeasure and wrath. The active agent in hypnotic behavior is the motive force of these latent needs rather than any power in the hypnotist, who serves at most as a kind of projection screen. It is safe to add that if the situation awakens latent anxiety or aggression hypnosis is effectually prevented.

A latent motivational factor of somewhat different nature is proposed by Schilder. He believes that the desire for omnipotence, routed from the forefront of the child's mind in his contests with reality, continues as a latent need which influences fantasy and may sometimes be projected upon real figures in the outside world. The hypnotist is in a peculiarly appropriate position to draw such a projection.

"His abilities," says Schilder, "are found in the fact that alterations take place in the external world at his mere wish. For the hypnotized, at least, he is the great magician, who alone is capable, by his wish and will, to produce creative changes in the universe, to eliminate objects from the universe or supply them to it. In addition, he has great power over the bodily functions of the hypnotized." The subject misinterprets the operator's position in this way because of his own latent desire for magic power, and he yields himself "only for the reason that he wishes to have a share in the greatness of the hypnotizer."

He projects this infantile wish upon the operator, "and thus participates, by the path of identification, in a magic power which he could not otherwise ascribe to himself." In other words, hypnosis offers an opportunity for the enjoyment of vicarious omnipotence and thus receives the support of a rather common latent need.

Although the writer's experiments with hypnosis have never been designed to investigate latent needs, he has observed occasional evidence which supports Schilder's theory. Presumably a dominating attitude on the hypnotist's part is most likely to encourage fantasies of an omnipotent being. The very circumstance that the writer adopted instead an unpretentious, affiliative attitude brought out in a curious way the inherent tendency of hypnosis to arouse such fantasies. Several subjects in subsequent interviews expressed disappointment at the informal, matter-of-fact atmosphere which prevailed during the hypnotic sessions. One man considered the "casual way it was done a great hindrance," while another, who had been thinking of Svengali and a gaze "penetrating enough to terrify one into a mild submission," experienced a "let-down" when he found the hypnotist "not very foreboding in appearance." A third subject explained the failure of hypnosis in his case with these words:

> If the hypnotist were some different sort of person, if he were different from your own background, you would be more inclined. Some of these Orientals, perhaps, someone exotic, alien to our way of being, not just a plain human being such as we are used to in daily life. There should be the quality of respect and awe.

It is evident that given a little encouragement from the hypnotist subjects such as these would gladly project omnipotent fantasies and would feel more favorably disposed toward the trance.

Psychoanalytic writers thus propose several latent needs which might serve as motivating forces for hypnosis, and by implication some others which might prevent it. Since the investigations which yielded these hypotheses are as yet hardly sufficient to carry conviction, it is appropriate to inquire how a more rigorous scrutiny might be made. As a first approximation it can be assumed that latent needs for love, for compliance, and for omnipotence will be stronger in hypnotizable subjects than in those individuals with whom the operator fails. Admittedly this is a crude formula, for the revival of infantile attitudes surely depends on many subtle and elusive factors. It is conceivable, for instance, that the hypnotist's voice or manner might remind a subject not of his adoring parents but of an uncle who caused him some humiliation. Nevertheless one can expect it to be approximately true that if certain latent needs are important for hypnosis the subjects who possess them in greatest strength will prove on the average more susceptible. The next step would be the baffling one of estimating the strength of latent needs. Psychoanalytic writers insist that it is unconscious if not actually infantile motives which bring about hypnosis; conscious love for the experimenter, conscious awe, or a conscious desire for dominance, they suggest, are more than likely to create resistance. The diagnosis of latent needs is clearly a delicate operation which requires a consultation of trained observers; one person's judgment is of scarcely any value. Murray has proposed a variety of techniques for exploring unconscious tendencies and has worked out criteria for estimating the strength of needs. The necessary tools are thus at hand, but as yet there has been no systematic study of the relation between latent needs and hypnosis. Until such a study yields more definite information it seems both plausible and probable that latent needs are sometimes aroused and that they sometimes determine the outcome of hypnosis. It is quite unnecessary, however, to assign them a unique and universal role. To do so would be to make the highly arbitrary assertion that hypnosis appeals exclusively to latent tendencies in personality, leaving untouched the needs which are manifested in daily life. If motivation is not all on the surface, neither is it all underground, and the student of hypnosis can do no better than keep a watchful lookout at both levels.

D.   RELATON OF NEEDS TO HYPNOTIC BEHAVIOR

So far we have made no attempt to analyze the relation between needs and behavior during hypnosis. In the days of Mesmer no one supposed that there was any relation; the magnetic fluid which emanated from the operator acted with an irresistible force quite regardless of the victim's frame of mind. Modern theories in which suggestion takes the place of animal magnetism have continued to neglect the possible contribution of motives in the hypnotized person. No one, perhaps, has swung to the opposite extreme and believed hypnosis to be wholly a matter of motivation, for it is recognized that the hypnotized person experiences his behavior as involuntary, automatic, and as if divorced from the usual play of personal motives. What has seemed most important to understand is the aptitude or capacity which makes it possible to produce automatisms on so large a scale, to suspend one's own needs so as to respond directly, as it were, to those of the hypnotist.

It should not be forgotten, however, that needs have a part in *automatic* behavior, even if that part is not the familiar and obvious one which they play in everyday directed conduct. When it comes to comprehending this part, the presence of a peculiar and little understood aptitude naturally offers an imposing obstacle. It is extremely difficult to isolate the factors; indeed, this is quite impossible when the attempt at hypnosis fails, for one is then left utterly without criteria for determining whether inimical motives or absence of aptitude produced the decisive effect. Fortunately the situation is not as hopeless when hypnosis is successful, so that the presence of the requisite capacity is guaranteed. The crucial instances for understanding the role of motives are those in which hypnosis occurs on one occasion but not on another, the only plausible difference between occasions being a change in the need pattern. Two classes of such data may be mentioned. (*a*) It sometimes happens that individuals who at first are insusceptible become excellent subjects when changes are made in the pattern of motives. We have already cited Prince's patient for whom hypnosis became possible only after a challenge to courage. Barry, MacKinnon, and Murray report the instance of a young man who could be hypnotized only by that one of three operators to whom he had given his confidence in personal matters of great privacy. The writer may mention from his own material an occasional belated success achieved by asking the subject to turn each suggestion into a vehement autosuggestion. Sometimes a change of hypnotist produces a surprising effect. The writer once experienced two failures with a college senior about whom it was known that he despised his father but was very fond of his younger brother. He was accordingly placed in the hands of a sophomore hypnotist, and proved to be highly susceptible. It would doubtless be possible to multiply these examples almost endlessly from the records of other students of hypnosis. (*b*) Sometimes hypnotized subjects abruptly refuse a repugnant suggestion and awaken from even a deep trance contrary to the operator's intention. It is unnecessary to rehearse the evidence for this familiar proposition. The question of legal responsibility for acts committed under hypnosis has prompted a great number of observations and experiments which repeatedly show that subjects can overcome suggestions genuinely displeasing to them. This conclusion, considered final for many years, has recently been challenged by Rowland, whose ingenious experiments with invisible glass give the impression that subjects will sometimes accept suggestions which expose them to serious danger. But it is possible, as Rowland allows, and quite in accord with findings such as Bramwell's that the subjects believed the operator would never, in a scientific laboratory, expose them to anything worse than the deceptive appearance of danger, a belief which in point of fact was perfectly correct. It is of course unsafe to make the flat assertion that hypnotized subjects can always under any circumstances resist repugnant suggestions, but there is little danger in the statement that they can usually do so.

From these considerations we are entitled to draw at least one conclusion: unfavorable motives almost always prevent hypnotic behavior from taking place. If a pattern of needs is regnant at the outset, which makes the subject prefer not to be hypnotized, the operator's efforts are foredoomed to failure, and if such a pattern becomes regnant during the trance the chances are strong that suggestion will lose its efficacy. Needs, whether manifest or latent, are vested with extensive powers of veto over hypnotic suggestions. On the positive side, a regnant pattern of needs which disposes the subject favorably toward hypnosis may be regarded as a virtually indispensable condition for its success. The evidence forces us to these conclusions, but it does not require us to go further and assert that the depth of hypnosis is directly related to the strength of favorable motivation, that a light trance betokens feeble motives and a deep trance imperious ones. It may well be that the positive power of needs is limited to ratification by simple majority of whatever the hypnotist proposes; thereafter the measure executes itself through the little understood machinery of automatism. We shall do well at this point to abandon further speculation. Insight into the nature of automatism must obviously precede a more exact understanding of the role of motives, and such insight is not yet at hand.

E. CONCLUSIONS

In the preceding section it was concluded that no one can be hypnotized against his desire. If a pattern of needs is aroused which disposes the subject unfavorably toward hypnosis the operator is certain to fail, and even if the trance is already well under way a repugnant suggestion is apt to be effectually resisted. Favorable motives, on the other hand, create conditions without which hypnosis cannot take place, but their strength is probably not correlated with degree of susceptibility. Hypnosis is more than a motivational problem, and it is precisely at this point that an aptitude or innate peculiarity of some kind becomes decisive.

What, then, in view of all the foregoing considerations, does a rank order on hypnotic susceptibility mean? Does it express different quantities of a single psychologically significant variable? This is certainly not the case; many factors are thrown together and their identity lost in the assigning of hypnotic scores. We may review as follows the motivational factors which have been the topic of this paper. The hypnotic subject is confronted by a situation which must be conceived not as a test but as an unusual kind of personal relationship. The central press is *dominance,* in a form which is at once extreme yet provisional. The character of this press is modified by the particular purpose of the session and by the operator's attitude, which may range from coaxing to portentous domination. It is further modified by preconceptions sown in the subject's mind by rumors and literary plots, often too well rooted to be removed by instructions. The press of hypnotic dominance is likely to arouse the need for *deference,* the strength of which correlates positively with susceptibility, or the need for *autonomy,* the strength of which correlates negatively. But there is a great deal of individual variation in the tendencies which are awakened, so that manifest needs like *passivity, exhibition, sex,* or *aggression* may sometimes occupy the foreground. At the same time hypnosis, by reason of its unusual nature, makes an appeal to certain needs which have become latent as the subject outgrew childhood. There is reason to believe that three latent infantile needs sometimes function as motivating forces favorable to hypnosis: the need for *love,* such as a child feels toward its parents, the tendency toward *passive compliance* in the presence of an elder, and the wish to participate in *omnipotence.* A latent need for *aggression,* on the other hand, works like a manifest one to oppose the operator's purpose. Positions in the hypnotic rank order can be predicted with a certain success, as the writer has reported, by examiners who know the subjects well enough to take some account of these diverse possibilities. Otherwise the only correlations which can be expected are with the needs most directly and commonly aroused, *deference* and *autonomy,* and these correlations will be small. It is doubtful whether the analysis of motivational factors can be pushed any further except by intensive study of the subjects as individuals.

Meanwhile there remains untouched the question of hypnotic aptitude. The foregoing arguments have made it plain that one cannot regard hypnotic scores as expressions of the degree to which this aptitude is possessed. It is impossible to factor out the motivational variables, and the method of correlation must forthwith be abandoned. There is one way, however, in which the effect of motivational factors can be considerably reduced, perhaps enough to permit an approximate isolation of the aptitude. In order to achieve this result it is recommended that all completely unhypnotizable subjects be discarded. This does not imply that some of them may not possess a minimal degree of the aptitude, only that one cannot be sure of the absence of unfavorable motivational factors. It is further recommended that from the remaining subjects there be formed two distinctly separated groups; the "somnambulists" or deep trance subjects in whom marked amnesia, anaesthesia, and hallucinations can be produced, and the lightest trance subjects who cannot attain these phenomena even after several trials, but who show eyelid and limb catalepsies which may be accepted as tokens that their motivation is generally favorable. It can be postulated of these groups that the first possesses hypnotic aptitude in marked degree, whereas the second possesses it to no more than a moderate extent. There should accordingly be significant differences between their average scores on tests which really measure the hypnotic aptitude.

---

*From *The Journal of General Psychology*, 24, 145-162. 1941.

CONTROL EXPERIMENTS AND THEIR RELATION
TO THEORIES OF HYPNOTISM*

R. M. Dorcus, A. K. Brintnall, and H. W. Case
University of California

EDITOR'S NOTE

This article has two distinct values. In the first place, it stresses the need for better controlled experimentation. Several of the preceding studies included in this anthology are criticized. In the second place, it reveals how important the attitude of a subject may be. It even implies that one may question whether anyone is ever really hypnotized.

During the past 10 years the majority of the experiments dealing with hypnotism have been carried on in educational institutions, and as a result college students have been used as subjects. The conclusions concerning both the nature of and the effect of hypnosis, drawn from many such experiments, are open to criticism on several grounds which we shall consider presently. Two methods of control experimentation have in general been followed: (a) Performances of subjects in the waking state have been compared with those of the same subjects in the hypnotic state. (b) Performances of subjects in the waking state have been compared with those of other subjects in the hypnotic state. It might be added that most experimenters have adopted the first procedure. Both of the procedures have been standard practices in psychological investigations, but certain inadequacies have been recognized in these procedures in other types of experimental investigation such as the effects of alcohol, drugs, and tobacco smoke. The earlier experiments on the effects of such exogenous products utilized essentially the types of control experiments which have been outlined. It was soon recognized that a very important factor was being neglected, namely, the attitude of the subject or subjects. Attempts were then made to introduce control smokes and disguised drugs. Even though they have not been entirely successful, they have in part mitigated the influence of the attitude of the subject.

Since the various theories of hypnosis depend to a considerable degree upon the adequacy of control experimentation and because of the possible nature of hypnosis, precautions of a more stringent nature than those usually employed in psychological investigations are necessary.

The three following experiments selected from the many that could be pointed out illustrate the futility of drawing conclusions concerning the effects of, or the nature of, hypnotism from experiments without adequate control.

One investigator attempted to show that regression took place under hypnosis. He compared the I.Q.'s (derived from the Stanford-Binet) of college students in the waking state with the I.Q.'s of the same subjects in the hypnotic state, after the subjects had been given the suggestion, "*You are now three years of age.*" The report states that the subjects approached the six-year level, and the author concluded that regression actually occurs. It would seem that almost any conclusion could be derived from this investigation. If we accepted the experiment uncritically, it would have a decided bearing on certain theories.

Other investigators (2) have shown that recall of verse or prose learned a year previously in the waking state is greater in the trance state than in the waking state. The subjects were presumably naive as regards the problem to be investigated at the time of the original learning. I should like to point out, however, that all of them had been tested for susceptibility to hypnosis, which raises some doubt as to their naivete. The controls used thus far in this experiment are not open to serious criticism. However, the subjects were asked to recall materials under hypnosis and in the waking state. No check was made to determine whether the subjects believed that recall is better under hypnosis or in the waking state and this point is really vital for proper interpretation of results.

Hull makes a possibly serious error in interpreting this experiment. He says, "The experiment goes far to justify in a controlled and quantitative manner the claims of clinical observers that hypnosis is somehow able to bring about a recall of more or less remote memories." While Hull may be correct in his interpretation, we cannot be certain that we are dealing with anything more than attitude. If we assume that hypnosis and attitude are one and the same then his interpretation would still be appropriate. This is not the usual definition of hypnosis, however.

A third investigator has demonstrated that color blindness as measured by the Ishihara Test can be hypnotically induced provided the subjects are properly hypnotized. That is, the claim is made that the reason certain other experimenters have failed to secure color blind responses under hypnosis is due to improper technique of induction. In spite of elaborate technique of induction in the investigation under consideration, the experimenter has not taken adequate precaution actually to determine whether the color blindness is feigned or real. We have no way of knowing whether the subjects' responses involve active suppression of sensations or whether there is some failure of integration of visually aroused sensations. It would, of course, be possible to answer this question, in part, with adequate control experiments.

In this study, we will report on two different types of work, although both of them have bearing on the nature and reliability of hypnotic phenomena. In one part of the study we have attempted to ascertain certain information concerning the dissemination of information about hypnosis among college students which, of course, influences their attitudes and in turn has an influence on the outcome of experimentation. We have secured answers to the following questions from 669 students at the

University of California at Los Angeles; 425 of them were women and 244 were man (Table 1).

TABLE 1

	No	Do Not Know	Yes
Have you ever been hypnotized?..............98.6%			1.34%
Has anyone tried unsuccessfully to hypnotize you?			8.6%
Have you ever seen anyone hypnotized?......			28.0%
Have you read anything concerning hypnosis? 46.0%			54.0%
Have you ever discussed hypnosis with anyone? 29.0%			71.0%
Do you believe hypnosis is possible?..........11.0%		10%	79.0%
Do you think you could be hypnotized?........38.0%		26%	36.0%
Do you think people will come out of hypnotic condition spontaneously?................14.0%		26%	60.0%
Do you think people will remember what took place while under hypnosis?.............64.0%		21%	15.0%

It is fairly obvious that college students are not naive subjects for hypnotic experiments, and it seems true also that the attitudes that they hold will probably affect the outcome of at least some kinds of work.

In the second part of the study, we wanted to discover how subjects actually did recover from the hypnotic trance in the absence of definite suggestions. For this purpose 20 subjects in whom tactual anesthesia, rigidity, and positive visual hallucinations could be induced, were selected. They were hypnotized and were told to stretch out on a cot. After having the subject relax, an assistant came in the room and said aloud to the experimenter, "*You are wanted on the telephone about an appointment down town.*" The experimenter replied aloud so that the subject could hear the conversation that he had forgotten an appointment down town and would be gone for the remainder of the day. Both the assistant and experimenter hastily left the room. The subject in the interim was kept under observation from an adjacent room through a peep hole. A control group of 25 subjects was treated in a similar fashion except that they were asked to sign up for an experiment, the nature of which could not be discussed beforehand. They were taken into the laboratory, asked to lie down on a cot, close their eyes and relax; and were told that after a few minutes of relaxation they would be given further instructions. In the period of supposed relaxation, the same conversation and technique about the appointment was carried out. It might be added that both the hypnotized and non-hypnotized subjects were interviewed before leaving the laboratory and were asked not to discuss the experiment in any way with their classmates.

The time elapsing between the experimenter's leaving the room and the subject sitting up to leave the room was recorded. The distributions of time for the control and experimental groups were fairly comparable (Table 2) although the times for a few members of the hypnotic group exceeded the longest time in the control group. Questioning revealed the fact that the behavior of both groups were influenced by similar factors in so far as they had important engagements, thought the experiment was over, or were waiting for the experimenter to return.

TABLE 2

Distribution of Time Elapsing Between the Experimenter Leaving the Room and the Spontaneous Arousal of the Subject

Hypnotic Group		Control Group	
Minutes	No. of Subjects	Minutes	No. of Subjects
0-10	6	0-10	9
11-20	5	11-20	5
21-30	1	21-30	7
21-40	0	31-40	2
41-50	1	41-50	0
51 and over	7*	51 and over	2*

*Longest time for any control subject 53 minutes. The seven of the hypnotic group requiring the longest times exceeded the maximal times for any of the control group.

While many theorists attempt to explain hypnosis in terms of dissociation, narrowing of the field of consciousness, or altered nervous state, there is much evidence that seems to indicate that these explanations are unsatisfactory. We should like to emphasize the importance of further investigation into the whole problem of attitude, as it is related to hypnosis. It is even possible that the phenomenon as such will disappear along with voodoo and hexing if the majority of people no longer hold it is possible. Even the concept of narrowing of consciousness seems to be invalid in view of the fact that the hypnotic subjects in the absence of definite instructions tend to awaken of their own volition and tend to incorporate into their thinking the important factors in their normal existence.

*From *Journal of General Psychology*, Vol. 24, 217-221.

AN EXPERIMENTAL INVESTIGATION OF THE POSSIBLE ANTI-SOCIAL USE OF HYPNOSIS

By Milton H. Erickson

Editor's Note

A series of recent experiments have been made to determine whether a hypnotized subject, in view of the active role he assumes, can be made to commit anti-social and self-injurious acts. The evidence is divided. Experiments by Young, Wells, and Brenman have found positive evidence for this thesis. On the other hand, a number of experimenters have arrived at negative conclusions. Dr. Erickson reports on 35 cases with very little success on his part to induce the subject to either commit anti-social acts or to carry out suggestions that were injurious.

The possibility of the misuse of hypnosis for anti-social or criminal purposes constitutes a most controversial question, not only for the payman but also for the psychologist, the physician and the psychiatrist interested in its study, its nature and its uses and applications. To settle this question is difficult, since it involves three inseparable factors of unknown potentialities—specifically, the hypnotist as a person, the subject as a person, and hypnosis as such, to say nothing of the significant influence upon these three, both individually and collectively, of the suggestion and the performance of a questionable act.

We know that it is possible, without recourse to hypnosis, for one person to induct another to commit a wrong, a fact we may explain loosely as the influence of one personality upon another. Hence, the question arises, "Can hypnosis, as a form of influence of one personality upon another, be utilized for wrongdoing?" Actually, however, the problem is not this simple, since in any hypnotic situation there exists not only the hypnotic relationship, but also interpersonal relationships entirely apart from the hypnotic, however intimately these various relationships are bound together in a single situation.

Hence, any experimental approach to the question requires an emphasis upon one or another of the significant factors to determine its intrinsic importance. In this paper, an effort will be made to emphasize primarily the hypnotic elements, and thus, to determine how much hypnotic suggestion itself can accomplish in inducing wrong behavior.

Recently, Rowland has made inquiry into the general hypnotic literature on the question of the possibility of inducing hypnotic subjects to perform harmful or objectionable acts, and has found that Hollander, Loewenfeld, Schilder, and Young were essentially agreed that there was little likelihood, if any, of such a possibility.

He then devised two experiments to discover if deeply hypnotized subjects could be induced to expose themselves to danger or to try to harm others. The one experiment consisted of having the subjects pick up a rattlesnake, variously described to them as a rubber hose and as a snake, lying in a carefully constructed box, the front of which was made of invisible glass and gave the impression of being open. The second experiment consisted of having the subject throw fluid he knew to be acid at the experimenter's face, which was protected in an unnoticeable way by invisible glass. Three of four subjects did as asked in the first experiment and both subjects used in the second experiment did as instructed while 42 persons in the waking state could not be induced to attempt the performance of the first experiment. The author presents these data as evidence of the possible misuse of hypnosis and offers, as a possible explanation of the results, a brief statement to the effect that the subjects' confidence in the hypnotist might have caused them to forego their better judgment. In addition, the author emphasizes the need to reexamine the entire question of the possible misuse of hypnosis.

That these experimental findings are valid as to their apparent significance is to be questioned, for the reason of the serious oversight, except for slight hints summarized in the tentative explanation offered for the results, of the definite and highly important subject-hypnotist relationship of trust and confidence, which could account fully for the findings. Particularly does this seem true for the situation in which these experiments were performed, aside from the consideration of the possible discovery by the subjects of the actual protection against harm afforded by the experimental apparatus. In this connection, Schilder and Kauders have made an excellent survey of the literature and offer, in relation to various aspects of the entire problem of the misuse of hypnosis, a wealth of general opinions based upon their own experience and that of others. They declare, "But we must not forget that the hypnotized person is always aware of the general situation, that he is conscious of the fact that an experiment is being made on him, and that he must be well aware that the hypnotizer is not inducing him to commit an actual murder, if the hypnotizer is a man of respected social position."

Furthermore, it is doubtful if any definite answer to the general question can be obtained except by an experimental situation in which the suggested anti-social act really can become an accomplished fact, obviously and unmistakably so, and without the protection afforded by a falsified situation which can serve only to vitiate or negate the experimental procedure for both subject and investigator.

While some recognition has been given to various aspects of this entire problem, a general survey of the literature discloses no systematic, comprehensive experimental study of the question, and also, that the available information tends to be limited either to general statements based upon the personal experience of reliable investigators or to reports centering around limited experimental situations of rather extreme character, Rowland's study for instance, without sufficient attention being given to the highly important factors of trust and confidence in the experimenter, the subject's probable realization of the actual use of concealed protective measures, and the general tendency, emphasized so strongly by Schilder and Kauders, for subjects to look upon any hypnotic situation as essentially an experimental procedure, particularly so in any formal laboratory setting.

GENERAL COMMENTS ON EXPERIMENTAL PURPOSES AND PROCEDURES AND ON THE SUBJECTS AND THEIR IMMEDIATE REACTIONS TO THE EXPERIMENTS

In this paper, it is proposed to report a series of experiments, performed over a period of years, bearing upon this important problem of the misuse of hypnosis, in which an earnest effort was made to avoid the difficulties involved in experimental settings as such, and to meet the absolute need for realism. To achieve these ends, informal situations for the most part were utilized, and acts of an extreme nature were avoided. Instead, definitely objectionable acts of a relatively minor anti-social character were employed, since such acts could reasonably be made to serve the investigative purposes and to yield significant, informative and indicative data.

The actual experimental procedure was, in general, simple in character, and consisted chiefly of seizing upon favorable opportunities and situations to suggest hypnotically some form of objectionable behavior, sometimes directly, sometimes indirectly. For some of the more complicated and difficult experiments, an elaborate technique of suggestion was evolved in which extensive allowance was made for the subject's personality. In all instances, every effort was made to induce either an actual performance or an approximation of the suggested act, so that, whatever the degree of the experimenter's responsibility and guilt or the extent of possible protective measures, there would still be the unescapable fact of the subject's own participation in an undesirable performance directed either against himself or against others. Also, whenever possible, control experiments were made in an effort to secure similar behavior in the waking state.

Practically all of the experimental procedures cited were repeated on several subjects, but only the more informative and representative examples are given, although it may be added that the instances omitted actually confirm those cited and that the findings were essentially the same for all types of subjects. No attempt will be made, because of the large number of experiments, to give all the experimental details; rather, a concise summary will be offered except in those instances where the subject's behavior is peculiarly informative.

The material to be presented is based upon the findings obtained from approximately 50 subjects selected from a total of more than 75. Among these subjects were children and adults, normal persons and some who had recovered from psychotic episodes, and they ranged in intelligence from feeblemindedness to the superior adult level, but the majority were either college students or graduates. They were all well known to the hypnotist, many had been utilized repeatedly for other hypnotic work, and all were well trained to accept any type of suggestion and to develop profound somnambulistic trances, as well as complete amnesias for all trance experiences.

However, despite their well-established trust and confidence in the experimenter, almost invariably the experimentation reported here caused them to develop intense resentments and antagonisms toward him. Only their realization, subsequently, of the scientific purposes of the work, aside from their general understanding of the hypnotist and the high degree of trust and confidence they had in his official position, served to effect a resolution of their resentments. Even then, there were some who thereafter limited any further participation in hypnotic experiments to strictly impersonal procedures.

Another important fact concerning their anger and resentment was that the subjects tended to develop and manifest much more intense feeling at the hypnotic level of awareness than at the conscious waking level. Many of the subjects in the waking state readily and easily forgave the experimenter, when informed of the situation, only to manifest in the trance state a full continuance of their anger. Also, the emotions of the hypnotic trance, despite the general state of suggestibility and the actual existence of a favorable waking attitude, were much more difficult to deal with than those of the ordinary waking state. Rarely did the subjects show equal degrees of resentment in both the waking and hypnotic states and still more rarely was the waking displeasure greater than the trance emotion. Also, it is of interest to note that certain of the subjects actually inflicted punishment and humiliation upon the experimenter in retaliation for his objectionable commands, the possibility of which has been noted by Schilder and Kauders.

INQUIRY INTO GENERAL POST-EXPERIMENTAL ATTITUDES, OPINIONS AND REACTIONS OF THE SUBJECTS

Before proceeding to the actual experiments, it may be desirable to present the results of post-experimental inquiries to serve as a general background for an understanding of the experimental findings. Exceptions to these general statements will be found in the individual experimental accounts.

In this connection, before the subjects had been given any recollection of their hypnotic experiences, and as a post-experimental measure, since previous experience had shown that such inquiries tend to make subjects suspicious and hesitant about participation in hypnotic work, inquiry disclosed that approximately 40 percent of the subjects employed believed that they could be induced in the trance state to perform objectionable acts of a definitely minor character if the acts were directed primarily against themselves, and that among these were many who had rejected such suggestions unconditionally with no attempt made either to evade the demands placed upon them or to alter the performance so as to render it unobjectionable. About 50 percent were most emphatic in denying such a possibility, and in this group largely were those who had seized upon the opportunity offered by the anti-social suggestions to inflict punishment upon the experimenter, while the remainder tended to be, on the whole, rather doubtful. All, however, were emphatic in denying the possibility of being induced hypnotically to commit anti-social acts of a major character.

Following this, despite the consistent failure to induce experimentally anti-social behavior of a genuine or effective character, certain of the subjects were given a full recollection of only their actual experimental behavior, and inquiry disclosed that many were emphatic in their declaration that only their trust and confidence in the experimenter could account for their submission to the experimental procedures, aside from the question of accepting and possibly acting upon the suggestions. Others declared that they must have been confident at the time that protective measures were actually in force and that "things were really different than they seemed." Still others explained that they must have had a general realization that the author probably had secret legitimate purposes behind his requests which made it possible for them to accept suggestions out of the question under any other circumstances. A few explained that they had probably been willing to do whatever was asked because they regarded the situation as having legitimate scientific implications, but that, even so, they must have found the requests to be "impossible" because of the violation of their personal code. And some others offered only the naive explanation, "Well, that just goes to show you how I really would act."

When instructed further to recall their feelings and attitudes when given the objectionable task, as well as their actual behavior, the results were essentially a confirmation of their previous statements and gave the impression of being a confusion of their immediate and of their retrospective understandings.

The remainder of the subjects were instructed to recall as a single task both their feelings and their behavior of the trance state, but, probably because the experimental situation demanded action rather than reflection, little that was informative could be obtained, except for statements of feelings of anger, resentment, hesitation, negativism, and unwillingness, and any elaboration of these statements was made in terms of their immediate understandings. It did not seem possible for them to differentiate between their understandings of how they felt at the time of the experiment and at the time of the post-experimental questioning.

Inquiry about the possibility of being induced to commit some seriously dangerous or culpable act because of implicit trust in the hypnotist and a certainty that there were adequate protective measures elicited the significant reply that hypnotic suggestion did not and, as they knew from personal experience, could not render the subject an obedient, unthinking automaton, as, in their opinion, the experimenter had discovered adequately. Also, they emphasized that invariably they scrutinized carefully every suggestion offered, primarily as a measure of understanding it fully to permit complete obedience and not for the purpose of taking exception to it, and that, if they were at all uncertain of it, their hypnotic state would force them to await either more adequate instruction or a better understanding by a direct, thoughtful, and critical consideration of the command. They added that this tendency would be all the more marked in the case of unusual or potentially dangerous suggestions and situations.

Inquiry about the possibility of being manipulated unfavorably or skillfully tricked by an unscrupulous hypnotist, who had won their full confidence, disclosed the common belief that they could be deceived to a certain degree, but not seriously, probably less so than in the waking state, because of the reasons given above and because the limitations of the hypnotic trance would constitute a protection in itself, since it is limited in time and situation and restricts so markedly environmental contact, and hence, would preclude the dangers of over-confidence likely to obtain in the waking state.

In addition, inquiry on these points among a large number of experienced subjects not used in this type of experimentation, disclosed their beliefs to be identical with those given above, and they also declared that a successful deception by an unscrupulous hypnotist would have to be one more readily achieved in the waking state, and then, that it would not be a function of the hypnotic condition, but, rather, that the hypnosis would be, as Schilder and Kauders remark, nothing more than "a particularly non-effective technical auxiliary" for inducing antisocial behavior.

EXPERIMENTAL FINDINGS

In presenting the experimental findings, an effort has been made to select material from as many different subjects as possible and to classify and group the various accounts in accord with their primary significance. However, many of the reports illustrate several points, as will become apparent to the reader. Also, while written as single accounts, the reader will note many instances in which the account is a summary of experiments and variations of those experiments upon a number of subjects.

No attempt will be made to offer a general discussion of all the material, since, for the most part, the reports are relatively clear. Rather, brief comments, wherever pertinent, will be made in direct relationship either to the individual experiment or to types of experiments, and these comments will be limited to the general problem of this paper, although the reader may observe repeatedly experimental illustrations of various dynamisms of behavior.

Finally, to avoid needless repetition of the fact, the statement may be made that, except where specifically stated otherwise, all the subjects were in profound somnambulistic hypnotic trances, and profound amnesias were developed in each of them for all trance experiences until the purposes of the experimentation warranted their waking recollection of all or part of the trance events. Thus, experimentation in the waking state could follow hypnotic experimentation without the subject's conscious awareness that it constituted a repetition of a previous experiment, and, in some instances, amnesias were produced for waking events to permit repetitions of waking acts.

Experimental Accounts

EXPERIMENTS INVOLVING PHYSICAL OR MENTAL INJURY TO THE SELF

Account 1:   The subject was shown hand electrodes and the flow of current was demonstrated by the experimenter's receiving a shock obviously disagreeable and violent in effects. He was then instructed emphatically and insistently to experience the same shock. This he refused, explaining that the experimenter's own discomfort and violent muscular reactions had satisfied all his curiosity about it. An attempt to compel or force him into obedience failed, although he did make several tentative attempts to pick up the electrodes. Finally, after much insistence by the experimenter, the subject became antagonistic and rejected the whole procedure as foolish and unnecessary.

Subsequently, with the subject in the waking state, the experimenter repeated the entire performance, but the subject still refused to receive a shock, giving essentially his trance explanation. Finally, he consented to take a lesser shock, when casually shown the use of a resistance coil. He demanded, however, that the experimenter prove the lessening of the current by receiving another shock. After he had experienced a mild shock, an attempt was made to induce him, still in the waking state, to permit a strengthening of the current. This he refused.

Again hypnotized and the original procedure repeated, he agreed to receive a mild shock, but insisted upon a preliminary demonstration of its mildness, checking additionally on the adjustment of the resistance coil. Argument that the experimenter's own performance demonstrated the harmlessness of the entire procedure elicited the explanation that nothing worthwhile could be accomplished by such self-punishment and that a mild shock was sufficiently unpleasant to warrant no further experimentation. *Account 2:* The subject was told to develop an anesthesia of his hand and then to prove it by holding a lighted match underneath his index finger. Ordinarily a hypnotic subject will refuse unconditionally to permit a testing of a hypnotically induced anesthesia by measures he regards as too injurious or destructive. This subject, however, readily did as asked, holding the lighted match to his finger until he smelled the odor of burning flesh. Commenting on this, he threw the match aside and asked irritably if the experimenter thought his purposes warranted such results. When answered in the affirmative, the subject replied that such had been his opinion. He then asked that the experimenter awaken him and give him a full conscious recollection of the incident.

Several days later, in the waking state, he discussed his experience with fellow medical students, emphasizing his loss of pain sensation. One of the students asked him if he could develop an anesthesia spontaneously. Becoming interested in this, the subject began making suggestions to himself that his hand would again become anesthetic, finally testing the self-induced anesthesia with a lighted match. The other students declared that he was probably wilfully enduring pain to uphold his argument. In answer, he attempted unsuccessfully to control his pain reactions to a lighted match applied to his non-anesthetic hand.

On another occasion, the subject in the waking state became interested in the ability of psychotic patients to endure pain in smoking a cigarette to the last puff and proceeded to duplicate the performance, willingly enduring a severe burn on his lips as a result, thereby illustrating his behavior when the question of hypnosis was not involved, either directly or indirectly.

Account 3: The subject, a 12-year-old girl, was given suggestions to the effect that a certain box was actually a hot stove. She accepted these suggestions and, upon request, sat upon the illusory hot stove, squirming, twisting and protesting that she was being burned, and begging to be allowed to get off. All of her behavior was fully suggestive of the reality of the experience to her.

Two weeks later the experiment was repeated, with the modification that on this occasion extremely careful suggestions were given to effect a realistic illusion of the selected box as a hot stove. This achieved, she could not be induced to sit on it. Yet, when another box was simply described as a hot stove and she was told to sit on it, she promptly did so, repeating her behavior of the original experiment. Nevertheless, she could not be induced to sit upon the more realistic illusory hot stove.

On another occasion an attempt was made to induce this same subject to sit upon an actual hot stove. She obeyed the request by mistaking another article of furniture for that stove and sitting upon it instead, giving every evidence of discomfort and distress. No amount of effort could make her approach the real stove, even when protective measures were provided that could be recognized by the subject.

As a variation, using this subject and a number of others to permit adequate control of each step of the procedure, an attempt was made to induce the placing of the hand on a hot stove, first casually and then later effectively described as being cold. Only an approximate performance could be secured, that of holding the hand briefly an inch or so above the stove and declaring that it was actually in contact with the stove. The induction of an anesthesia in the chosen hand led to a preliminary testing with the non-anesthetic hand and resentment over the attempted deception. When, by careful suggestion, the subject was deprived of all self-protective measures, an unconditional refusal resulted.

Account 4: During some experimentation on crystal gazing, a subject was told, by chance, to visualize the most important event of the year 1925, as a measure of keeping her busy while the experimenter directed his attention elsewhere. Promptly, as the crystal images began to develop, the subject began to manifest extreme emotional distress, and there occurred a marked loss of rapport with the experimenter. With difficulty, hypnotic contact was re-established with her and sufficient information elicited to disclose that she had visualized an occurrence of marked psychic traumatic significance. Thereafter it was necessary to reassure this subject about hypnosis, and she could not be induced to do crystal gazing unless first instructed firmly to see only pleasant happy scenes, and this demand continued to be made even after she had spontaneously requested from the experimenter a psychotherapeutic review of her unhappy experience.

Since this incident, the experimenter has had many similar experiences, especially with patients seeking psychotherapy, but also with subjects employed only for experimental or demonstration purposes.

Comment: These four accounts illustrate clearly that the hypnotic subject is not a blindly obedient automaton, that he does possess a good critical ability, and that there is full capacity for self-protection, both in the immediate sense and in relation to the future. In addition, the need to know what the subject will do in the ordinary waking state, and the profound need for realism in the experimental situation are clearly shown. Also, one needs only a few such experiences as given in the last account to realize how easily a good hypnotic subject or patient may be lost by having them face too precipitately a painful experience.

INVOLVING DAMAGE OR LOSS OF PERSONAL PROPERTY

Account 5: This subject smoked secretly, but knew and did not object to the fact that the experimenter was aware of her habit. One day, when she was in his office, noting that she had with her a gift handkerchief which she prized highly, the experimenter hypnotized her and gave her a cigarette to smoke, counseling her earnestly that should someone happen to enter she should keep secret her smoking by crumpling the cigarette in her handkerchief, thus concealing the evidence. She was not receptive to the idea, explaining that such a procedure would burn her handkerchief, but it was argued insistently that that measure might well be kept in mind. However, she continued to smoke, not taking the suggestions seriously. Suddenly, the experimenter summoned the occupant of the next office, but so maneuvered that, while the visitor's back was toward the subject upon entrance, his discovery of her was imminent, thus confronting her with an immediate and compelling need to dispose of her cigarette by the method suggested. As the visitor entered, the subject flushed angrily, glanced at her handkerchief, made several tentative moves to follow the suggestions given her, then carefully and deliberately tucked the handkerchief into her sleeve and continued to smoke, despite the fact that she particularly did not want that visitor to know of her practice. When this reaction had been noted, the visitor was manipulated out of the office without a betrayal of her secret. Nevertheless, she gave the experimenter an angry scolding and criticized him harshly for his conduct and for his deliberate attempt to make her ruin her handkerchief, demanded to be awakened, threatened to awaken spontaneously if this were not done at once, and declared her intention of never again being hypnotized.

Only after she had been given a complete understanding of the situation was it possible to win back her confidence, and it was necessary to do this in both the hypnotic and the waking states, despite her waking amnesia for the experience.

Account 6: This subject possessed a prized book which had been greatly admired and often solicited by a friend as a gift, but only an implied promise that on some auspicious occasion it might be made a gift had been elicited. In a deep trance, extensive systematic efforts were made to induce the subject to keep that implied promise, either at once or by a specified date, with even the privilege of naming the date, but the most that could be accomplished was a repetition of her waking promise, namely, that sometime the book might be made a gift. Approximately a year later the book was made a gift, but to another friend not mentioned in the trance, who also desired it greatly.

Comment: In Account 5, the subject was painfully and sharply trapped by the situation and apparently given no alternative except obedience to the urgent suggestions given her. Nevertheless, she made a deliberate and painful choice of behavior in contradiction to the hypnotic commands, and, despite the continuance of the trance state, she exercised fully her normal waking prerogatives by denouncing the experimenter and depriving him of his control over the situation, emphasizing the latter by compelling a justification at both the hypnotic and the waking levels of awareness.

In the next account, although the general idea suggested was entirely acceptable, the subject could not be induced to act upon it except under conditions and circumstances to be self-decided in the waking state. The final outcome suggests an actual defeating of the hypnotic suggestions.

GIVING OF ADVERSE INFORMATION ABOUT ONESELF

Account 7: While engaged in mischief, a young man injured himself seriously, necessitating surgical intervention. Before full treatment could be administered efficiently, it was necessary to know the exact nature and method of his accident. Questioning at length by the experimenter's colleagues elicited an obviously false and misleading story because of the embarrassing and humiliating character of the injury, nor could the emergency of the situation be impressed upon him sufficiently to induce him to tell the truth. Accordingly, the experimenter was asked to hypnotize him, since he was one of the experimenter's well-trained subjects, and thus to secure the essential information. The subject went into a deep trance readily enough, but persisted in telling the same false story as he had in the waking state, despite instruction about the seriousness of the situation. Finally when the experimenter refused to accept his story, the patient offered the argument that the experimenter was a doctor and really ought to understand. Accepting this contention, the experimenter instructed him, while still in the trance state, to listen carefully to the experimenter's understanding of the probable course of events and to correct any misstatements. In this indirect and unsatisfactory way, sufficient correct information was reluctantly and incompletely yielded to permit proper treatment, although, the persistence in a general misstatement of facts continued.

Even after recovery, the subject persisted in his false story in both waking and trance states, although he knew that the surgical intervention had disclosed the truth.

Nor is this case unusual, since similar behavior is frequently encountered in the therapy of neurotic conditions, even when the patient earnestly desires help. Likewise, with normal hypnotic subjects detected in a lie, a systematic and careful attempt to secure the truth in the trance state will frequently elicit only a stubborn persistence in the falsification unless a justification, adequate for the inquisition and satisfactory to the subject as a person, can be proved. Otherwise anger and resentment, concealed or open, is likely to develop, together with loss of trust, confidence and hypnotic services. This situation is difficult to alter by any straightforward objective explanation, since the highly subjective character of the situation renders objectivity difficult to achieve.

Nevertheless, under conditions where the subject's personality situation warrants it, hypnotic measures are exceedingly effective in eliciting adverse information about the self and it frequently happens that the subject will disclose the truth unreservedly in the trance state, but, in a most inexplicable fashion, will persist in his right to a negation of the truth and absolute misstatements in the waking state.

Comment: Despite the shift of responsibility, the submissiveness of the hypnotic subject, and the peculiar significance and strength of the hypnotist-subject relationship, and the tremendous and recognized importance of obeying the hypnotic commands, the actual character and nature of the individual's waking patterns of behavior carried over into the trance situation. Apparently, from this and from general hypnotic therapeutic experience, the elicitation of adverse information about the self is a function not of hypnosis itself but rather of the total personality situation.

INVOLVING VIOLATION OF THE SUBJECTS' MORAL OR CONVENTIONAL CODES

Inducing Subjects to Lie

Account 8: Attempts were made to induce a number of subjects to tell deliberate lies to persons placed in rapport with them, the lies to cause both petty annoyance and marked inconvenience, or even definite difficulties. In all instances the efforts failed, although all of the subjects could be induced to tell "white lies," but, even so, they all reserved the privilege of correcting or nullifying the lie should it lead to even the slightest inconvenience for the victim. Thus, one subject, induced to make a slip of the tongue in informing a friend about the hour set for a ride home from the office, nullified the act by an apparently casual waking decision to accompany that friend home.

However, it was found that, if the subjects were given sufficient reason, they could be induced to promise to tell lies in the deep trance state of character protective of themselves and of others, but marked limitation was placed by the subjects upon this willingness, and their lies were again restricted to those of an insignificant character when they were forced to act upon their promise. In addition, they invariably reserved the privilege of correcting or nullifying their misstatements, and, in all instances, the lies were corrected subsequently, either directly or indirectly.

But of particular significance was the discovery that when the subject could be induced to lie effectively, it was necessary for the subject to be in a trance state. Despite every measure of technique, it was found to be impossible to bridge the gap between the hypnotic and the waking levels of awareness to permit a meaningful waking reiteration of the lie.

Efforts made to induce lying in response to post-hypnotic suggestions invariably led to unsatisfactory results, namely, the defeating of the purposes of falsification, even when the lies were of a protective character. Inquiries about this afterward in the trance state disclosed that the subjects objected strenuously to post-hypnotic lying and they explained that they preferred to work out another and truthful method of either dealing with the situation or evading it. Nor could any amount of suggestion alter their attitudes, since they argued that a waking knowledge of the desired behavior would actually aid them because of increased contact with the environment, if there were a justification for the lying.

In those instances where they were induced to tell lies post-hypnotically with some degree of success, the results were totally unsatisfactory, since each of the subjects performed his task in a compulsive and inadequate fashion, rendering the falsity of his statement at once apparent. An adequate explanation of the failure of lying as a post-hypnotic performance may be found in the peculiarities of post-hypnotic behavior as such, which does not come within the scope of this paper.

Comment: As shown in previous accounts, subjects can tell lies while in the trance state for reasons of their own, but, apparently, the situation becomes totally different when the hypnotist tries to induce them to tell lies in the trance state. In such case, apart from the conflict aroused by the violation of the subject's personal code by the attempt to induce lying and the self-protective reactions engendered by this, the separateness of hypnotic and waking levels of awareness apparently renders lying in the trance state, however successful in a limited sense, only an alien intrusion into waking patterns of behavior to be rejected at the earliest opportunity. One is at once impressed by the significant bearing of the above findings upon the generally recognized folly of dealing only with a single limited aspect of the total personality.

In such procedures as the above, one is only setting, under the time- and situation-limited circumstances of the hypnotic trance, a restricted aspect of the personality at variance with another and more dominant aspect, and asking that lesser aspect, contrary to its nature and habit, to act directly in the field of conscious awareness, an impossible task, apparently, to judge from the experimental findings.

Inducing the Drinking of Liquor

Account 9: A subject, known to have scruples against drinking liquor, was urged to take a cocktail. Every suggestion to this effect failed, although she did explain, under pressure, that she might do so if she were awake. When it was argued plausibly that the entire purpose was to have her take the drink in the hypnotic state to see if she could detect having done so after awakening, she failed to be convinced of the desirability of the act.

After awakening, however, she was persuaded by renewed argument to taste the cocktail, but she declared that it was distasteful and pleaded to be excused from the task, explaining that she would, despite personal objections, drink the rest of it if to do so were really necessary. She was promptly hypnotized and informed most urgently that it was highly essential for her to finish the cocktail. She refused to do so unless she were awakened, arguing that if drinking the cocktail were really important, it would be better for her to drink it in the waking rather than in the hypnotic state.

Similarly, an attempt to induce intoxication failed completely in a subject who drank moderately and who objected strenuously to intoxication, despite an admitted strong personal desire to experience such a state. The explanation offered by this subject for his absolute refusal to take more than the customary amount of liquor was simply that to become intoxicated would be strictly a matter of personal interest and desire, possible of satisfactory achievement only in the waking state, and that the experimenter's interest in intoxication during the trance state was of no moment or pertinence.

On the other hand, a subject who had previously been intoxicated in the waking state and who desired the additional experience of becoming intoxicated while in the trance state, just as unequivocally refused to take a single drink until he had first been hypnotized.

Comment: Apparently, the need to satisfy the wishes of the total personality and the need to participate as a total personality in an objectionable, questionable, or special performance takes entire precedence over the wishes and commands of the hypnotist.

VIOLATION OF PERSONAL PRIVACY
Physical Examinations

Account 10: Several of the author's sisters, as has been mentioned briefly elsewhere, were hypnotized separately and instructed that they were to be given a complete physical examination in the presence of their mother, for which they were to undress completely. Each refused unconditionally. An explanation was requested, and they responded by declaring that even though the experimenter was their brother and a doctor, they did not think it fitting for him to make such a request, and no measure of persuasion succeeded.

Subsequently, in the waking state, the same issue was raised with each of them and each consented, hesitantly, to the request. Questioned upon rehypnotizing as to this apparent inconsistency in their attitudes, they explained that being examined when they were awake gave them a sense of better contact with the entire situation, but that in the trance state, being asleep, they felt that they would not know what was going on.

Similarly, a hypnotic subject suffering from a painful pelvic condition came to the experimenter for examination. The suggestion was given her that she could be hypnotized and given a hypnotic anesthesia which would relieve her of much pain and distress. She refused unconditionally, despite the presence of the attending nurse, until the promise was made to produce the anesthesia as a post-hypnotic phenomenon, so that she could be more satisfactorily in contact with reality during the entire time of the examination and treatment. Apparently, the highly personal character of hypnosis in such a situation renders it less acceptable than a drug anesthesia, as the experimenter has found on a number of occasions.

Comment: Whatever the strength and nature of the hypnotic relationship, it does not alter the sanctity of one's personal privacy. This belongs, apparently, to the waking state upon which it depends for protection. Had a violation of the stipulation regarding the examination been attempted in Account 10, an awakening from the trance would have occurred, since an attempt at examination would have been equivalent to a cue to awaken. One may judge from the above that the process of being hypnotized is perceived by the subject as a peculiar alteration of his control over the self, necessitating compensatory measures in relationship to any occurrence seeming to imply a threat to the control of the self.

Giving Information of an Intimate Character

Account 11: The subject was asked deliberately to disclose the name of the girl in whom he was most interested. This he did readily. Later, in the waking state, he asked for an account of all trance occurrences. Disclosure of the question about the girl's name elicited violent anger and he declared that his trust in the experimenter had been destroyed. When he was convinced by adequate proof that he had made the same disclosure some weeks previous in the waking state, a fact he had forgotten, his anger abated, but thereafter he refused to participate in hypnotic work except for strictly impersonal procedures, and any attempt to violate that condition, even indirectly, resulted in a prompt and angry awakening from the trance. Nor could this state of affairs be altered by careful hypnotic suggestion designed to correct his attitude.

In this same connection it is not an unusual experience in medical or psychiatric practice to have patients seeking any type of therapy, particularly psychotherapy, withhold or distort information bearing upon their problems because they feel the details of personal history to be of too intimate a character or too embarrassing to reveal, as has been noted above in Account 7. When recourse is had to hypnosis during the course of therapy, as a measure of securing information, the same tendency to withhold or to distort information is to be found, and this despite the fact that the patient may actually and urgently be seeking aid and has a clear realization that there is a legitimate reason for yielding the specific information. Usually, however, hypnotic questioning serves to elicit the information more readily than can be done in the waking state, but the entire process of overcoming the resistance and reluctance depends on the development of a good patient-physician relationship rather than upon hypnotic measures, and the hypnosis is essentially, in such situations, no more than a means by which the patient can give the information in a relatively comfortable fashion.

Comment: Although there had actually been no violation of personal privacy, the questioning was so construed in the waking state. Yet, despite refutation, this temporary misunderstanding permanently limited the extent of subsequent hypnotic work and precluded any alteration of the state of affairs by hypnotic suggestion. The relationship of these findings to unfortunate errors in psychotherapy is at once apparent.

Exhibiting the Contents of One's Purse

Account 12: On several occasions and under various circumstances, female subjects were asked to exhibit the contents of their purses and definite systematic attempts were made to build up in each a compulsion to do as requested. In each instance, however, the attempt failed and the explanation was obtained repeatedly that they considered such a request an unwarranted intrusion upon their privacy.

When this procedure was repeated on them later in the waking state, one subject yielded sufficiently to exhibit a part of the contents, but the others regarded the request as unreasonable. When told that there were justifiable and legitimate reasons for the experimenter's seemingly rude request, they replied that whatever his scientific purposes might be, he would have to be satisfied by their refusal.

However, these same subjects in the waking state would not resist the experimenter's picking up their purses and examining the contents. Rather, they took the sardonic pleasure in reducing the experimenter, by the implications of their manner, to the position of a prying busybody.

When a similar attempt was made to investigate their purses while they were in a second trance state, they resented and resisted it strenuously, nor could they be induced to account adequately for the inconsistencies of their waking and trance reactions.

This same general experimental request, in relationship to the contents of their pockets was readily and even proudly acceded to in both waking and trance states by small boys and by little girls with purses. When, however, an attempt was made to induce adult male subjects to exhibit the contents of their purses, they reacted as did the female subjects, or else yielded to the request in such fashion as to humiliate the experimenter greatly. *Comment:* A direct but inconsequential aggression upon the subjects' privacy was resisted even after it had been permitted in the waking state. One has the feeling that, as a result of their hypnotic state, they sensed a certain feeling of helplessness reflected in intensified self-protection, as has been noted in the comment on Account 10.

EXPERIMENTS INVOLVING HARM TO OTHERS
Physical Harm to Others
Account 13: Some college students had played the prank of feeding a large quantity of cathartic candy to an unpopular and

greedy student, who was also openly disliked by the experimenter and his hypnotic subject. Sometime later this subject was given a package of cathartic gum and instructed to replace with it a similar but harmless package of gum in the unpopular student's desk, so that unwittingly he would again become ill. The subject refused unconditionally, stated that the student had already been made sick once and that, while he would not mind a repetition of the prank, he preferred that the experimenter himself play the trick.

No amount of urging could induce the subject to change his mind, although it was discovered that he had been one of the original pranksters. Questioned about this, the subject explained that he had already satisfied his dislike fully and, hence, that there was no need of repeating the prank. When the experimenter offered to do it, the subject looked on with obvious amusement, but he could not be induced to share in the performance, nor did he seem to have any realization or expectation that the experimenter would secretly correct this act. Yet, at a later time this subject, in the waking state, did pass out cathartic gum to his unsuspecting friends.

Account 14: An explanation was given to a subject of the crude joke in which one inhales cigarette smoke deeply and then, professing to blow it out of his eyes to distract the victim's attention, dexterously burns the victim's hand.

The subject was urged to play this joke upon a suitable victim, and he was asked to go through a mock performance with the experimenter as a measure of ensuring a smooth enactment. Instead of a mock performance, the subject deliberately burned the experimenter's hand. No comment was made on this, and a discussion was held as to the proper victim, but one proposal after another was rejected. Finally, the subject declared an absolute unwillingness to do it on anybody except the experimenter, explaining that a cigarette burn was a nasty, unpleasant thing, that there was no humor in the joke and that the whole thing was not worth doing.

Inquiry subsequently disclosed that the subject felt justified in burning the experimenter's hand as a punishment for trying to take advantage of him, but that he did not feel that anybody else should be made a victim of so crude and painful a joke.

Account 15:   As a practical joke, it was suggested to a subject that a third person be induced to lift a box having metal handles, which were actually electrodes connected with a source of current. The experimenter then demonstrated on himself the effect of the shock, which was definitely violent and disagreeable.   However, the subject could not be induced to test the shock himself, and, when an unsuspecting victim was secured, he refused to close the switch, despite his willingness and readiness to turn on the current when the experimenter was lifting the box.   He explained his refusal on the grounds that the experimenter's full acquaintance with the apparatus and obvious willingness to take the shock justified his turning on the current, but that the unexpectedness of a violent shock for an unsuspecting victim would be a most questionable and unwise thing.   Yet subsequently, in the waking state, he joined with his fellows in using this apparatus to shock unsuspecting victims.   Even then, he could not be induced to go through the performance in the trance state, declaring that to do so would be only a blind automatic performance lacking in any element of humor and that, at best, he would not be a participant but only an instrument, a role for which he had no liking.

Account 16:   An exceedingly spoiled and pampered young woman had the unpleasant habit of slapping anyone who offended her even slightly.   When she was in a deep trance state an assistant was placed in rapport with her, with secret instructions to make definitely offensive remarks to her.   When he obeyed these instructions, she flushed angrily, turned to the experimenter and declared that the assistant was probably acting in response to the experimenter's request and that, by rights, the experimenter should have his face slapped, and that his face would be slapped if the assistant continued to make disagreeable remarks.

An attempt was made to persuade her of the experimenter's innocence, and also, that regardless of his innocence or guilt, she ought to slap the assistant, since he really had free choice in the matter. She declared, however, that she preferred to do her slapping when she was awake and that unless the trance procedure were changed she would awaken herself and would refuse to do any further hypnotic work, and it was found necessary to accede to her demands.

Comment: In these four accounts, not only did the subjects resist suggestions for acts actually acceptable under ordinary waking conditions, but they carried over into the trance state the normal waking tendency to reject instrumentalization by another. However, acting on their own sense of responsibility, there was no hesitation about aggressive behavior directed against the experimenter, but apparently the submissiveness of the trance state and the instrumentalization effected by the hypnotic suggestions of aggression against others rendered such suggested acts so impersonal and lacking in motivation as to be completely objectionable in the trance state.

Verbally Abusing and Giving Adverse Information About Others

Account 17: The subject was instructed to make a number of cutting disagreeable remarks to a person strongly disliked by that subject, and also to persons actually liked. However, she refused to perform either of these tasks in the trance state, declaring that she would not hurt her friends' feelings in any such fashion, and explaining that if she said unpleasant things to people she disliked, she preferred to be awake so that she could enjoy their discomfiture.

When it was suggested that she make disagreeable remarks

to disliked persons as a post-hypnotic performance, she again refused, explaining that if she said unpleasant things she wanted to be the one who originated them, and that it would be done only at her desire and at an opportunity that she selected, and not in response to the experimenter's request. Despite much urging, she could not be induced to alter her attitude.

Yet, in an obviously experimental setting, where it was plain that everybody understood the total situation, this subject, as well as many others, was found entirely willing to accede to such requests and even to take advantage of the opportunity to say things more disagreeable than necessary, but to secure such a performance, there is always a need for the protection afforded by a recognized experimental situation. However, even under obviously experimental conditions, many subjects will refuse to accede to this type of request, explaining that they might inadvertently hurt someone's feelings.

Comment: While the suggestions themselves were not repugnant to the subject, the general situation was, and the subject reserved full rights and demanded the privilege of obeying only under conditions of full conscious awareness. Yet, at a mere experimental level, where the purposes of the act are defeated by the nature of the setting, full obedience may be obtained. Again, resistance by the subject to instrumentalization is apparent.

Account 18: A subject, known to be aware of certain unpleasant facts concerning an acquaintance whom she disliked greatly, was questioned extensively in an effort to secure from her that information. She refused to relate it, even though, previous to the trance, she had on several occasions been on the verge of imparting that information to the experimenter, and had been deliberately put off. She did explain that perhaps sometime when she was awake she might disclose the facts, but that she would not do so in the trance state. No manner of suggestion served to induce her to yield, even though the experimenter's secret knowledge of the entire matter permitted the asking of leading

questions and the relating of a sufficient amount of detail to justify
her fully in the feeling that she would betray little or nothing.
After much pressure, she finally expressed a willingness to tell
after awakening, if the experimenter could convince her in the
waking state of the legitimacy of his request. Her offer was
accepted, but when the attempt was made she evaded the situation
by a deliberate falsehood, which, if the experimenter had persisted
in his inquiries, would have served to force him into a position
where he would have had to embarrass and humiliate her by the
exposure of her falsehood.

Comment: Not only did the subject resist the hypnotic commands, but also she withstood a situation which ordinarily in the
waking state would lead to capitulation, and, in addition, she
effected, at an unconscious level of thought, a contretemps pre-
cluding any further action by the experimenter. In this instance,
at least, the subject was more capable of resisting the experimenter's commands in the trance state or by unconscious measures
than she was in the waking state.

Offenses Against Good Taste and the Privacy of Others

Account 19: A subject was asked to tell risque stories in a mixed
group. This request he refused unconditionally. Subterfuges of
seemingly hypnotizing the other members of the group and giving
them instructions to become deaf failed to convince the subject
of the reality of the performance. Finally, suggestions were
given him to the effect that the others present had left and that
he was now alone with the experimenter and could tell the stories.
The subject apparently accepted this suggestion of the absence
of others, but declared that there was something peculiar about
the room, that there were inexplicable sounds to be detected and
he refused to accede to the request.

On a later occasion, the subject was rendered hypnotically blind
and taken into a room where others were quietly present. When
asked to tell a risque story, he explained that he could not because
he was not confident of the nature of the situation.

On still another occasion he was rendered hypnotically blind and hypnotically deaf, with prearranged tactile cues calling for different types of behavior, among which was the relating of a certain objectionable story. Finally, the signal for the story was given him, but the subject demanded that the experimenter assure him honestly, by a tactile cue which he specified, that there was nobody else in the room. Only then would he relate the story.

When an account of this was given to him later, with the implication that others might have been present, the subject remarked sardonically that any embarrassment deriving from the situation belonged solely to the experimenter and to any others present.

Comment: The need for realism in the actual situation, the capacity for self-protection in even a recognized experimental setting and the ability to allocate responsibility is obvious.

Account 20: A subject was instructed to open her companion's pocketbook, to secure a cigarette, and to give it to the experimenter, this to be done with the full awareness of her companion, but without express permission. She refused to do so despite urgent demands and angry insistence. Since these measures failed, she was given a post-hypnotic suggestion to the effect that after awakening she would notice the experimenter fumbling with an empty cigarette package and that she would then openly abstract a cigarette from her friend's purse. She agreed, but rather hesitantly. After awakening, the proper cue being given, she made several abortive attempts to obey the command, and finally took refuge from the situation by lapsing back into the trance state and explaining that she "just couldn't do it, it wasn't nice, it wasn't proper and it was too discourteous." It was pointed out to her immediately that the companion's full awareness of the situation and failure to manifest any objection rendered the request legitimate. Nevertheless, she persisted in her refusal.

Subsequently, she was awakened with a complete amnesia for the trance and the post-hypnotic experience. During the course of a casual conversation, the experimenter asked her for a cigarette. When she replied that she had none, he suggested that her companion had cigarettes and this statement was confirmed by her friend. She was then asked if she would open her companion's purse and secure a cigarette. Her first reaction was one of being shocked at the impropriety of the request, but finally she yielded to repeated demands, first thinking the matter over and then reasoning aloud, "If you ask me to do a thing like that, you must have a good reason, and she (the friend) certainly looks as if she were waiting for me to do it, and doesn't object, so, with your permission (addressed to the friend) I will do it. If I didn't think you (the experimenter) had a good reason, I wouldn't do it."

Shortly afterward she was re-hypnotized, reminded of the entire course of events and was again asked to secure another cigarette. She explained that she could do it better if she were awake, and, when the experimenter persisted in his demands that she do it while still in the trance state, she again refused. Nor would she repeat her waking performance in response to further post-hypnotic suggestions, declaring that once was enough and that the whole thing was entirely unnecessary.

Account 21: Another subject was instructed emphatically, but unsuccessfully, to examine the contents of her friend's purse. Finally resort was had to post-hypnotic suggestion and when this failed, she was given post-hypnotic suggestions to the effect that after awakening she would absent-mindedly pick up her friend's purse under the impression that it was her own (care had been taken to arrange that the friend's purse could be mistaken easily for the subject's) open it and become so puzzled and bewildered at seeing unfamiliar objects in her purse that she would examine them in an effort to discover how they happened to get there. After awakening, during a casual conversation, the proper post-hypnotic cue was given. She immediately mentioned that she felt like smoking, casually picked up her friend's purse and started to open it, but, as she did so, remarked, "What's the matter with the clasp on my purse? It's suddenly got awfully stiff. Why this isn't my purse!" and then, recognizing it, put it down and picked up her own, apologizing to her friend.

Upon being re-hypnotized, the subject explained that she simply could not do what had been asked, but added that she had "tried hard."

An attempt to repeat these two experiments, 20 and 21, in the absence of the owner of the purse was resisted strenuously, and the experimenter's own attempt to examine the purse was met with anger and extreme contempt. Similar results were obtained with several other subjects.

Account 22: The subject was engaged in a casual conversation about how little things tell a great deal about the personality. From this, comment was made upon the contents of small boys' pockets and then it was suggested that the contents of the experimenter's purse might be most revealing. She was then urged to take his purse, empty it of all its contents and to make a critical examination of them. The subject was most unwilling to do this, but after extensive urging, she finally yielded, declaring, "You must have some purpose in this or you wouldn't want to make me do it, and it's going to be your own hard luck if I do. I will do it, even though I don't want to. I suppose you are carrying on an experiment and I will just help you out the way you want me to. Another thing, you probably planned this so there isn't going to be anything in your purse you don't want me to see." Having made these remarks, she performed the task, but with obvious distaste and reluctance, and constant urging was required to induce her to scrutinize each object.

Comment: In the three accounts, 20, 21 and 22, the subjects either rejected the suggestions or transformed the performance into one entirely excusable though obviously distasteful. Such was the strength of their objections in the trance state that they would not permit the experimenter to perform the act required of them in accounts 20 and 21 except at serious risk to himself. In brief, not only did they control the situation for themselves, but they also limited the experimenter in his own aggressive behavior against others not present and who presumably would never be aware of that aggression.

Account 23:   Over a period of months, a hypnotic subject was instructed, in accord with a carefully planned technique of suggestion, to read his roommate's love letters, without the subject's knowledge that the experimenter had secretly made contact with that roommate and had arranged for the leaving of personal letters readily accessible.   On the occasion of each hypnotic trance, the subject was asked urgently if he had performed his task, and every effort was made to convince him of the legitimacy of the act as a worthy scientific procedure, related to the investigation of the ability to remember unpleasant things, and connected, in turn, with an investigation of memory processes as affected by hypnosis.

Nevertheless, the subject failed to obey instructions, and offered to do any number of disagreeable tasks which could be used as a memory test and which involved himself only.   Finally, a promise was secured from the subject that he would do as asked on a particular evening if the experimenter would be present. His demand was met and the subject, in the deep trance state, was told to find a letter, actually readily accessible, and to read it. Extreme difficulty was experienced by the subject in finding that letter.   He overlooked it repeatedly and searched in all the wrong places, since no overt move was made by the experimenter to direct his search.   Eventually, he had to be forced to find the letter and to open it.   He immediately discovered that he could not read it because he had mislaid his glasses.   In searching for his glasses, he succeeded in mislaying the letter, and when both the glasses and the letter were at hand, he opened the letter in such fashion that he was confronted by the blank sides of the pages. These he kept turning around and around in a helpless fashion, explaining that the pages were blank. After being told insistently to turn the pages over, he yielded, but did this in such fashion that the writing was then upside down. When this error was corrected, the subject developed spontaneously a blindness and became unable to read. When the blindness was corrected by suggestion and the letter again presented to the subject, the blindness returned and it finally became necessary to discontinue the attempt.

Some weeks later, the roommate, again under instruction from the experimenter, remarked to the subject, "I just got a letter from my girl that I want you to read." The subject replied, "I would like to. It's a funny thing, but for a long time I have wanted to read your mail. I don't know why. I've just had an awfully strong urge and it has disturbed me a lot, and I will be glad to do it and get that urge out of my system." He then read the letter, of which fact the experimenter was notified by the roommate. On the occasion of the next trance, the subject was asked the general question about having read his roommate's mail. He stated that he had done so one day in the waking state at the roommate's but not at the experimenter's request. He was then questioned extensively for the content of the letter, but he was found unable to remember any of it. When it was suggested that he re-read the letter, he agreed, but demanded insistently the privilege of asking his roommate's permission first, nor would he consent to re-read the letter unless this concession were made.

Comment: Despite a hypnotic technique of suggestion sufficient to hold an offensive task before the subject for a period of months, an exceedingly plausible and acceptable justification, and obviously worthy motives, the entire attempt was so complete a failure that he could not be induced hypnotically to repeat the waking performance authorized in a socially acceptable manner except under the precise conditions of that waking performance. Yet extensive knowledge of him disclosed him to be no more conventional than the average college student.

Acceptance of Complexes Implying Misdeeds Against Others

Account 24:   Before presenting the material of the next four experiments, which have been briefly reported in a study of the induction or implantation of artificial complexes, a preliminary explanation may be offered. These four experiments centered around the procedure of causing hypnotic subjects to believe that they had already committed an objectionable act. While developing an adequate technique of suggestion for this complex implantation, it was discovered that, to be effective, that is, to elicit genuine rather than realistic responses, the complex had to be about an act supposedly already accomplished in the relatively remote past only, and all attempts to build up a complex about some unfortunate act that they would inevitably perform in the future failed. Each explained, when the latter type of suggestions was attempted, that they could not conceive of the possibility of doing such a thing in the future. Yet, these same subjects, told they had actually done the same thing in the past, could be induced to accept the suggestion and would then respond in a highly significant fashion, as has been reported in the experiment mentioned above. The significance of these findings in relationship to the suggestion of criminalistic behavior to hypnotic subjects is at once apparent.

Another consideration of equal importance is the fact that the subject must necessarily have a waking amnesia for the complex material. Conscious recollection of the story, unless so vague, incomplete and inadequate as to render it meaningless, will effect a complete understanding and a rejection of it. Attempts to induce a belief in a complex at both waking and hypnotic levels of awareness invariably lead to a complete and resentful rejection of the complex story. The outcome of a conscious recollection is illustrated fully in *The Study of an Experimental Neurosis Hypnotically Induced in a Case of Ejaculatio Praecox,* in which the subject first recalled the complex as a reality experience and then immediately recognized its nature, nullifying completely its reality. Hence, although a subject may be induced to believe that he has committed some reproachable act, he must not be allowed to become consciously aware of this belief. Its acceptance as a truth apparently depends upon its remoteness from the possibility of conscious examination, and its effect upon the personality is comparable to that of repressed experiences.

Since the four experiments were all of the same general character, they will be presented as a single account.

Subjct A was given a complex centering around the belief that he had accidentally burned a hole in a girl's dress through carelessness in smoking. He accepted the complex, reacted strongly to it, complained the next day of a severe headache, quit smoking, gave away his cigarettes, and was hostile and resentful toward the experimenter and uncooperative in regard to future hypnosis. Rapport was reestablished with difficulty, and thereafter for some months, despite the removal of the complex and the giving of insight, he was unwilling to act as a hypnotic subject unless convinced of the value of the scientific purposes to be served.

Subjects B and C were given separately complexes to the effect that, in their eagerness as medical internes to learn the technique of the cisterna puncture, they had inadvertently caused a patient's death, which they failed to report. Both accepted the complex in part, but rejected certain points for various plausible reasons, and their exposition of these was then followed by a complete rejection of the complex. Both reacted with intense resentment toward the experimenter, although friendly feelings were reestablished when they were acquainted fully with the experiment. Also, both then expressed regret about failing to meet the experimenter's purposes by their rejection of the complex. Nevertheless, when another attempt was made later to induce in them a second complex centering about a culpable act, both rejected it unconditionally with essentially the same succession of events as occurred in relation to the first complex. Of particular interest is the fact that one of these subjects was used in the experiment in Account 2 above. Apparently, his intense curiosity did not extend to this type of painful experience.

Subjects D and E, occupational therapists, were given complexes to the effect that they had, through carelessness not in itself seriously culpable, been directly responsible for a serious injury to a patient. Both accepted the complex, reacted with great intensity to it, became markedly hostile and resentful toward the experimenter, but cooperated with him in the trance state because of his secret knowledge of their supposed misdoing. After the complex had been removed and insight given, both demanded that no further experiments of that nature be done on them, and thereafter they tended to scrutinize closely any suggestions given them in the trance state.

Subject F, a nurse, was given a complex to the effect that she had inadvertently applied the wrong medication to a patient's wound, with serious results. When an attempt was made to describe the extent of the unfortunate consequences, it was found necessary to minimize them somewhat if the subject were to be induced to accept the complex. Later, after the complex had been removed and an understanding of the situation had been given, the nurse explained spontaneously that her acceptance of the complex had actually been based upon a somewhat similar mistake nearly committed during her course of training, and she remarked that the experimenter had been fortunate in seizing upon something that could be directly related to a real incident of her past, since otherwise, she could not conceive of ever having been so careless.

Comment: The fact that such complexes as the above could be induced only in relationship to the past is highly significant in itself. Apparently, it is easier to conceive of oneself having already done wrong than to consider the possibility of committing a wrong in the future. An indirect criterion of the validity of the experiment is to be found in the account of Subjects B and C, who, even after being acquainted fully with the experimental nature of the procedure, rejected unconditionally the second complex.

Finally, these experiments serve to demonstrate that, while there is a good possibility of making a hypnotic subject believe, in the trance state only and not in the waking state, that he has done an objectionable act, he cannot be induced to believe that he will do such an act.

OFFENSES AGAINST THE PROPERTY OF OTHERS
Damage, Destruction or Loss

Account 25: It was suggested to a subject that a practical joke could be played on a certain unpopular girl who was highly critical of the habit of smoking and who professed falsely never to smoke. The joke as outlined was to the effect that the subject should light a cigarette and then, watching her opportunity, pick up a handkerchief which the disliked girl had on her desk and crumple the cigarette in it, so that those aware of the joke could discover it and accuse that girl of smoking secretly and of being surprised in the act and driven to conceal the evidence in this manner.

Adequate arrangements were made secretly with the proposed victim to permit a favorable situation for the perpetration of the joke. However, when the time came to act, the subject refused, declared that it was unfair and wrong to destroy that girl's handkerchief by burning it, even though the girl was a liar, and argued that there must and would have to be a better way to carry out the joke. No amount of urging could induce the subject to accede to the proposal, but she was entirely willing that the experimenter perform the act. Even so, she could not be induced to encourage the experimenter or anyone else in such a performance.

Account 26: A subject, employed as a stenographer, was typing the final copy of a colleague's paper, a task which she had been instructed by her superiors to complete at a specified hour. While so engaged, the subject was hypnotized and a great variety of suggestions was given her to compel her to type inaccurately and to make a poor copy, with the excuse offered that the poor quality of her work could be accounted for by haste and over-anxiety. These suggestions failed and she could not be induced to do anything of a destructive character, despite the fact that she knew the experimeter could and would, by virtue of his official position, protect her from any possible consequences. The only results of the suggestions were a temporary decrease of her speed in typing and a general increase in the care with which she worked.

Account 27: A subject was instructed to destroy or throw away certain important papers lying at hand on the desk of a disliked superior. All circumstances were arranged to make the general situation entirely favorable for the performance. Despite repeated and insistent efforts, all suggestions were rejected, although there was no objection to the experimenter's offer to do the task.

Account 28: The subject was instructed to abstract from a colleague's desk certain important papers and to mislay them in some inaccessible place, thereby causing serious inconvenience to their owner. Despite insistence and emphatic suggestion, the proposal was rejected. Post-hypnotic suggestions were given to the effect that later in the day, while securing legitimately from that desk certain other papers, there would be an accidental and unnoticed picking up of those documents. Thus, in an absent-minded way, there could be an actual and guiltless mislaying of the papers.

There resulted only an obedience to the first part of the post-hypnotic suggestion, namely, securing and filing away the proper documents, but the others, while picked up at the same time, were promptly sorted out and returned.

Comment: In the four above accounts, various factors of justification for the performance, the existence of adequate protection, a degree of willingness to do the suggested act at a waking level, and, in Accounts 26 and 28, the possibility for total exculpation on the basis of accident all failed completely to permit a performance of the suggested acts.

INDUCING SUBJECTS TO COMMIT THEFTS

Account 29: A subject was presented with a specious argument about the possibility of developing marked finger dexterity as the result of hypnotic suggestion and it was proposed to use him for that purpose, to which he readily consented. It was then suggested that he pick his roommate's pockets, and long, detailed instructions and careful practice were given him, particularly about how to stand, how to distract his intended victim's attention, and how to rely upon his own subconscious understandings of dexterity to pick pockets unnoticeably.

The subject objected most strenuously to the entire plan, but finally yielded to the specious arguments offered him. On the selected occasion, with provision made for the distraction of the roommate's attention through his close examination of an attention-compelling object, the experimenter and the subject crowded against the victim closely, jostling him in an apparent eagerness to join in the examination. As this was done the subject proceeded with the pocket-picking but did it so crudely and so roughly that it was impossible for the victim, who was fully aware of the situation, to avoid noticing what was occurring.

Nevertheless, the subject insisted that he had performed the act gently and delicately and nothing could convince him that he had been rough and forceful in all of his movements. Similar results were obtained upon repetition with this subject, despite his realization then that it was an experimental situation.

Similar findings were made with other subjects, among whom was one whose favorite practical joke was picking the pockets of his friends and distributing his loot among the pockets of the group, and then, by some clever subterfuge, causing a discovery of the trick. In the trance state, he declared an entire willingness to do this when awake, since then he "would know everything going on" but he flatly refused to do it as a trance performance since he would be out of contact with his environment and since it would not be a joke but a highly questionable performance carried on at the behest of another.

Comment: The apparent acceptance of the suggestions for pocket-picking was made entirely meaningless by the character of the performance, and the persistence in this type of performance, even after the nature of the act had been revealed, disclosed that the unconventional aspect alone of the misdeed was sufficient to preclude a satisfactory execution. Likewise, the attitude of the jokester makes clear the sense of limitation that the hypnotized subject feels in relation to his environment. Also, there is an adequate demonstration of the ability of the hypnotized subject to recognize readily the entirely different significations of a performance when executed as a prank and when done as an act of simple obedience.

Account 30: During a casual visit, a subject displaying his empty package, asked the experimenter for a cigarette. The experimenter apologized for not having any, induced a deep trance and suggested that the subject purloin from the adjacent office a package of cigarettes habitually left on the desk, since the owner would have no real objection. Thus, both he and the experimenter could enjoy a smoke and the whole situation could then be forgotten. The subject expressed entire willingness to do this if confession might be made to the owner of the cigarettes. When this concession was refused, the subject rejected all the suggestions, even though the experimenter offered to replace the cigarettes with a full package later.

Subsequently, while the subject was in the waking state, in

response to his original request for a cigarette, it was suggested that he might, as a joke, purloin cigarettes from that same office. To this the subject consented readily, went to that office, and secured two cigarettes, one of which he gave to the experimenter with marked insistence that it be smoked while he smoked the other. Later, it was found that the subject made full confession of his act to the owner of the cigarettes.

Comment: An act, not entirely acceptable in the waking state, as shown by the insistence upon inculpating the experimenter and the making of amends was found completely unacceptable in the trance state, despite the knowledge that restitution would be made.

Account 31: A poverty-stricken college student was instructed repeatedly in a series of trances extending over a period of weeks to purloin small sums of money left lying carelessly about by his roommate, with whom secret arrangements had been made. Elaborate suggestions and rationalizations were employed, but always without avail. Yet, on the occasion of each new trance state, although invariably he pleaded to be excused from the task, he could be induced to renew his previous promises to obey. Finally, it became necessary to discontinue the experiment because the subject's intense resentments were effecting a breakdown of the profound amnesias for the trance experiences which had been established by the experimenter, both as a measure of promoting the suggested act and as a means of preventing the subject from discovering the purposes of the repeated hypnotic trances.

Subsequently, it was learned that, during the course of the experiment, the subject had made numerous vague inquiries among the experimenter's colleagues concerning the experimenter's character, for which conduct he could give no reason at the time. When later the subject was given an account of the experimental procedure, he was very much relieved, protested that the experimenter should have known that hypnosis could not be used to make a thief of anybody, and he declared that he could now understand his past "peculiar unhappy feelings about you" which had distressed him greatly at the time and which had caused him to seek reassurance about the experimenter's character.

Comment: Apparently, in attempting to induce felonious behavior by hypnosis, the danger lies not in the possibility of success, but in the risk to the hypnotist himself. What might have happened had an adverse opinion been given of the experimenter is interesting only to speculate upon, since general knowledge of hypnotic reactions suggests that an unfavorable statement would have served to abrogate the suggestions for an amnesia of the trance events. The probability of this will be shown in Accounts 34 and 35.

EXPERIMENTS INVOLVING THE DIRECT ABUSE BY THE HYPNOTIST OF THE SUBJECT'S CONFIDENCE

Account 32: A subject was induced by careful suggestion to believe as the truth a statement originally known by the subject to be false. The outcome was a firm and effective expression of belief in its veracity in subsequent trance states, but a full recognition of its falsity in the waking state. All action on the statement was limited to the waking state, since, during hypnosis, the burden of any action was shifted upon the experimenter. Efforts made to have the conviction of truth carry over into the waking state failed, apparently because there had to be a meeting of conscious objections to the statement at the level of conscious awareness.

Comment: Yet the "poisoning of the mind" by subtle lies in the ordinary waking state will lead to the development of complete belief, both conscious and unconscious. Apparently, the time and situational limitations of the trance state serve to preclude a similar development of belief for both the hypnotic and the waking levels of awareness.

Account 33: Another subject was carefully given malicious misinformation about an acquaintance, and this was systematically and convincingly confirmed by the experimenter's colleagues. There resulted in the waking state the development of a definite attitude of dislike, distrust and avoidance, coupled with a marked alertness and an intense interest and curiosity on the part of the subject concerning that acquaintance. Within a few days, however, the subject complained to the experimenter of having felt vaguely but distressingly uncomfortable for some unknown reason since the occasion of the last hypnotic session and demand was made for rehypnotizing as a measure of relief. This request was granted, but an attempt was made to evade the issue. The subject, however, demanded that a full waking recollection be given of the communications of the previous trance, explaining only that "it just has to be done."

When this was finally done, the subject reacted in a relieved but bewildered way, finally declaring, "Well, if that's true, and they all said it was, why did you have to tell me when I was asleep? Even if they did say it was true, I don't believe it. I can't believe it. I'd have to find out for myself and just telling me when I'm asleep wouldn't make me believe it. You'd have to tell me when I'm awake so I would know it. You can't believe a thing if you don't know it and you told me when I was asleep so I wouldn't know it. If you want me to believe a thing you will have to tell me so I'll know it when I'm awake and not just when I'm asleep. If it is true, I'll find out about it and then I'll believe it, but this way, why it's no more than a nasty story. What were you trying to do?"

A full statement and proof of the victim's awareness of the experiment clarified the situation, and subsequent hypnotic work met with no difficulty, the subject accounting for this on the grounds that the whole experience had been merely unpleasant and of no importance except scientifically, and that there had never been any true credence of the story.

Comment: Apparently, to judge from the subject's remarks, such a communication as the above to a subject in the trance state lacks some attribute or quality of reality essential for credence. Despite the acceptance of the story in the state of hypnotic submissiveness, the failure of the inclusion in such acceptance of processes of conscious awareness and of conscious responses to the information deprived the story of any significant credence value.

Account 34: A second subject, utilized for a repetition of the above experiment, showed essentially the same course of behavior, with the exception that no direct requests were made for a second trance. Instead, frequent apparently purposeless visits were made to the experimenter's office, with vague hesitant complaints offered about feeling generally depressed and unhappy, all of which were received with casual indifference which led finally to a rather sudden resentful departure by the subject.

About an hour later the subject burst into the office in a violent rage and a most difficult situation followed. In the period of time after leaving the office, there had developed slowly and then with increasing rapidity a full spontaneous recollection of the events of the trance session, a critical review of the entire situation and of the misinformation given, a complete repudiation of its veracity and the development of an intense anger toward the experimenter and everybody concerned. Finally, however, the exhibition of the experimental protocol and of the observations that had been recorded, and proof of the victim's awareness served to effect a satisfactory adjustment, aided, probably, by the subject's own scientific training and intense interest in clinical psychology and hypnosis.

In reviewing the whole experience a few days later, this subject offered essentially the same explanations as had been given by the first subject. In addition, the intensity of the angry outburst was explained as the reaction to the experimenter's violation of the hypnotist-subject relationship occasioned by his seeming indifference to the vague complaints of distress and by his virtual refusal to meet his responsibilities in a situation where all responsibility belonged entirely to him. As in the first case, no difficulties were encountered in further hypnotic work with the subject.

Comment: In addition to confirming the findings of the preceding experiment, this account is particularly informative in relationship to the general futility of this type of attempted misuse of hypnosis and to the seriousness of the risk encountered by the hypnotist in such attempts. Also, the outcome suggests what might have occurred if the experiment on theft in Account 31 had not been interrupted.

Account 35: One actual instance of intentionally unscrupulous use of hypnosis concerns a hypnotic subject employed in some laboratory experimentation by Mr. Blank, a capable hypnotist generally regarded as of a somewhat questionable character and who was known to dislike the author intensely. Over a period of weeks this subject manifested increasingly marked avoidance reactions toward the author, with whom there existed a casual acquaintance. After about a month of such behavior, the subject suddenly entered the author's office, rudely demanded attention, and burst into a tirade of "I don't like you, I hate you, I despise you, I've got no respect for you, I can't stand the sight of you, and I don't know why. That's why I've come here. I want to find out. I want you to hypnotize me and when I'm in a trance I want you to ask me so that I can tell you. It may not be important to you, but it is to me, and I want to know what it's all about."

Attempts to question him in the waking state elicited only the sullen insistent reply that he did not come to bandy words, that he came to be hypnotized so that he could find out something. However, he did add that he had never done or said anything against the author and that nobody else knew how he felt. He explained further that he was a well-trained subject and that he was certain he would go easily into a satisfactory trance.

Taking him at his word, the author induced a deep trance easily, recapitulated the remarks that had been made upon entering the office, and suggested that perhaps he could now know what he wished. The subject proceeded at once to tell a long, detailed story about how Blank, in almost daily hypnotic sessions over a period of two months, had subjected him to an endless recital of innuendoes, veiled remarks and subtle suggestions discrediting the author. He explained that, while he believed none of the remarks, he had found the situation increasingly intolerable, and that it had now become imperative to escape from it. Just how he might do this he did not know, since he did not wish to disrupt Blank's experimental work, which he believed to be excellent, as was actually the case. He then suggested that it might help to give him a full conscious recollection of these matters, since Blank always gave him insistent instructions never to remember consciously any of his trance experiences, with the explanation that such memories, whatever they might be, might interfere with the experimental work, even though it was purely physiological in character.

The subject's suggestion was accepted and acted upon, with a complete readjustment of his attitude toward the author and an intense anger toward Blank, but so adequately controlled was that anger that Blank's experimental findings on him continued to agree with those on other subjects. Upon the completion of that work, the subject refused to do any further work with Blank. Subsequently he explained that after his trance with the author, he had continued to have a full conscious recollection of all those events of his trances with Blank not connected with the experiment, and that in this way he promptly "washed them out" immediately upon awakening.

On a later occasion, another of Blank's subjects was hypnotized by the author, and inquiry disclosed that a similar attempt had been made upon him but that his reaction had been, "But I knew you and I liked you, so I didn't pay any attention to what he said, and when he kept on I just told him that I liked you and that you were a friend of mine and so he shut up."

Comment: Here there is an actual unscrupulous attempt to misuse hypnosis and yet, despite the extreme care with which it was carried on, it led to results unfavorable only to the hypnotist himself, without causing sufficient disruption of the subject's personality reactions to interfere with the legitimate hypnotic work being done with him by the unscrupulous hypnotist. The adequacy and the effectiveness of the protective measures employed by the subject, who was apparently susceptible to such abuse, is striking.

SUMMARY AND CONCLUSION

To summarize this investigation, one may state briefly that a great variety of experimental procedures was employed upon a large number of well-trained hypnotic subjects to induce them, in trance states or in response to commands and suggestions given during trance states, to perform acts of an unconventional, harmful, anti-social and even criminal nature, these acts to involve aggressions against both the self and others, as well as to permit direct abuse of the hypnotic subject by the hypnotist. Every effort was made to meet the need for control investigations covering the possibilities of waking behavior, for realism in the experimental situation, and for adequate and varied techniques of hypnotic suggestion. The findings disclosed consistently the failure of all experimental measures to induce hypnotic subjects, in response to hypnotic suggestion, to perform acts of an objectionable character, even though many of the suggested acts were acceptable to them under circumstances of waking consciousness. Instead of blind, submissive, automatic, unthinking obedience and acquiescence to the hypnotist and the acceptance of carefully given suggestions and commands, the subjects demonstrated a full capacity and ability for self-protection, ready and complete understanding with critical judgment, avoidance, evasion, or complete rejection of commands, resentment and objection to instrumentalization by the hypnotist, and for aggression and retaliation, direct and immediate, against the hypnotist for his objectionable suggestions and commands. In addition, many demonstrated a full capacity to take over control of the hypnotic situation and actually did so by compelling the experimenter to make amends for his unacceptable suggestions.

Had the above experiments been conducted as obviously experimental investigations, it is entirely possible that the subjects would have given realistic performances in such protected situations, but under those conditions, the outcome would not have been a function of the hypnosis itself but of the general situation. In that type of setting, one might deceive a subject into performing some objectionable act, but the deception would not be dependent upon the hypnosis. Rather, it would depend upon entirely different factors and the hypnosis, as shown repeatedly above, could easily constitute an actual obstacle to a deception based upon other factors.

Hence, the conclusion warranted by these experimental findings is that hypnosis cannot be misused to induce hypnotized persons to commit actual wrongful acts either against themselves or others, and that the only serious risk encountered in such attempts is incurred by the hypnotists in the form of condemnation, rejection and exposure.

*From *Psychiatry: Journal of the Biology and Pathology of Intersonal Relations*, Vol. 2, No. 3, Aug. 1939.

THE PRODUCTION OF BLISTERS BY HYPNOTIC SUGGESTION: A REVIEW*

FRANK A. PATTIE, *The Rice Institute*

EDITOR'S NOTE

Can hypnotic suggestion produce blisters? Many psychologists deny the effect of mind over body. Others believe that it is possible only with hysterical subjects. Still others think that it can be achieved with normal people.

The following article contains abstracts of all the cases on record of the formation of blisters by hypnosis. Unfortunately many of them were observed a long time ago and not under ideal laboratory conditions.

Can organic functions which are not under voluntary control by modified or controlled by hypnotic suggestion? This fundamental question must be answered by every author of a theory of hypnosis.

Some of the experiments and clinical observations purporting to show that certain functions (such as those of the digestive glands and the kidneys) not under voluntary control can be modified in the trance are discussed by Hull. In discussing the production of gastric secretion when hallucinations of eating are suggested, he points out that certain other experiments show similar reactions in the waking state if the subjects merely talk about eating. The gastric secretions, in other words, are actually under indirect voluntary control. Hull also reviews an experiment in which herpetic blisters (cold sores) were produced in the hypnotic state by suggesting (1) the itching sensation which usually precedes the appearance of a cold sore and (2) an extremely unpleasant emotional experience. Inasmuch as the suggestion of itching was not sufficient to produce the sore, it may be concluded that the emotional state lowered the physiological resistance of the subjects and that the sores were a direct consequence of this lowering. In fact, the authors of the experiment, by determining their subjects' opsonic index, showed this to be true. It is not difficult for Hull to explain all of the experimental results which he reviews by reference either to the principle of the conditioned reflex or to some intercurrent emotional state. But he omits any reference to reports of cases in which a cold object, applied to the skin with the suggestion that it is hot, has produced a blister. The processes which produce blisters on the skin are certainly not under direct or indirect voluntary control.

There is a widespread skepticism about the possibility of thus producing blisters. This attitude is in part due to the belief that the subjects in the experiments were not carefully watched between the giving of the suggestion and the exhibition of the blister and in part to a suspicion that they, with the zeal characteristic of hypnotized and hysterical subjects to give the experimenter the results desired, made the blisters by actually injuring their skin. If this skepticism can be traced to any particular publication, it is most likely due to the article of von Schrenck-Notzing in 1896; the author, after having obtained positive results with poor control of his hysterical subject, decided to bandage her arm during the time between the suggestion and the appearance of the blister, whereupon the results were negative and there was evidence that the subject had tried to injure the arm. Another experiment with the arm in a plaster cast was also negative in result.

The following paragraphs contain abstracts, arranged in order of publication of the original articles, of all of the literature that the writer has been able to find on this subject. The abstracts have been made as full as possible with respect to the control of the subjects between the stimulation and the appearance of the skin reaction.

1886 Focachon, a pharmacist who was in touch with Beaunis

and Bernheim. Subject: a hystero-epileptic woman, 47 years old, whose crises had disappeared under Focachon's hypnotic treatment. The subject was hypnotized at 11 a. m. Eight postage stamps were applied on the left shoulder, and she was told that a blistering plaster was being applied. A slight dressing composed of several strips of adhesive plaster and a compress was put over the stamps; its purpose was to impress on the subject the idea that a blister would develop. Subject was watched until night, at which time she was put to bed, still in the trance, and told that she would not awake until 7 a. m. She slept in a room locked by the experimenters. At 8:15 a. m. next morning the dressing and stamps, which were intact, were removed. The place where the stamps were applied was yellowish white in color and surrounded by a zone of redness and swelling about 5 mm. wide. Blisters were not noticed until later on the same day, after subject had made a train trip from Nancy (where the experiment was performed in the presence of Bernheim and others) to her home. Sixteen days later the skin area was still "en pleine suppuration." Similar stamps applied to the skin of another person for 18 hours produced no irritation.

1888 Von Krafft-Ebing. Subject: Ilma S., an hysterical woman used also in Jendrassik's experiments. In the trance, a metal letter K (dimensions not given) was pressed on an area situated somewhat centrally from the left shoulder blade. Suggestion: that next morning the area touched would be blood-red, but there would be no itching. Professor Lipp then bandaged the chest and back so that the area touched was absolutely inaccessible. The bandage was sealed in four places. A cover-bandage was then applied and sealed in two places. Lipp kept the seal. Next morning Lipp and other physicians examined the bandages and seals, which were intact. On the place touched there was an irregularly shaped area 5.5 by 4 cm. in size. From this spot the epidermis had become detached. The immediate surroundings were red. Two other areas, corresponding to the non-vertical lines of the K, were also present; on them the epidermis was loosened and could be pulled off easily. Nothing is said about control of the subject during the night.

1888 Jendrassik. In his best-controlled experiment on Ilma S., Jendrassik states that a blister developed five hours after stimulation and that during this interval the subject was watched while she was occupied with some hand work. The blister, however, did not develop where it was supposed to, on the left upper arm, but in a symmetrically located place on the right upper arm. The subject had hysterical right hemianesthesia.

1890 Rybalkin, a student of Bernheim and a physician in St. Petersburg. Subject: a 16-year-old boy, a major hysteric with anesthesia of almost the whole body. In the trance, he was told that upon awakening he would accidentally touch a stove (actually cold) and that a burn would result on his arm. Some minutes after contact with the stove there was redness without swelling at the place. A bandage was put on, and the subject went to bed "under the eyes" of the observers. At the end of the sitting, three hours later, there was a considerable swelling, accompanied by redness and a papulous erythema. A bandage was now applied; next morning two blisters were found. Nothing is said about control during the night, and the paper says no more than is indicated above about the watching of the subject during the sitting of three hours, at which several persons were present.

1906 Doswald and Kreibich. The latter author was a distinguished dermatologist and a prolific writer in his field. Experiment A. Subject: Dr. U., a clinical assistant, easily hypnotizable and having a delicate white skin and lively vasomotor reactions. After three preliminary experiments, which produced erythemas in two cases and nothing in one, the main experiment was done thus. U. was touched lightly on the forearm with a match stick, and the suggestion was given that a blister would form as quickly as possible. After waking U. (apparently immediately afterwards, but the time is not stated), the two experimenters watched the place continuously, and no one touched it. After three minutes, the place and its immediate surrounding were a delicate rose color, and after another six minutes the epidermis had raised itself to form a thin-walled, flabby blister about the size of a bean. After 48 hours, the blister was excised without tearing its top. The histological findings, which showed epithelial necrosis characteristic of neurotic skin gangrene, are described in detail.

Experiment B. Subject: a nurse, not hysterical, easily hypnotized. Two years before she had suffered from neurotic skin gangrene. Since that time, after warm baths or severe mental excitement there would appear on her skin red spots and wheals. In deep hypnosis she was touched with a match stick and told that a blister would form immediately. The place touched, the inner surface of the left upper arm, was covered with a stiff cardboard tube which went over the elbow and into the axilla. It was tied with bandages, which were signed with an ink-pencil. Inside of the cardboard tube there were put a definite number, known only to the experimenter, of porcelain balls, "which gave a definite color reaction by the drying out of a non-stimulating chemical substance." (The rationale of the control with the balls is by no means clear.) At 4 p. m. (it is not stated when the experiment began), the bandage was perfectly intact. Since it was too tight, it was removed. The balls were counted and all were recovered. On the skin there was a red spot of the size of a crown coin. A delicate pink color around this area indicated a more extensive hyperemia. In the middle of the red spot there was a yellowish-white bloodless area; its paleness resulted from edema of the papillary body. The same bandage was put on and removed next day, 24 hours after the suggestion. The area was excised. The histological findings were consistent with what the authors have described in connection with neurotic skin gangrene as dilatory erythema. Over the whole area the epidermis is connected with the cutis, at no place raised in the form of a blister, and in the epidermis there are the most varied degrees of epithelial necrosis. Further histological details are to be found in the original article.

1909 Heller and Schultz, of the dermatological clinic of the City Hospital, Frankfurt-am-Main. Subject: a carpenter, 19 years old, extraordinarily suggestible, who had been used as subject by several lay hypnotists; he could slow down his heart beat in the trance to about 30 beats a minute. Delicate skin, dermatographia of medium grade, but no urticaria factitia or other signs of a specially labile vasomotor system. At 11 a. m. a mark coin was laid on the back of the left hand, and he was told that a painless burning was occurring which would produce a blister by 5 p. m. When the coin was lifted, a red spot on the skin was noticed, corresponding exactly with the size of the coin. Professor Herxheimer, director of the clinic, bandaged the hand with a cover of cotton-wool, closed on all sides, and sealed the knots. The subject was now awakened and felt no pain. At 5 p. m. on removal of bandage, there was a round, red, and slightly raised efflorescence of the exact size of the coin. The left half was like a wheal and was of a brighter red, and in the lower left quadrant the epidermis was raised to form an irregularly shaped, flat, hard blister. The bandage was again put on. Thirty hours later, the blisters had flattened but the redness was still plain. After five days the blister had healed with a bright red scar. The authors say that they were justified in concluding that their case did not correspond to urticaria facticia, in which scars never occur, but that it involved epithelial necrosis.

1909 Podiapolski, a physician of Saratov, Russia. Subject: a healthy peasant woman, a good somnambulist who five years previously had been relieved by hypnosis of hysterical loss of voice due to fright. At that time Podiapolski had produced a blister and had published an article about it. In 1908 he read of a discussion of the Societe de Neurologie (Paris), in which

Raymond affirmed and Babinski denied the possibility of producing blisters. This controversy renewed his interest, and he called a conference of five physicians to plan an experiment in which all precautions should be taken to guard against fraud or error. Subject was put into deep hypnosis in a hospital in the presence of three other physicians. At 1 p. m. two burns were suggested in a place on her back that would be hard to reach. Stimuli: a coin and the convex bottom of a metal thermometer case, applied with light pressure. Subject was not allowed to see them or to know what they were. Subject was then placed on a perfectly smooth couch without any projections and left there to sleep. Every possibility of intentional rubbing was removed, and a nurse was employed to watch her without interruption. In addition to the nurse, Poliapolski and two other physicians were in the room nearly all the time. At 4 p. m., subject was brought out of the trance. At 8 p. m. two erythemas were noticed, which were not exactly in the places stimulated. At 10:30 subject fell asleep until midnight, when she awoke and complained of pain and said that a blister on her back had opened up. This was found to have occurred. She had been sitting as she habitually sat, without leaning back, in accordance with the habit developed by Russian peasants, who usually had only backless benches in their houses. Subject could even fall asleep in a sitting position with no support but her left hand. She did not remain for a moment without being watched, and "those on watch duty literally did not remove their eyes from her." No attempt to injure herself was noticed. The stimuli were applied at the upper and lower corners of the shoulder blade. One of the blisters was about 3 cm. from the spot stimulated; the other was 1 cm. off. There was a round, red field, slightly swollen and corresponding to the size of the coin, with 3 or 4 small blisters inside it. The effect of the application of the thermometer case was a single blister, which had burst.

1912 Smirnoff of Moscow. Subject: a strong and healthy

peasant girl, 19 years old, whom Smirnoff had treated successfully with hypnosis for toothache. First experiment: a triangular collar button, which Smirnoff pretended to heat over a lamp, was laid on the rear surface of the upper arm. Subject was kept in the trance 15 minutes after the suggestion. Shortly before her awakening, a reddening of the skin was seen, elliptical in shape, with the long axis lying in the same direction as the long dimension of the button. The redness was somewhat lower than the place touched by the button. Fifteen minutes later, a white blister formed, around which the redness extended for 4 cm. Second experiment, 4 days later, in the presence of Podiapolski and another physician. Stimulus: a flat copper letter C (dimensions not given). Painful burning was suggested. Trance was prolonged an hour after stimulation. Towards the end of the hour redness, 4 cm. in diameter, was noticed, not at the place of stimulation but around the "burn" produced in the first experiment. This effect soon disappeared, and another erythema appeared between the old "burn" and the place just touched. The place occupied by the new redness became gradually whiter and more swollen and in the course of two hours after the suggestion, a white blister formed, about 1 cm. long. Simulation is ruled out, since "the whole process went on before the eyes of the observers."

1915 Wetterstrand. The experiment was performed in the presence of Alrutz, a psychologist, and Sederholm, a dermatologist, in 1903. Subject: an hysterical woman, 55 years old. Suggestion given at 10 a. m. that burning sealing wax was being poured on a place on the volar side of the right forearm. There is no account as to what stimulus, if any, was applied. Subject complained of pain. A round glass plate held in metal and rubber rings, 4 cm. in diameter, was tied over the place. The glass was 7 mm. above the skin. The ends of the bandage that held the plate on the arm were sealed. At noon, the suggestion was given that a blister would form by 2 p. m. At that time "a possibly beginning reddening" was seen. The bandage was removed, and an adhesive plaster bandage with a dome-shaped celluloid pane was put on. Around this a gauze bandage was put; its ends were sealed with sealing wax in two places and signed. It is not stated when subject was brought out of the trance. Next day, 11 a. m., subject returned and reported pain; the bandage was intact. Twenty-four hours later the fully intact bandage was removed. Blisters could be seen through the celluloid plate in the adhesive plaster, which also was intact. A protocol from the dermatologist is given, testifying briefly with respect to the bandages and the appearance of the blister.

1917 Hadfield. Subject: Leading Seaman P, being treated for "shell shock" in a naval hospital. First experiment. The suggestion was given in the trance that the anterior aspect of the forearm was being touched with a red-hot iron and that a blister would form. Subject was watched for three hours, part of the time in the waking state and part in the trance. The arm was then bandaged with a large roller bandage so that it would be impossible for subject to interfere; the bandage was pinned with a safety-pin and the pin sealed with sealing wax. The subject was then sent to the ward, suffering great pain. He returned in six hours from the beginning of the experiment. A blister had formed on the spot touched, a white patch of dead skin in the center with a small amount of fluid underneath and hyperemia around it.

Second experiment, with stricter precautions. The lateral aspect of the upper arm was used. "I was never personally left alone with the patient; the patient was never left alone and I personally never touched the arm of the patient, this being done by another surgeon present, whilst I made the verbal suggestions. Throughout the day the patient was watched, and at night he was not only watched by the night nurse but his arm was securely bound up and sealed as before." Next morning, 24 hours later, the bandage was removed in the presence of three surgeons. The seal and bandage were intact. On the spot that had been touched there was "the beginning of a blister as before, which gradually developed during the day to form a large bleb with an area of inflammation around." The longer time required in the second experiment is attributed to the fact that for some hours the arm was exposed to cold air and also probably to the extra thickness of the skin on the upper arm.

In 1920 Hadfield reported experiments on reducing the temperature of the skin of a very susceptible subject, on whose skin he could also produce blisters. He gives no details on the blister-formation, as the case was similar to the previous one.

1927 Schindler. Subject: a woman, 38 years old, who had suffered for six years from extensive and painful ecchymoses, spontaneous in appearance and hysterical in origin. The trouble was diagnosed as hysterical after several years of ineffective somatic treatment. After a good many trials, it became possible to produce ecchymoses by hypnotic suggestion at spots indicated to the subject in the trance. In one experiment, an area on the forearm was marked off with a grease pencil. A thick plaster cast was then put on, extending from the middle of the upper arm and enclosing hand and fingers. After two days the cast was removed, and the ecchymosis was found, corresponding quite closely to marks. In one of these experiments, she was told that the place pointed out would "burn." The purpose of this suggestion was not to produce a blister but merely to insure the production of the ecchymosis. The ecchymosis appeared, but in its center there was a blister containing several drops of clear serum. On the next day there was a hemorrhage into the blister. The following entries are from the clinical record:

Jan. 20, 1921. At present spontaneous blisters appear daily, without suggestion, on the most varied parts of the body, always on the top of an ecchymosis. They progress, in general, as did the first one. However, now and then the bleeding into the blister does not occur.

Jan. 26, 1921.   The production of a blister can now be controlled to the minute.   It shoots up before the eyes of the doctor at the appointed time and is fully developed in five minutes. Such a blister is suggested, and a plaster cast with a watch glass is put on.   The blister appears and is demonstrated in the medical society.

Jan. 28, 1921.   Today a blister appeared without previous ecchymosis.

The above entries constitute the whole of the regrettably short record relating to blistering.   The patient was entirely relieved of her symptoms by hypnosis and change of environment, although the particular psychogenesis of the trouble could not be found out.

Some articles that are scientifically without value are not abstracted.

To summarize: Of the 11 subjects mentioned above, three were normal, two were normal but had suffered from hysterical aphonia and neurotic skin gangrene respectively, and six were hysterical.   Hadfield's second subject is not counted because of the absence of details concerning the control.   The time required for the development of the skin reactions varies enormously — from 10 minutes to 24 hours for the blister, from a few seconds or minutes to seven hours for the erythema.   In two cases it is stated that the skin response did not occur exactly at the area stimulated.   In the last 55 years there have been only 10 articles written in which investigators have reported the formation of blisters and given a reasonably full account of their procedure and control of the subject.

The writer, after all this evidence, still finds himself in an attitude of suspended judgment, an attitude due mostly to his inability to understand by what physiological processes suggestion — or the central nervous system — could produce *localized and circumscribed* erythemas or blisters.   The results of actual thermal or mechanical stimulation of the skin are due (1) to an increase in the permeability of the walls of the capillaries and a consequent exudation of fluid and (2) to dilation of the arterioles. The first effect is caused by a local liberation of histamine (or a similar substance) in the injured tissues. The second effect is due to axon reflexes. Both of these processes are independent of the central nervous system. In addition to these two processes, the skin may be in certain circumstances subject to the influences of antidromic impulses. These impulses, set going by irritation of the dorsal root ganglion of the spinal cord, produce the vesication observed in herpes zoster. In the laboratory antidromic action can be produced by artificial stimulation of the ganglion. There seems to be no evidence that antidromic impulses ever occur except in these two cases. Even if they were held responsible for hypnotic vesication, one would still have to explain how these impulses are produced by cerebral influence and how they could produce localized effects.

It may be objected that one should not deny the existence of a fact or what appears to be a fact merely because it cannot be explained in the light of present physiological knowledge. To this objection the answer may be made that the alleged fact needs stronger experimental evidence than the clinical observations given above afford. The observers have looked for blisters, which are the final result in a process involving several stages. If in certain rare cases blisters have been produced, we should reasonably expect to find, in a large number of cases, skin reactions that do not go so far as vesication but end in erythema. Further research should be carried out on a large number of subjects in order to see if such slight skin reactions to suggestion can be detected. In order to eliminate the effects of mechanical stimulation, a spot of light from which all heat rays have been filtered should be used as a stimulus in some of the experiments. In order to detect the slightest degree of erythema, photography with the proper type of film and filters should be used in order to detect vasomotor changes in the skin that are too slight to be visible to the eye. The surface temperature inside and outside of the "burned" area should be taken. Other precautions will suggest themselves to any one trained in experimental technique. Only further research will dispel the doubts concerning this fundamental problem of hypnosis.

*From *The Journal of Abnormal and Social Psychology*, Vol. 36, 1941, pp. 62-72.

EXPECTANCY VERSUS PERFORMANCE IN HYPNOSIS*

WESLEY R. WELLS, *Syracuse University*

EDITOR'S NOTE

What is the relation of suggestion to hypnosis? Is belief necessary and does our expectation affect our performance while hypnotized?

This article demonstrates that expectancy and actual performance are independent variables. Since skeptics are often hypnotized and believers often fail to be hypnotized, and since the subjects' beliefs and expectations were at variance with the actual performances, it follows that the suggestion theory of hypnosis seems untenable.

There is frequently a failure in hypnotic experiments to observe that expectancy of the subject and the actual hypnotic results are independent variables. Often the former is made out to be the cause of the latter by noting only those instances in which expectancy and performance happen to agree and by ignoring the instances in which they are diametrically opposed. This is well illustrated by Crane's summary of an experiment. Crane says:

> In London some years ago an experiment was performed with five soldiers to determine the influence of their mental state upon their physical strength. They gripped a dynamometer as hard as they could to register their maximum hand-grip strength. For the five men the average was 101 pounds. Then they were hypnotized, after which they were told that they were very weak and feeble. They were again given the dynamometer and told to grasp it as strongly as possible. Their average now was only 69 pounds. Then they were given the opposite statements, namely, that they were powerful, Herculean, after which their average strength of hand-grip was 140 pounds.
> . . . The belief that they were strong actually increased

their physical strength almost 40 percent above their normal capacity, while the belief that they were weak reduced their strength 30 percent below their best record.

The reading of the above passage by Crane prompted me to undertake a repetition of the experiment, but with this difference, that the two factors, belief or expectancy of the subject as to his increased or decreased strength and the actual increase or decrease of strength should be made by hypnotic methods to vary inversely, thus disproving the proposition stated by Crane that it is the belief or expectancy of the subject which brings about the variation in strength in such an experiment.

A. HISTORICAL ORIENTATION

The setting for this experimental problem is the suggestion theory of hypnosis. The essence of suggestion is the production, by indirect methods, of belief or expectancy, as illustrated by medical suggestion where, e.g., the patient who has been put to sleep previously by hypodermic injections of a sleep-producing drug is finally put to sleep by the injection of sterile water, if lied to and made to believe that the usual sleep-producing drug is being administered. In the 1880's, when the suggestion theory of hypnosis as promulgated by the Nancy school became widely accepted, most hypnotists were physicians who in general used suggestion, as physicians are so prone to do, attempting to induce expectancy of hypnotic results, along with an hypnotic technique devoid of suggestion, usually without recognizing the two aspects of their procedure as distinct and separable. In 1890 Wm. James summed up this suggestion theory of hypnosis in a sentence, as follows: "The prime condition of success is that the subject should confidently *expect* to be entranced."

In 1898 Boris Sidis subjected the suggestion theory of hypnosis to devastating criticism. *"Dissociation is the secret of hypnosis,"* he asserted, and he stated that the method of hypnosis "varies ... inversely as indirect suggestion." Sidis' point, however, was not quite that of the present paper, which stresses the element of expectancy or belief as the core of suggestion while being irrelevant to hypnosis.

Alongside a general tendency to accept expectancy as the cause of hypnotic results, there are recorded observations running counter to the expectancy theory throughout the history of hypnotism from the time of James Braid. Braid, the founder of scientific hypnotism and the first to use the term, as early as 1851 described cases contradicting the expectancy theory. Braid wrote as follows:

> I have been quite charmed by an article which appeared in the number of *Chambers' Edinburgh Journal* for the 8th of last month . . . The writer of the article alluded to had been a decided sceptic, and had accompanied a gentleman of his acquaintance, who was equally sceptical as himself, to a *seance* in a private family . . . The said friend offered to submit to the trial on himself, for the purpose of proving the fallacy of such pretensions; however, *the result was very different from his anticipations,* for the proud sceptic and derider was converted into a complete victim . . . From what has been stated by Professor J. Hughes Bennet, it appears that several members of the Medical Society of Edinburgh, who *were most sturdy sceptics,* were also victimized upon submitting to such trials . . .
>
> The potency of this method was proved by me at a public lecture in Manchester, before an audience of about eight hundred individuals . . . I requested strangers, who had never been operated upon, to come forward and try the effect of my process. Fourteen adult males came forward . . . One . . . was a powerful mechanic, who was sent down, bribed by a medical man, to resist me, and this he tried by not complying with my conditions; but, nevertheless, when I at length signified that I observed he was acting falsely, he set about it with a look of grim defiance, when he was speedily caught, and became one of the best examples of the power of my process that evening. Another, a most intelligent gentleman, was so sceptical, that before coming down he said, *"seeing* was *not* believing" with him, but that he must *feel* it before he would believe it,—he became a beautiful example.

The literature of hypnosis of the 1880's is filled with instances like the following from Moll which show, as in the cases from Braid, that hypnotic results may be contrary to the expectation of the subjects. Moll gives the following case:

I ask a man before I hypnotize him to tell me of something which, in his opinion, would never be found in my room. He says he would never believe there was an owl in my room . . . He wakes and says he sees the owl plainly; it is chained by the foot . . . It is so real to him that he hesitates to put his finger on the spot where he imagines it to be.

A few months ago I duplicated this experiment of Moll's as follows:—Miss *Be,* a subject previously developed to the somnambulistic stage, who could subsequently be put into the deepest hypnosis in a few seconds, was asked if there was someone who she knew could not possibly come into my office. She replied that her cousin *Ma,* who was serving in the Navy in the Pacific, could not possibly come to the office. Thereupon I put her into deep hypnosis, and in less than a minute she saw and began to converse with her cousin. Her first exclamation was, "Why, *Ma,* how did you get here?"

Bramwell had this to say:

I have failed with subjects who firmly believed I could hypnotize them, and that they were specially susceptible. On the other hand, I have succeeded with many who were convinced that they could not be influenced. Liegeois says it is not necessary for the subject to have faith . . . Forel states that people who laugh and say that they cannot be hypnotized are often easily influenced.

In three earlier articles I have described experiments of my own in which hypnotic results have been obtained contrary to the expectations of the subjects. In fact, so far as the first hypnotizing of subjects is concerned, the usual attitude of college students as subjects is one of skepticism. Skepticism is one of the most important motives in developing new subjects. Subjects frequently are willing to come to be worked on primarily to prove that they cannot be hypnotized, as in cases cited above from Braid. R. W. White, in his study of motivation in hypnosis, overlooked skepticism, the desire of the subject to prove that he cannot be hypnotized, as one of the important motives in actual practice in experimental hypnosis. Other things being equal, I would always choose a skeptic as a hypnotic subject. One cannot really fail with a skeptic, and one cannot really win with a believing subject. If one fails to get hypnotic results with a skeptic, the subject takes it as a matter of course, not criticizing the operator. If one succeeds in getting the skeptic into deep hypnosis (and skepticism does not interfere in the least), then one has really proved something. With a believer, on the other hand, if one gets good results the subject takes it as a matter of course, and the operator is apt to suspect malingering on the subject's part. If one fails to get results with the believing subject, then the subject tends to blame the operator for having inadequate methods.

The rule in the use of a straight hypnotic method is that hypnotic phenomena come first and belief comes afterwards as a result of the hypnotic phenomena. Here are three illustrative cases. With subject *Ph* I tried to produce contractures of the right arm and hand. I said to him, "You cannot raise your right hand. Try and you will see." He spoke up and said, "I can raise my right hand but my left hand is stuck down." I said, "Yes, your left hand is stuck down, but your right hand is stuck down also. Just try to lift it." He tried to lift it, found that he could not, and said, "Well, I'll be d——d!" He had believed that he could lift his right hand until he tried and failed. In the case of subject *Xy*, whom I was hypnotizing for the first time, I produced contractures of the hands, making them clasped so that *Xy* could not separate them. This was the first hypnotic phenomenon except contractures of the eyelids that he had experienced. He was so surprised at his inability to separate his hands, not believing in advance, nor even yet, that such a thing was possible, and he struggled so violently in trying to separate his hands, that he finally slipped out of the chair on to the floor, all the time struggling to get his hands apart. Of course he was finally convinced; he believed after the event, not before it. In a third case I was trying for the first time to get hallucinations with subject *De*. I said to him that when I had counted to 10 he would hear band music just as if there were actually a band playing nearby. When I started to count he shook his head. I interpreted this at the time as an indication that he believed it would not work, and afterwards he confirmed that this was what he had intended by shaking his head. But even before I reached the count of 10 he nodded his head and said that, after all, he did hear band music. He did not believe until *after* the hallucination had appeared that it could be made to occur.

Miss Brenman and Knight have reported a case similar to the last three cases above. In this case the subject "made no attempt to conceal her deep scorn for the procedure." Finally, in the twelfth hour, the subject was told for the first time that she could not open her eyes. "She laughed and said, 'Nonsense,' and proceeded to try." Thereupon "she found to her amazement that she could not."

This historical orientation has dealt with several aspects of the relation between expectancy and performance, in some cases referring to the first hypnotizing of skeptical subjects, and sometimes referring to the production of specific hypnotic phenomena in previously hypnotized but still skeptical subjects. The series of experiments in Section B is concerned with one specific problem, the control of strength of handgrip in previously developed subjects without a corresponding expectancy but instead with the contrary expectation.

B. Experiments on Ten Subjects

The following experiments were carried out during a period of four years on the best of available subjects selected by group hypnosis on college classes, except for the one subject *Mo,* and then developed to the somnambulistic stage by individual work. All the subjects except *Mo* were undergraduate students in my classes. This one exception was a graduate student, whose hypnotic history is given below. An average of three or four hours of individual work was spent in developing each of the subjects to the point where he could be put into deep hypnosis quickly, usually at the mere count of seven, as a result of previous hypnosis.

The procedure with each subject was as follows: First, his normal maximum strength of grip was measured by three trials with each hand. Then he was put into hypnosis. In the case of the first three subjects each subject was told in hypnosis that in the second test of strength, following hypnosis, he would be completely paralyzed when he tried to squeeze the dynamometer, though having normal control of his hands for other purposes. Each subject was told that he would believe, however, that he was stronger than in the first test, the prehypnotic one, for whatever reasons might occur to him, such as practice. He was told that he would not notice anything peculiar about the condition of his hands in this test. In none of the tests was the subject allowed to observe the dynamometer record, which was read by my assistant and set down in his notes. The subject was brought out of hypnosis with amnesia for the hypnotic period, his expectancy and his actual strength of grip being controlled by subconscious processes.

Profiting by my experience with the first three subjects, I improved my method in the later experiments. Each of the last seven subjects was told in the first hypnotic period that after he came out of hypnosis both arms and hands would be completely paralyzed, hanging limply at his sides, without strength enough even to clasp a sheet of paper, and that I would hold the dynamometer during the test. I stated that he would observe nothing peculiar in this, and that he would have the feeling of greater strength and greater exertion, as in the instructions to the first three subjects.

After the first posthypnotic test of strength and recording of the subject's report as to his belief regarding his strength, the subject was put into hypnotic state No. 2. He was then told that in posthypnotic Test 2 he would actually be somewhat stronger than in the prehypnotic test as a result of greater actual exertion on his part. He was told that he would believe, however, that he was weaker than normal, for whatever reasons might seem plausible to him, such as fatigue. Then he was brought out of hypnosis with amnesia for the two hypnotic periods and for the intervening period during which the first posthypnotic test was made. It is obvious that such an experiment cannot be done except with subjects in whom complete amnesia can be produced, not only for a single hypnotic period, but also for non-hypnotic periods as well. That amnesia can be made 100 percent complete with good subjects has been proved in another series of experiments.

After the second posthypnotic test of strength and report of the subject's expectancy had been made, each subject was put into hypnotic state No. 3. In this hypnotic state all hypnotic control of strength and of expectancy was removed, in order that effects of fatigue and of practice alone might be measured. Then the subject was brought out of hypnosis with amnesia for the three hypnotic periods and for the two interhypnotic periods, remembering only one previous test, the prehypnotic one, and remembering being hypnotized only once. The fourth test of strength was then made.

It should be too obvious to require mention that in all four tests equal encouragement was given to each subject. Every time before the subject gripped, or tried to grip, the dynamometer, 24 times in all, he was told, "Do the best you can."

The results were as follows:

Subject Miss Sp. Miss *Sp* was an excellent subject, with a centile rank well above 90. She was developed to the somnambulistic stage in one individual session of two hours a few days

prior to the experiment. Prehypnotic test:— R., 12, 18, 13; L.,
21, 19, 18; av., 16.83; av. best R. and best L., 19.5. Posthypnotic
Test 1:—R., 0, 0, 0; L., 0, 0, 0. She believed she was stronger
in this test. She said, "I felt a greater strain in arms and shoulders." Posthypnotic Test 2:—R., 20, 25, 23; L., 24, 23, 23; av.,
23; av. best R. and best L., 24.5. She believed that she was
weaker. "I felt tired," she said. Posthypnotic Test 3:—R., 19,
18, 17; L., 22, 16, 17; av., 18.17; av. best R. and best L., 20.5.*

For ordinary purposes in dynamometer tests, as Whipple states,
only the highest record for each hand is used. For such a problem as the present, however, involving so many tests, the average
of all six trials in each test is the best single measure for the test.
I have recorded the complete results above, computing the average of the highest right-hand and highest left-hand performance
combined as well as the average for the six trials in each test.
Only the average of the six trials in each test is used in Table 1.

TABLE 1

Strength of Grip in Kilograms, Average of Six Trials in Each Test

Subject	Prehypnotic Test	Posthypnotic Test 1 Expectancy, Greater Strength	Posthypnotic Test 2 Expectancy, Less Strength	Posthypnotic Test 3
1. *Ba*	40.42	10.42	40.75	39.33
2. *An*	21.75	0.42	25.33	17.75
3. *Mo*	40.92	0.58	45.17	40.92
4. *Br*	43.33	0.00	41.50	36.83
5. *Ca*	37.58	0.00	47.50	40.25
6. *Ha*	28.66	11.00	28.83	25.66
7. *La*	13.00	0.00	23.17	10.33
8. *Be*	12.17	0.00	15.00	10.33
9. *Bs*	27.67	0.00	28.00	26.67
10. *Sp*	16.83	0.00	23.00	18.17
Average	28.23	2.24	31.83	26.62

* The preceding nine cases have been omitted.

A further check on the accuracy of the subjects' reports of their expectancy in posthypnotic Tests 1 and 2 was provided when amnesia for all three hypnotic states and for the two interhypnotic periods was removed in later hypnosis. This was done with nearly all the subjects, and they were brought out of this final hypnotic state with all amnesia removed. Then they were able to review at leisure the whole course of the experiment. Every subject in whom the amnesia was thus removed confirmed the genuineness of the feeling of increased strength following the first hypnotic state and the feeling of weakness following the second hypnotic state. The memory of just how strong they had felt in posthypnotic Test 1, and of how weak they had felt in posthypnotic Test 2, was so vivid that at first some of them doubted my statement when I told them that the dynamometer records showed that their performance had been just the reverse. It was interesting to see some of them studying my assistant's notes on the results of the tests before they would fully accept the fact that they were weaker, in most cases completely paralyzed, in posthypnotic Test 1, and stronger, in some cases very much stronger, in posthypnotic Test 2.

All 10 subjects were sufficiently hypnotizable so that complete control of expectancy in posthypnotic Tests 1 and 2 was achieved. In all 10 cases partial or complete paralysis (complete in six cases) was produced in Test 1, when the subjects believed they were stronger than normal. Subjects *Ca, La,* and *Sp* showed the most striking increase of strength in posthypnotic Test 2, when the subjects believed they were weaker than normal. All the subjects except *Br* showed at least a slight increase in strength in this test in comparison with the prehypnotic test. If posthypnotic Test 2 is compared with the average of the two hypnotically uncontrolled tests, the prehypnotic test and posthypnotic Test 3, then all the subjects, including *Br,* showed the greatest strength in posthypnotic Test 2. This last comparison is the most valid since it takes into account fatigue from the prehypnotic test against which the subjects were working in posthypnotic Test 2, by comparing the results in subjects fatigued in one test with the average of results in unfatigued subjects (the prehypnotic test) and doubly fatigued subjects (posthypnotic Test 3). Fatigue resulting from posthypnotic Test 1 may be ignored, since the subjects were either completely paralyzed or too nearly so to fatigue themselves.

Averages of the results in the four tests for the 10 subjects are given in Table 1. Averages are misleading in hypnotic experiments unless care is taken to exclude from the averages results from subjects not sufficiently hypnotizable. In the present instance, however, all the subjects were hypnotizable enough so that averages may be found useful.

It should be added that, unless counteractive measures are taken, such experiments can be done only on naive subjects, subjects unfamiliar in advance with the nature of the experiment to be performed. If a subject had seen the experiment done previously on another subject, then he would suspect, when posthypnotic Tests 1 and 2 were being made, that the same inverse relationship between expectancy and strength would probably exist in his own case as in the case that he had seen. He would then allow for this by predicting just the opposite, in the way of performance, of what really seemed to him likely. But subjects are not hypnotizable enough for such an experiment, or for any difficult hypnotic experiment, unless complete amnesia can be produced, not only for the hypnotic period itself, but also for non-hypnotic incidents and periods of time. Thus subject Miss Sp had seen the experiment done on Miss Bs less than two weeks earlier. However, in this case amnesia was produced in Miss Sp in the first hypnotic period of the experiment, lasting through the whole experiment, for all that she had observed in the experiment on Miss Bs, and for all that she might ever have read or heard about this or similar experiments. This enabled me to proceed, having made Miss Sp artificially naive, by hypnosis, and thus a suitable subject. The results showed the success of the method.

Also with all the other subjects, as a precaution I produced amnesia in the first hypnotic period for anything they might ever have read or heard about such an experiment as that in which they were about to participate.

It is pertinent to add a comment regarding the difficulty of hypnotic experiments. Nine of the 10 subjects described in this article were selected by group hypnosis involving over 300 college students, during a period of five years. All of these except Miss *An* were selected during four years, but Miss *An* had been selected the previous year. *Mo* had been selected and developed by another hypnotist several years earlier, as stated above. Miss *An* and *Ca*, though selected in group hypnosis by me, had been developed individually by other hypnotists, as related above. I developed the other seven by individual hypnosis. There were only three other subjects, Miss *Gw*, Miss *Ge*, and *Tu*, whom I developed during these four years to the point where they might have served for such an experiment. I regretted my inability to include them in this experiment. I did use them in other research experiments, but pressure of college work, the approach of final examinations, etc., made it impossible for them to spare time for this experiment. Group hypnosis is by no means infallible in selecting the best subjects. I spent a great deal of time trying without success to develop other subjects to complete somnambulism during the four years.

If enough time were spent, up to 20 or 25 percent of college students might be developed sufficiently for such experiments, but this would require an immense amount of work. I know a psychiatrist who has used hypnosis therapeutically for more than 15 years, and in all this time he has not succeeded in developing a single patient to the somnambulistic stage. Numerous articles appear in the journals based on experiments done on the best subjects available, but none of them somnambulistic and suitable to indicate what real hypnotic phenomena are. The vast majority of people simply are not and cannot be made good enough hypnotic subjects for experimental purposes.

Janet, in 30 years, developed only 120 somnambulistic subjects from nearly 3,500 patients on whom he tried hypnosis. Even the great masters, Liebeault and Bernheim, were unable to develop more than 20 percent of subjects to the somnambulistic stage marked by complete amnesia such as is needed for most experimental work.

Many years ago during one college year I developed to the somnambulistic stage 16 out of 51 subjects, all men, but this percentage is well above my general average. By good luck I happened to find an unusual percentage of highly hypnotizable students in the particular classes from which these subjects were selected. I was then younger, with more time and strength for such work than now. In 24 years of hypnotizing students, chiefly for instructional purposes in abnormal psychology classes, I have developed less than 100 completely somnambulistic subjects.

C. IMPLICATIONS OF THE PRECEDING EXPERIMENTS, AND FURTHER EXPERIMENTS

The first and most obvious implication of these experiments is with regard to the suggestion theory of hypnosis. In spite of observations to the contrary in the literature of hypnosis for nearly 100 years, such as are referred to in Section A of this article, the theory that hypnotic phenomena result from expectations of the subjects, constituting the core of the suggestion theory, still permeates the literature. One of the most flagrant illustrations of this error is in the widely used elementary textbook by Ruch. If more psychologists working in the field of hypnosis would only take pains to improve their methods so as to get hypnotic results without bringing about expectancy, or better, by encouraging skepticism in their subjects, then hypnosis might truly become an honest science and an honest art, uncontaminated by the art of suggestion.

Occasionally, to be sure, the beginning subject expects in advance that hypnotic phenomena will occur in him, but certainly in experimental work with college students skepticism is the prevalent attitude, and a most healthy one. The art of hypnosis as distinguished from the art of suggestion can be demonstrated best if skeptics are deliberately chosen as subjects in preference to those who expect to be hypnotized. Especially should the fallacy of neglect of negative instances be avoided. Specifically this means that attention should be directed to hypnotic phenomena which run counter to the subject's expectations, instead of neglecting such instances and counting only the cases where expectancy and hypnotic results happen to agree.

It is as if a surgeon had operated only when an anesthetic such as ether had been used in conjunction with some other substance such as rose perfume. By failing to distinguish experimentally between ether and rose perfume, and by insisting always that rose perfume be used as a part of the total anesthetizing agent, he might come to think that he had proved rose perfume to be a really essential part of the mixture. Hypnotists who use the art of suggestion, always attempting in their procedure with subjects to bring about expectancy, are like the surgeon who always uses rose perfume as a part of his anesthetic.

Medical suggestion at its best, in the hands of competent physicians whose presence and whose practices inspire in the patient a well-founded confidence in recovery, deserves the high praise given it by the great physician Sir Wm. Osler. But this is medical suggestion and not hypnosis. At its worst, medical suggestion, resorting to tricks of the bread-pill method, is, in Ewer's words, "somewhat contemptible."

Jolles defines suggestive therapeutics as a "technique of deceiving patients into believing that they are receiving medical rather than mental aid." "The general technique," he says, "is to build up a great deal of expectation by planting suggestion after suggestion." Some physicians and psychologists seem to think that hypnosis is only an elaborately developed art of suggestion, working only by developing expectancy. Then in their practice they sometimes incorporate contemptible aspects of the bread-pill method with its explicit or implicit lying. Hull's procedure, on one occasion, as described by himself, is a good illustration. Hull was trying to get contractures of the arms of six medical psychology students in a group experiment. He said, "Now I'll touch a center in your arm." Since there are no nerve centers in the arms, such a statement is explicitly untruthful, apparently being made to develop expectancy by indirect means. Hull also stated, "Now *I'm* going to hold your arms." Here again is an untruthful statement, seemingly intended to cause expectancy by appealing to the common superstition that there is an external mental influence involved in hypnosis. The pathetic aspect of such a procedure is that it is all so unnecessary, since suggestion is neither a necessary nor a useful adjunct of hypnosis. Hull did get contractures in some of his subjects, but the result was independent of the expectancy or the skepticism of the subjects, as the experiments described in Section *B* of this article prove.

Incidentally, the hypnotic results reported by Hull in this instance were very slight, lasting no more than 10 seconds in the best subject. Using a strictly non-suggestive technique, I have on numerous occasions of group hypnosis of beginning subjects obtained contractures lasting 10 minutes or more, or until removed by hypnotic methods, in one case nearly an hour after the termination of the group experiment and then only on request of the subject, who complained of pain in his tightly clasped hands and begged for relief. This last subject, selected in this way for high hypnotizability, was easily developed individually to complete somnambulism, and was *Subject 2* of my posthypnotic amnesia experiment.

A second implication of such experiments as the ones described in Section *B* is in the field of psychopathology. It is not uncommon for some psychiatrists and psychologists as well as the general public to regard functional illnesses such as hysterical paralysis, blindness, etc., as only imaginary,—as if the patient were not really paralyzed or blind, or at least as if, granting that the patient is really ill, the illness is a result of a prior belief that the illness was going to occur. Brennan, e.g., describes Breuer's case of *Anna O,* whose symptoms included paralysis of an arm. Brennan calls this paralysis "an imagined inability to use one arm."

Six of the 10 subjects of Section *B* had complete paralysis of both hands, and the other four had partial paralysis (two of these four had complete paralysis after the first trial in posthypnotic Test 1), while they all believed they were stronger than usual. In these experimental cases, of course, the belief as well as the paralysis was caused by hypnotic methods. The hypnotically induced paralysis would have been the same if no effort had been made to control expectancy. In such a case the subjects, when asked in advance of tests if they had noticed any weakness of their hands, would typically and truthfully have said, "No." Then, when they attempted to grip the dynamometer, they would have discovered, if not prevented by previous hypnosis from making the discovery, that they were paralyzed. They would have believed that they were paralyzed only after they had tried unsuccessfully to use the dynamometer. If a patient merely believed he was paralyzed, without actually being paralyzed, then he would be suffering from a delusion, not from paralysis; and usually he could be cured of his false belief merely by being asked to use, and by using, the hand previously believed to be paralyzed.

I have frequently produced paralysis of a hand, the paralysis to persist posthypnotically, without any attempt to control the subject's expectation. Then I have customarily asked the subject after hypnosis if he felt all right physically or if he had suffered physical impairment as a result of hypnosis. He has almost always said, "Yes, I am all right." Then I have asked him to do some act involving the use of the paralyzed hand and he has discovered, much to his surprise, that he is paralyzed. Belief follows the paralysis and is not a cause of it.

It often happens in nature's laboratory, in clinical cases of dissociation analogous to cases of experimentally induced dissociation, that a person wakes up some morning and tries to get out of bed, expecting to walk as usual. He falls to the floor because of (functionally) paralyzed legs. At first he just cannot believe it. He feels sure that he is all right, and he tries repeatedly to walk. The paralysis may persist, however, for years. I have seen one case of functional paralysis of the legs which had confined the victim to a wheel chair for 14 years. More usually the paralysis passes away in a matter of hours, days, or perhaps months, or it is cured by psychotherapy of some sort. While it lasts, however, the victim comes to believe (unless he is indeed psychotic), and to believe truly, that he is helpless. Typically, in clinical as well as in experimental cases, the belief follows the paralysis; it does not antedate the paralysis in the form of expectancy.

The onset of Professor W. E. Leonard's distance phobia is a good illustration of this point. Leonard collapsed at the Indian Mounds, where he experienced hallucinations, without delusions, of a chariot and a negress in the sky. When he reached home he thought he was dying. He felt better the next day, however, and started out for a walk, not anticipating any hindrance to such a plan; but at a distance of a hundred feet from the house he found himself "in horror of being so far away," and was compelled to rush back home. This one experience was not enough to teach him to expect any later recurrence of such a phobia. Consequently the second morning he started out again to take a walk, and soon experienced a phobic collapse just as on the previous morning. This was the beginning of a distance phobia which never left him as long as he lived, nearly 33 years after the onset of the phobia as above described. Gradually he learned from experience that a collapse was inevitable if he ventured too far from home, but expectancy was not the cause of the phobia for the simple reason that expectancy was not present in advance of the onset of the phobia.

I recently duplicated this sort of thing experimentally with Subject *Sp* (the last subject of Section B), as follows:—I put Miss *Sp* into deep hypnosis and told her that, after being brought out of hypnosis, she would go into a second state of deep hypnosis instantly if a certain fellow-student, Miss *Kl*, touched her upon the left shoulder. Miss *Sp* was brought out of hypnosis with complete amnesia for the hypnotic period. Consequently she did not expect to be hypnotized by Miss *Kl's* touch. She had never been hypnotized this way before. Several other students touched her with no effect; but when Miss *Kl* touched her left shoulder Miss *Sp* fell immediately into deep hypnosis as a result of an hypnotically implanted subconscious mechanism. If this had happened enough times Miss *Sp* would have learned finally to expect to be hypnotized when touched by Miss *Kl*, but expectancy would not have been the cause of the hypnosis in the later instances any more than at the start.

In another experiment, with Subject *Su*, I produced an hallucination of pain in one hand. I told him in hypnosis that, after he came out of hypnosis, with amnesia for the hypnotic period, he would again experience the hallucination of the pain in his hand for one minute whenever Miss *Sm*, another student in the class, asked him a question. The first time that Miss *Sm* asked him a question he could not have anticipated that pain in the hand would follow, for his amnesia for the hypnotic period was complete. The pain occurred, however, as a result of the operation of a hypnotically induced subconscious mechanism analogous to the subconscious mechanism which brought on Leonard's phobia. In the course of the next hour Miss *Sm* several times asked *Su* a question. Each time he would attempt to answer it civilly enough, while experiencing an unusual pain in his hand, much to his consternation. After a few such occurrences he discovered that he was somehow allergic (figuratively speaking) to Miss *Sm's* questions, and he learned to expect pain in his hand whenever she asked him a question, just as Leonard learned to expect a phobic collapse if he ventured too far from home.

D. SUMMARY AND CONCLUSION

This article is devoted primarily to the description of experiments on 10 selected and highly developed hypnotic subjects in whom strength of grip and expectancy were controlled by hypnosis. Complete or partial paralysis was produced in all the subjects while their hypnotically controlled belief was that they were stronger than usual. Then their strength of grip was increased while their hypnotically induced belief was that they were weaker than usual.

These results contradict the suggestion theory of hypnosis, as illustrated by an experiment described by Crane, in which the two factors of expectancy and hypnotic performance are commonly said to be related causally,—hypnotic phenomena being regarded as caused by expectancy.

Implications of the results of these experiments are pointed out, not only in regard to the distinction between the art of suggestion and the art of hypnosis, but also in regard to the relation of expectancy to disability in clinical cases of functional illness. Further hypnotic experiments pertinent to these two points have been described in Section C.

*From *The Journal of General Psychology*, 35, 99-119. 1946.

HYPNOTIC IDENTIFICATION OF
AN AMNESIA VICTIM*

By L. F. BECK, *University of Oregon*

EDITOR'S NOTE

In addition to constituting a study of the use of hypnosis in the identification of a victim of amnesia, this article reveals the active role the subject can play while in a trance. Instead of being an automaton or robot without any will of his own, he can not only participate actively, but can actually malinger under hypnosis. The active part this subject took, even to the point of trickery, indicates the point to which wishes and attitude may enter into the hypnotic trance.

Medical and psychological literature contains a host of facts which show that mnemonic processes can be profoundly modified by hypnosis. In general, however, the hypnotized person has been depicted as an automaton, and memory disturbances hypnotically induced have been attributed to the instructions the hypnotizer gave. Some consideration has been given to the fact that a somnambulist will not carry out grossly immoral or criminal suggestions, but for the most part the role of attitudes, wishes, and motives in the behaviour of a hypnotic has been neglected. This paper, besides shedding additional light on the course and complexity of hysterical amnesia, attempts to show that a hypnotized person actively participates and can discriminate selectively, even to the point of trickery in order to foster a wish.

At midnight, July 29-30, 1935, a young man appeared at the police station in Eugene, Oregon, and stated that he knew neither his name nor the location of his home. He said that at eight o'clock that morning he suddenly discovered himself on a strange street in a large city, and that a pedestrian informed him that he was in Portland, Oregon (a city 125 miles from Eugene).

He experienced no aches or pains at the time of his 'awakening,' and a cursory physical examination at the police station in Eugene revealed no bruises on his head or body. He was attired in a well-pressed, light grey suit and carried a paper sack which contained a pair of swimming trunks bearing a Red Cross life-saving insignia. There was a cleaner's mark 1702w44x on the lining of his coat, and a laundry mark, KEL, on his shirt. Search of his pockets produced only a nickel, two pennies and a new Yale key.

The man claimed that his experiences of the day were as follows: he roamed the city of Portland from about 9 to 10 a. m. During his wandering he discovered the Pacific highway, along which he walked for some time. Eventually he was given a short ride in an auto, after which he resumed his walking. A second car picked him up and this time he rode 60 miles. At the termination of this second jaunt, he said he went swimming in a river, using the trunks which he carried in the paper sack. A third ride brought him to Eugene. The last driver, a traveling salesman, asked if he was 'broke,' and learning that he was, gave him a dollar. With the money he purchased a lunch, attended a movie, bought a few glasses of beer, and had seven cents' change in his pocket when he voluntarily called at the police station at midnight!

The police took the man to the county jail where sleeping accommodation was available. He spent the night there. The following day the writer was called in consultation on the case, and an examination was conducted at the jail.

The young man's memory for impersonal things and events was undisturbed. He knew, for example, the names of various cities, animals, automobiles, baseball teams, railroads, highways, foods, clothes, watches, contraceptives, cigarettes, and liquors. He wrote legibly and could read well. A discussion about contraceptives provoked considerable embarrassment, a fact showing that the man's affective reactions were at least partially intact. He was certain that he could dive, swim, and drive a car, but he could not remember having engaged in any of these activities. All of the points which should be checked in lubricating a car were quickly named, yet he could not recall having worked in a gasoline station or serviced a car. He insisted that he must have gone to school, but he didn't know where. Whether he had parents, a wife, siblings, a girl friend, or even a name were merely so many unanswerable questions.

The initials, K.E.L., on his shirt collar, suggested the first remedial technique.[1] He was asked to write all of the given names of which he could think. He began with Kenneth and ended with Lawrence. None of the names, however, seemed particularly familiar to him, nor did any have a significant emotional tone. Surnames produced essentially the same result. He then was requested to relax completely and to think of nothing especial. Under these conditions he consistently reported images of high, timbred mountains. He could not name them, although he seemed to recognize a certain familiarity about them. As the city of Eugene is surrounded by mountains, the possible significance of this association was not comprehended by the writer at the time.

Following this initial equivocal survey, the man reclined on a couch and was hypnotized with customary verbal commands and optical fixation. Eye and arm catalepsy were induced quickly, and a profound trance was achieved within two minutes. The patient, however, became extremely agitated, clenching his fists, grimacing, rolling his tongue, and breathing deeply and irregularly. When asked his name, he failed to answer and grew even more disturbed. Repeated interrogation brought no reply, and it seemed as though he was too excited to speak. Suggestions of relaxation quieted him sufficiently to allow him to manipulate his fingers upon command. Thereupon, a pencil was placed in his hand and he was instructed to write his name on a piece of

---

1. It was subsequently learned that K.E.L. were the initials of a cousin who had loaned a shirt to the patient.

paper at his side. Automatic writing immediately appeared and the name 'Marian' was slowly and carefully written. At the completion of the task the pencil fell from the patient's hand and he began to roll and toss. Suggestions of quiescence again were given, the pencil was replaced, and the writer inquired 'Marion who?' Slowly the hand produced 'Kingsley.' Inquiry about the residence of Marion Kingsley brought 'Moscow, Idaho,' together with much apparent internal conflict. In fact the patient had become so disturbed by this time that it was considered unwise to question him further. It is interesting to know that Moscow, Idaho, is a city situated near high, timbered mountains, a fact which might explain the patient's frequent report of timbered mountains during free association.

The customary verbal commands were given in order to produce awakening, but they seemed to have little, if any, effect. Finally the commands were reinforced by forcibly opening the patient's eyelids and slapping his face. Within a minute he showed some signs of awakening. While in the hypnoidal state, he was asked who Marian Kingsley was. He immediately uttered the words 'My wife,' and added, 'Oh, Mary Ann!' He explained that Mary Ann was the name of his two-year-old daughter.

When he had completely awakened he remembered the above names as well as most of his previous associations with them. He knew, in addition, the names of his father and mother, and recalled the important points of his childhood in Moscow. Yet he could not recollect his first name, and it was not until two hours later when asked what name he signed on his marriage license, that he was able to remember his given name, Charles.

At the patient's request a telegram was sent to his parents in Moscow telling them of their son's plight, and requesting whatever pertinent information they could give about the case. A return message stated that Charles Kingsley had left Moscow about four months previously and had presumably been living with relatives in Salem, Oregon (a city 75 miles from Eugene on the road to Portland). When confronted with the telegram, the patient said he knew that he had relatives in Salem, but was confident that he had never lived with them. A close check of the man's memory for recent events showed that the last incident he clearly remembered was leaving Moscow for Twin Falls, Idaho, in his automobile about March 1, 1935. Inasmuch as the patient had not been questioned at all in the first hypnotic trance about events occurring in this four-months period for which he seemed still to be amnesic, a second hypnotic session was held. Direct questioning in this second trance supplied no conclusive evidence, either spoken or written, that the patient remembered having been in Salem. Repeated interrogation did bring to light through automatic writing the following new facts: (1) his wife had given him the bathing trunks that he carried in the paper sack; (2) he left his car in a garage in Moscow; (3) he bought his grey suit in Boise after leaving Moscow for Oregon; and (4) he came to Oregon by 'bumming' rides on the highway. Facts (2), (3) and (4) are incidents which fall within the four-months period for which he still was presumably amnesic. The significance of this will appear later.

The following day the patient was taken to see his relatives in Salem with the hope that his memory would be aided by talking to them. Upon his arrival he recognized all of his relatives, but to each one he exclaimed, 'Why, the last time I saw you was in Moscow!' To his brother who had come to Salem one month before, he declared: 'You were in the hospital in Moscow with pneumonia when I left!' The relatives gave the information that Charles had lived with them for nearly four months, and just the previous week had gone on a motor trip with the family to the seashore.

The patient had made several friends during his brief visit in Salem, but none of them was now recognized. With the aim of forcing recognition, he was hypnotized in the presence of a young man who had been a very intimate friend. The patient was commanded during the trance to open his eyes and was asked if he knew the friend. He stared at the man for a moment, and gave some facial indications of recognition, but suddenly he swooned and slumped over a desk at which he was sitting. No recollection of this occurrence was carried over into the waking state. A subsequent hypnotic session produced essentially the same result.

To our surprise, this friend testified that Charles had been with him in Salem Sunday night and until almost noon on Monday, the morning that the patient (at midnight) had claimed to have awakened from his trance at 8 a. m. in Portland. (Portland is a city 50 miles from Salem.) As far as the friend could tell, the patient's memory had been intact at noon Monday. The brother produced a postal card written by the patient in Eugene and posted at 6.30 p. m. Monday. The card was correctly addressed to the Salem relative and requested that some clothes be sent to General Delivery at the Eugene post office. The card carried the following additional message: 'This Co. is nuts. We started to work Salem and then they changed their mind and sent us to Eugene. Got a hot prospect to-day if it goes thru will be sitting OK in a couple of weeks. They are feeding me.' Inquiry about the company, as well as the 'hot prospect,' proved each to be non-existent, but it is pertinent in this connection that the patient had considered selling roofing material in a Salem store, and even had agreed to report for work at 8 a. m. Monday. He had failed to appear at the store, however.

DISCUSSION AND INTERPRETATION

The patient's flight from Salem is suggestive of an hysterical fugue. Yet he was not completely amnesic at the end of the fugue, for after arriving in Eugene he had correctly addressed and mailed the postal card to his brother in Salem.

Apparently he had 'bummed' his way from Salem to Eugene on the highway, which of course disprove his statements about waking up in Portland. The story he related at the police station might even be called a yarn, for he was taken over 75 miles of the highway which he said he had traversed from Portland, and failed to recognize any part of it. Presumably he had unwittingly supplied some of his story by a process of retroactive paramnesia and the remainder from his imagination. There is evidence that he had been in Portland about four months previously, and probably a portion of the material of that initial visit was displaced in time and had become an integral part of this episode. Likewise the strange tale that he wrote on the postal card about his job and the 'hot prospect' had some factual support, for he had considered working on a commission basis in a Salem store, but obviously the facts had been grossly distorted. Furthermore, he must have ridden in automobiles to Eugene, but his starting point was Salem, not Portland. It was impossible to determine whether the patient had gone swimming as he claims, but so far as the writer could ascertain, neither the paper sack nor the woolen bathing trunks showed any signs of having been wet that eventful Monday afternoon. Possibly, therefore, his statements about swimming as well were based upon some previous incident, or were supplied imaginatively.

The fundamental basis of the patient's affliction seemed to have been his domestic troubles in Moscow. He had lived happily with his wife for nearly three years, but his father-in-law had disapproved of the marriage and had on several occasions tried to persuade his daughter to leave the patient. Finally, in February, his wife did return to her parents and immediately started divorce proceedings. Shortly thereafter, the young man lost his job, became despondent, and commenced to gamble and to drink excessively. His worries and troubles became so severe that he left Moscow for Twin Falls, Idaho, about March 1, 1935. This date is significant, because not a single event subsequent to it was ever recalled in the waking state.

Behaviour during the hypnotic trance indicated strong emotion attached to all verbal associations with his family. During a trance mere mention of either his wife or daughter would profoundly disturb his breathing and he would toss about convulsively. He declared both during and after each hypnosis that he wanted to return to Moscow. It is the writer's belief that the patient had become so distraught over his domestic failure and his inability to find satisfactory work in Salem that all verbal reactions in any way related to the worry and fear for his wife and child had become blocked or dissociated.

But the question still remains as to the persistence of the localized amnesia. Why was the patient unable to recall events between March 1 and June 30, 1935?

Thirty-six hours before his fugue he had participated in an all-night party with a young lady and other friends. At 6 a. m. Sunday, which was the day before his attack, he became morose and left the party despite requests of friends that he remain. According to the young lady, 'he walked out without saying a word. He had never acted that way before.' It is noteworthy too that, according to his associates, he had repeatedly said that he would never return to Moscow. Yet without a doubt he wanted to, as shown by his reactions during and after hypnosis. It seems, therefore, probable, that the revival of memories of the young lady and his promises to her would have interfered with his return to Moscow and the reunion with his family. That he must have realized this fact is suggested by certain oddities in his behaviour during hypnosis.

In the first hypnotic trance the patient, when asked his name, responded by writing Marian. This unexpected result demonstrated that the patient was not reacting as an automaton, but was fostering a wish for his wife. In the second trance, the purpose of which was to pierce the localized amnesia, the patient persistently shook his head at all questions and steadfastly contended that he could not recall anything after March 1, 1935. Yet persistent questioning produced, through automatic writing, facts about his clothes, car, and trip to Oregon, all of which had occurred within the period of the localized amnesia. The reticence with which these few details were revealed led the writer to suspect that the patient was malingering under hypnosis. It seemed as if he were carefully selecting and reproducing only those facts which could in no possible way interfere with a return to his family. Additional support for this belief was gathered during the third hypnotic session when the patient, profoundly hypnotized, was asked to open his eyes and identify a friend whose acquaintance he had formed while in Salem and with whom he had been quite confidential. A change in the patient's countenance suggested recognition, but when questioned about the friendship he clenched his fists, began to weep, and suddenly slumped over a desk at the side of him. No unusual difficulty was encountered in awakening the patient, which indicates that psychological rather than physiological factors were the cause of the episode. The simulated syncope served as an escape mechanism, forestalling the recollection of conflicting mnemonic material.

That trickery as complicated as this can occur during hypnosis is demonstrated by a case of malingering reported by Pattie. Uniocular blindness was suggested to a young girl during hypnosis, and results on several refined tests of vision administered over a period of months indicated that her right eye was amaurotic during the trance state. By the use of a complicated filter test, deception finally was detected, but in the face of this evidence the girl vehemently insisted that she *was* blind. Demands for a confession were met with a clenching of fists, crying, tossing about, and a great deal of agitation in her vocal and facial expression. Eventually, under hypnosis, a confession was wrung from her, bit by bit, and there was abundant proof that her deceptive tactics were not a part of her normal waking life.

In disposing of our patient, it was decided to experiment somewhat, and to see what kind of a readjustment the man could make with the localized amnesia left intact. Arrangements were made for the patient's return to Moscow under favorable conditions, and a close check has been kept on his behavior there. A recent communication states that the man seems to be behaving much better and appears more hopeful than at any time during the previous two years.

*From *British Journal of Medical Psychology*, 16, 1936-37.

WHY WE DON'T KNOW MUCH ABOUT HYPNOSIS*

By MICHAEL BLANKFORT, *Princeton University*

EDITOR'S NOTE

This is a racy essay reviewing the history of hypnosis, and, while it does not add to the science of hypnosis, it forms an interesting finis to the subject.

About eighty years ago a professor of physiology in France said to his students that hypnosis was to psychology what vivisection was to physiology. Now that psychology has taken over hypnosis as part of its domain, has it done anything to justify the statement of the old savant?

From the time of the soothsayers to the latest discussions, hypnosis has always been tinged with an air of the supernatural, an atmosphere of the occult. Cagliostro and men of his tradition added mystery to mystery, hindering every effort to bring out of the cabbala the "marvels" of hypnosis. The problem, curious enough by itself, has been doubly obscured by the many early religious perversions of its uses, as well as by our modern Rosicrucians.

Moll introduces his justly famous book by listing some of the strange sects of the past that had made great rituals of hypnosis. The Montanists, a Christian people living two hundred years after Christ, also called the Truskdrugites from the Greek forefinger and nose, were accustomed to hold the forefinger to the nose during prayer. A little while of this and insensibility occurred similar in all respects to certain types of hypnotic trance. Among the best known convents of the Greek Orthodox Church was the Hesychasts or Omphalopsychists who lived on Mt. Athos. They hypnotized themselves by gazing fixedly at the umbilicus. This constituted their main religious diversion.

Paracelsus knew about it. Egyptian doctors wrote about it.

Chinese Magicians in West Borneo cured with it. Abyssinian fakirs made slaves with it. It is one of the world's oldest phenomena, and what have our scientists done about it?

Influenced by the tomfoolery of Mesmer's magnets and Braid's Neurohypnology, Charcot's unscientific theories concluded chiefly from observation on one poor dement, and the lengthy incredulous buncombe of clinicians, most modern experimental psychologists have consistently shied from the problem as though it were leprosy. With the exception of a few workers, some of whose experiments I shall discuss later, modern laboratories have looked down with scorn and disfavor on any attempt to experiment along these lines. Some universities have had men specialize in experimental hypnosis. There are about five in the United States. There are many reasons why these five are the only ones encouraging this type of experiment, but there are more valid reasons, perhaps, why others do not follow the lead.

From the very induction of an hypnotic state, the procedure makes it difficult for the tough-minded psychologist to dissociate the black history of hypnotism from its potentialities as an experimental subject. To introduce the hypnotic state operators frequently make use of passes of the hand and stroking. These smack of the vaudeville performer but sometimes they are essential to swift and complete induction. However, this is the first "psychological" objective made by the tough-hombre mechanist. Secondly, the experimentalist finds it very difficult to get enough subjects to make his essay worth while, because the ancient abracadabra is still potent enough to frighten. In this connection it is observed that most people and many "scientists" are still obsessed with the notion that by allowing themselves to be hypnotized, they are weakening that precious thing called will. Parents of undergraduates about to be used as subjects, object strenuously to "any irreligious, unethical, harmful and morbid practice like hypnotism." The whole sequence of objections frightens the experimenter. There are simpler problems to be done, he thinks, doing which he will not be liable to complaints of fond parents and ignorant administrators.

At one of the great large-city Eastern universities all attempts to hypnotize either for experimental or demonstrational purposes has been forbidden because once, long ago, a student had died, and it had been discovered that he was hypnotized during his last month. Sic transit . . . O Tempora! O Hypnosis!

There are other facts, more important ones, which practically force the psychologist to disregard hypnosis. They reside in the peculiar quality of the phenomenon itself. They make a hard problem even more severe. In the first place there is no objective yardstick by which one can measure the different stages of the trance. Throughout the literature there are many discourses concerning the number and qualities of the many stages, and none agree. Each writer arbitrarily classifies certain trance activities such as amnesia, somnambulism, etc., as being characteristics of certain stages. These, however, do not always hold true. These activities vary considerably and are influenced by the depth of hypnosis, the technique of the operator, the personality and training of the subject.

Although it has been generally accepted that suggestion plays a great part in hypnotic phenomena, if not the entire role, it is still a matter of conjecture whether it is induced by the operator, or by the subject himself. Or it may be a combination of both, not unlike our response to advertising where our potential desire is stimulated and at times almost created out of nothing by the suggestions we receive. The great problem of who suggests, the operator or the subject, hetero- or autosuggestion is still unsolved. It is important to get to the bottom of it because at the present time we are finding it difficult to determine just what part the operator plays in inducing the characteristic phenomena of the trance stages. We do not know whether these same phenomena are spontaneously part and parcel of the trance or artifacts of suggestion.

To explain hypnosis by saying that it is suggestion is to replace one unknown by another. The tendency to do so is evident in nearly all the standard textbooks. Suggestion being merely a word which describes certain types of stimuli and their corresponding responses, I find it extremely hard to accept it as an explanatory principle. We do not even know how suggestion works, what individual elements make one person more suggestible than another, or one suggestion more potent than its brother.

The objective which has been raised as to the fact that we can never tell when a person is shamming is not as important as might be expected. The somnolent attitude, the lethargic response, the vague movements contribute definite detection of the genuine state. Such tests as post-hypnotic amnesia or post-hypnotic suggestion are too complex to be faked. The mechanism of catelepsy which can be induced in hypnosis is also a sign that the subject is not having his fun.

A much more important objection lies in the fact that the operator is never sure whether his subject is going to allow him to suggest what he ordinarily would.

Young of Louisiana State College working on this problem showed that any subject *can* control the type and degree of suggesting he will take by making prehypnotic autosuggestions to himself. These experiments also demonstrate the power of autosuggestion. There is still time for scientific Coueism. The immensity of the research for scientific auto-suggestion is readily evident in psychoanalysis. It is apparent that there is a large common factor among such widely different subjects as psychoanalysis, hypnosis, and Listerine advertisements.

Here too the psychological brethren veer from the hypnosis question because it has been somewhat stained by psychotherapeutic uses. In psychotherapy suggestion is used to reintegrate a mind which has been suffering from a dissociative malady, by means of post-hypnotic commands. At the same time hypnosis depends on dissociation in order to be effective, so we find ourselves in a dilemma. How can we cure dissociation by inducing dissociation? It is obvious that nearly all of our daily habits are the products of dissociation. Because we are able to tie our tie while reading the headlines brings us no nearer to the psychopathic ward. The cry against hypnosis for therapy is just as unfounded. It is true that a poor, incompetent, and careless operator can cause a major mental-split. But then poor, incompetent, and careless operators must not be allowed to practice. Surgeons have been known to kill people by bungling with an artery.

Often the murmurs against hypnosis have taken the form of articles and lectures titled, "The Moral Dangers of Hypnosis." It has been shown, time and time again, that people will not do anything under the hypnotic trance, that they ordinarily would inhibit. Whether a long series of suggestions would be sufficiently powerful to break down resistance obviously has not been proven. Charles Baudouin in his Suggestion and Auto-Suggestion has answered competently the question of whether individuals can be compelled by hypnosis to do an immoral, unethical, or illegal act. He answers, "Yes, if the subject imagines this to be possible." He goes on to say, "Books that point out the dangers of hypnotism are more dangerous than hypnotism itself." In other words, if the subject feels that he is expected to do certain things, and knows that it is possible for him to do them, he can be influenced by an unscrupulous operator. Books, articles, and lectures which suggest to people that certain immoral acts are possible when suggested under hypnosis, instill in their audience a belief that it is potentially capable of doing them. Thus this belief makes it easier for the dishonest charlatan, or immoral operator to break down resistances. Reformers were always more vicious than the objects of their chase.

Before any study of hypnotic phenomena can be accepted the experimenter must make a comparative study of the individual in both states, the normal and the hypnotic. If the old clinicians had taken the trouble to ascertain the normal abilities of their patients, they would have been less impressed with their so-called "fact of hypnosis." Bergson's boy is an amusing example of this sort of thing. The youngster was found to possess the ability, after having been hypnotized, to read letters which were reflected from the eyes of a man standing in front of him. Young asserts that the boy probably had microscopic vision normally. Many other cases of hyperaesthesia which fill the books of Moll, Bramwell, and others, may be rejected on the grounds that there is no proof whether their subjects were *normally hyperaesthetic,* or not.

A few psychologists have realized the importance of comparative studies, Hull, Williams, Young and their co-workers. An excellent example of the value of their work is established by comparing Moll's opinion, expressed in 1889, on hypnotic catalepsy with Williams' experiment in 1930. Moll believed that an hypnotic cataleptic, i.e., one who manifests cataleptic symptoms when suggested, could not hold up his hand any longer than an imposter. For forty-one years theorists argued one way or the other, each depending on the publications of clinical reports affirming or denying the general question. Then Williams of Wisconsin experimentally proved that there is no characteristic difference between voluntary and hypnotic catalepsy in the gross average length of time during which an arm was held up, or in the falling of the arm. Slight differences have been found between the waking and the trance states with the conditioned-reflex, the ability to resist fatigue, and resistance to pain. Miss Huse of Wisconsin found there to be no variance between the two states in the recall of memory, although the material she used, as Stein points out, has a negligible emotional content when compared to that of psychopathic memory traces. This is an example of poor experimental conditions.

The first and last words which can be said of hypnosis is that it is the most interesting and most profound of all psychological material which has merited so little attention. The handicaps to research I have considered. They are not insuperable. The general fear and ignorance can be lowered if psychologists themselves would appreciate the phenomenon itself, apart from all its context of psychic research and spiritualist seances. Research may get free from the present encumbrances when psychologists who have had a thorough training in experimental psychology find themselves in hospital work, or near psychopathic clinics, where they can bring their training to aid in the solution of a very ancient problem.

*From *Journal of Abnormal and Social Psychology*, Vol. 26, Ap. 1931-Mr. 1932.

BIOGRAPHICAL NOTES

DR. LESTER F. BECK

DR. LESTER F. BECK has been a member of the instructional faculty of the University of Oregon for the past decade. During the war years (1942-46) he served as a specialist with the War and Navy Departments in the production and evaluation of training films for the armed forces. The potentialities of hypnosis as a psychological research instrument were first brought forcibly to his attention by a masterful demonstration and discussion of the subject which Dr. Milton Erickson gave at Brown University in 1933 for the assembled graduate students in psychology.

A. K. BRINTNALL

A. K. BRINTNALL was born in Valley City, Ohio, in 1914. He received his A.B. from Denison University in 1935, and attended Graduate School of The Johns Hopkins University 1935 to 1937. He received his Ph.D. from U.C.L.A. in 1939. Thereafter he has been an instructor in psychology at U.C.L.A., Associate in Psychology at the University of Illinois, Director of Field Research, Chicago office of the Psychological Corporation and currently is Manager, Labor Relations Department, Allis-Chalmers Manufacturing Company.

HARRY W. CASE

Attended the University of California at Los Angeles where he majored in psychology. Received A.B. in 1935, M.A. in 1937, and Ph.D. in 1940.

Teaching Assistant in Psychology at the University of California at Los Angeles in 1935-36 and 1937-39, and Research Associate in Psychology in 1939-40. Associate in Psychology at the University of Illinois in 1941-42. At the present time Research Associate in Psychology at the University of California at Los Angeles.

From 1942 to 1945 Assistant Engineering Personnel Manager for the Douglas Aircraft Company. From 1945 to present Personnel Procedures Specialist for the Safeway Stores, Inc.

PUBLICATIONS:

The Psychology of Military Leadership, L. A. Pennington, R. B. Hough and H. W. Case, Prentice-Hall, N.Y., 1943.

Mental Hygiene Problems in Industry, Roy M. Dorcus and Harry W. Case, *Review of Education Research*, Vol. XIII, No. 5, Chapter X, Dec. 1943.

Spacial Relations, Floyd Ruch and Harry W. Case, California Test Bureau—A test prepared for measuring an individual's ability to measure form perception.

Training in Industry on the Engineering Level, Harry W. Case. *California Industrial Education News Notes,* Vol. V, April 1945.

And numerous other publications.

ROY MELVIN DORCUS

ROY MELVIN DORCUS was born in Woodboro, Md., 1901. He received his A.B. from John Hopkins in 1922, his A.M. in 1924, and his Ph.D. in 1925. From 1925-27 he was an instructor in psychology at Johns Hopkins, an associate professor from 1927-37. Since 1937 he has been at the University of California, where he is now Professor of Psychology. Professor Dorcus has been managing editor of the Journal of Comparative Psychology, editor of the Comparative Psychological Monograph, and a member of many scientific organizations. His chief work has been in abnormal psychology, personality traits, mental traits of athletes, vestibular investigation, tobacco effects, and animal behavior.

MILTON H. ERICKSON

MILTON H. ERICKSON received his B.A., M.A., and his M.D. from the University of Wisconsin. He was a clinical and research psychologist at the Wisconsin State Board of Control, assistant physician at the Rhode Island State Hospital for Mental Diseases, and Chief Psychiatrist at the Research Service, Worcester State Hospital. Since 1934 he has been Director of Psychiatric Research and Training, Wayne County General Hospital and Infirmary, Eloise, Michigan, and Associate Professor of Psychiatry, Wayne University College of Medicine, Detroit, Michigan. He is a Fellow of the American Psychiatric Association, the American Psychological Association, the American Pathological Association, and the Society of Sigma Xi.

ELIZABETH MOORE ERICKSON

ELIZABETH MOORE ERICKSON (Mrs Milton H. Erickson) received her B.A. in 1936 from Wayne University, Detroit, Michigan.

RICHARD WELLINGTON HUSBAND

RICHARD WELLINGTON HUSBAND was born in Hanover, N. H., 1904. He received his A.B. from Dartmouth College in 1926, his M.A. from Stanford University in 1927, and his Ph.D. from Stanford University in 1929. From 1929-1941 he was Assistant Professor of Psychology at the University of Wisconsin. He was Assistant Professor of Psychology at Pennsylvania State College in 1941-42. From 1942-45 he was in the Industrial Relations Department, Carnegie Illinois Steel Corporation, Pittsburgh, Pa. During the past year he has been Professor of Psychology and Chairman of the Department of Psychology, Beloit, Wisconsin.

Dr. Husband is the author of *Applied Psychology, General Psychology,* and *Psychology Through Literature,* as well as some 40 research and technical articles published in professional psychological journals.

FREDERICK GEORGE LIVINGOOD

FREDERICK GEORGE LIVINGOOD, Dean and Professor of Education, Washington College, Chestertown, Maryland, was born at Punxsutawney, Pennsylvania, September 19, 1893. He is a graduate of Slippery Rock State Teachers College, Slippery Rock, Pennsylvania. Degrees include: B.S., Albright College (1922), Ed.M., Harvard University (1924), Ed.D., Harvard University (1925), and LL.D. (honorary), Albright College, 1941. Teaching experience: Farrell, Pa., public schools, instructor in the summer sessions of Albright College and Seton Hill College, Professor of Education and Psychology, Washington College since 1925; dean since 1940. Member of American Association of University Professors, National Society for the Study of Education, National Society of College Teachers of Education, American Psychological Association, national and state educational associations. Contributor to educational and psychological publications.

DR. FRANK A. PATTIE

DR. FRANK A. PATTIE received his A.B. from Vanderbilt, A.M. from Harvard, and his Ph.D. from Princeton. He was a National Research Fellow and later an instructor in psychology at Harvard. From 1929-31 he was an instructor in psychology at Rice Institute and has been an assistant professor of psychology since then.

Professor Pattie has published articles in the psychological journals in the fields of audition, animal learning, gregarious behavior of chicks, hypnosis, and stuttering.

LOYD W. ROWLAND

LOYD W. ROWLAND was born August 4, 1902, at Fort Worth, Texas. Most of his life was spent in the southwestern part of the U.S. Collegiate training: A.B., Baylor University at Waco, Texas (1925), M.A., University of Texas (1928), and Ph.D.,

University of Chicago (1935). Teaching experience: University of Tulsa, 7 years; Head of the Department of Psychology at Baylor University, 4 years.

At the present time he is Director of the Louisiana Society for Mental Health. He is much interested in the importance of a more dynamic approach to psychological problems, as well as in reexamining some of the experiments that are considered fundamental in our science, the "classical experiments," which though accepted are possessed of a flimsy experimental basis. Newer techniques will either establish or disprove them. He is also much interested in designing new, simple apparatus.

WESLEY RAYMOND WELLS

WELLS, WESLEY RAYMOND, Syracuse University, Syracuse, N.Y. Born Bakersfield, Vt., June 20, 1890.

University of Vermont, Ph.B., 1913. Harvard University, 1913-1917, A.M., 1914, Ph.D., 1917.

Assistant in Philosophy, Harvard, 1916-1917. Instructor in Education, Washington University, 1917-1919. Assistant Professor of Philosophy and Psychology, Colby College, 1919-1921. Professor of Philosophy and Psychology, Lake Forest College, 1921-1927. Acting Dean and Dean, Lake Forest College, 1922-1926. Professor of Psychology, Syracuse University since 1927.

Fellow, American Association for the Advancement of Science. Member, American Psychological Association, American Philosophical Association, American Association of University Professors, Phi Beta Kappa, Sigma Xi.

Author of 27 articles in psychological and philosophical journals, nine of which have been in the field of hypnotism, as follows:

1. Hypnosis in the service of the instructor. *Psychological Review*, 1924, 31, 88-91.

2. Experiments in waking hypnosis for instructional purposes. *Journal of Abnormal and Social Psychology,* 1924, 18, 389-404.

3. Hypnotizability versus suggestibility. *J. Abn. & Soc. Psychol.,* 1931, 25, 436-449.

4. The extent and duration of post-hypnotic amnesia. *J. of Psychol.,* 1940, 9, 137-151.

5. Ability to resist artificially induced dissociation. *J. Ab. & Soc. Psychol.,* 1940, 35, 261-272.

6. Experiments in the hypnotic production of crime. *J. of Psychol.,* 1941, 11, 63-102.

7. The hypnotic treatment of the major symptoms of hysteria: a case study. *J. of Psychol.,* 1944, 17, 269-297.

8. A basic deception in exhibitions of hypnosis. *J. of Abn. & Soc. Psychol.* (in press).

9. Expectancy versus performance in hypnosis. *J. of General Psychology* (in press).

ROBERT W. WHITE, PH.D.

ROBERT W. WHITE graduated from Harvard College in 1925 and subsequently taught at the University of Maine and Rutgers University. Upon returning to Harvard for graduate study he joined the group of workers at the Psychological Clinic. He took up the investigation of hypnotism, a tradition well established by the Clinic's founder, the late Dr. Morton Prince, and participated in the group studies of personality directed by Dr. Henry A. Murray, later published in the book *Exploration in Personality* (1938). He received the degree of Ph.D. in 1937 and continued on the Harvard teaching staff, serving as Acting Director of the Psychological Clinic during the war and being appointed Director in 1946.

His work with hypnotism has always been subsidiary to a larger interest in the dynamics and structure of personality. The therapeutic use of hypnosis has not been widely explored or practiced at the Harvard Psychological Clinic. On the other hand, its use to control variables in psychological experiments and its theoretical significance as a modification of those aspects of behavior variously called ego, will, intention, etc., are enduring topics of study and reflection.

PAUL C. YOUNG

PAUL C. YOUNG was born in Whitewright, Texas. Education: Norh Texas State Teachers College, David Lipscomb College, Bowdoin College (A.B.), University of Minnesota (M.A.), Harvard (A.M., Ph.D.). Teaching experience: Florida State College for Women, Acadia University, and Louisiana State University (since 1925). His main interests are abnormal and clinical psychology, mental hygiene, hypnosis. He is president of the Louisiana Legislative Council, an organization made up of 21 state associations interested in progress in public welfare. His published articles deal mainly with suggestion and hypnosis.

GLOSSARY

ABREACTION—The process of discharging pent-up tension by reliving the experiences that caused the emotional tension. The reliving may take the form of speech, action, feeling, or imagination.

AGRAPHIA—A pathological inability to write.

AMAUROTIC—Loss of sight due to a defect of the optic nerve.

AMNESIA—A functional disorder characterized by partial or complete loss of memory.

ANESTHESIA—Partial or complete loss of feeling.

ANIMAL MAGNETISM—Lines of force that were believed to be emitted from the body.

ANOREXIA—Refusal to eat or a loss of appetite.

ANTIDROMIC—Conducting impulses in a direction opposite to the normal.

APHASIA—A pathological impairment of the ability to use or to understand language.

APHONIA—Loss of voice.

AUTOMATIC WRITING—Act of writing with no conscious control or awareness.

CHEVREUL'S PENDULUM—A pendulum by whose motion the sex of the individual holding it is supposedly determined.

CIGARETTE TEST—A lighted cigarette is put between the fingers of a hypnotized subject to determine whether he can release his fingers when the cigarette burns him.

DELUSION—A false belief.

DEPTH SCORE—The depth or profundity of a trance as measured by a scale for hypnotic susceptibility.

DERMATOLOGIST—A doctor who specializes in the skin and its diseases.

DISSOCIATION—A splitting of the mind or the splitting off of certain activities from the control of the individual.

ECCHYMOSIS—The escape of blood from a vessel, or its discoloration due to it.

ELECTRA COMPLEX—An abnormal attachment of a girl for her father.

EPIDERMIS—The outermost layer of the skin.

EPITHELIAL—Pertaining to cellular substance of skin or mucous membrane.

ERYTHEMAS—Blushing or redness of the skin.

EXOGENOUS—Derived from outside the body.

FRACTIONAL AUTOHYPNOSIS—Hypnosis of one part of the body at a time, such as the foot or hand.

FUGUE—A flight while sleep walking.

GLOVE ANESTHESIA—Anesthesia or loss of ability to feel in the hand.

HALLUCINATION—A false perception that has no basis in reality.

HEMIANESTHESIA—Loss of feeling or sensitivity for either lateral half of the body.

HEMIANOPSIA—Half blindness, that is loss of vision in half of each retina.

HEMIPLEGIA—Paralysis of one side of the body.

HERPES—Skin disease marked by clusters of small vesicles.

HESYCHASTES—Members of a mystic cult of the Eastern Church.

HETEROHYPNOTIC—Referring to suggestion or directions by someone other than the subject.

HEXING—Practising witchcraft.

HISTAMINE—Uterine stimulant tending to reduce blood pressure.

HYPERMNESIA—Heightened or exaggerated ability to remember or recall.

HYPEREMIA—A congestion or superabundance of blood.

HYPNOIDAL—A primitive type of rest-state that is considered to be a transitional state between the normal and hypnosis.

HYPNOTHERAPY—The treatment of disease by hypnosis.

HYPNOTIC ABLATION—The technique of having the subject under hypnosis regress to an earlier age.

HYPNOTISM—The science of hypnosis; distinguished from hypnosis which is the phenomenon itself.

HYPOCHONDRIASIS—A morbid anxiety about one's health.

HYSTERIA—An unconscious adoption of a symptom of a disease to resolve a mental conflict.

HYSTERICAL BLINDNESS—A functional blindness unconsciously adopted as the resolution of a conflict.

I.Q.—An intelligence score derived by dividing the mental age of an individual by his chronological age, and multiplied by a hundred to eliminate decimals.

ISHIHARA TEST—A test for color blindness.

JAPANESE ILLUSION—A confusion of the sense of touch caused by the intertwining of the fingers.

KINAESTHESIA—Sensations accompanying movement of any part of the body.

MALINGER—To feign sickness or disability.

MALINGERING—The feigning of illness to shirk duty.

MESMERISM—Hypnosis thought to be induced by animal magnetism.

NARCOTIC—A drug that allays pain or produces sleep.

NECROSIS—Death of tissue.

NEUROGRAM—The impressions of lasting effect produced as a result of activity and serving as the basis for memory and personality.

OEDIPUS COMPLEX—An abnormal attachment of a boy for his mother. Psychoanalysts have recently been using the term to mean both the love of a boy for his mother and of a girl for her father. See Electra complex.

OPSONIC INDEX—The ability of the blood to resist bacilli.

PARAMNESIA—A false memory or recollection.

PHOBIA—A morbid fear.

PLANCHETTE—A form of the Ouija Board.

PSYCHONEUROSIS—A general term used to designate mild mental disorders of a functional type.

PSYCHOSOMATIC—Pertaining to mind and body, but specifically bodily symptoms due to mental or psychic causes.

RAPPORT—Harmony or accord between two individuals.

REGRESSION—The act of reverting to an early or more primitive level of behavior in order to avoid making adjustments to the present requirements of the situation.

ROSICRUCIAN—A society of philosophers claiming to have mystic powers or knowledge.

RORSCHACH TEST—A personality test consisting of inkblots which the subject is asked to explain. This test is used to evaluate personality and to detect personality disorders.

SODIUM AMYTAL—A drug used to produce hypnosis. It is slower in action than sodium pentothal.

SODIUM PENTOTHAL—A drug used to produce hypnosis. It has a much faster action and shorter duration than sodium amytal.

SOMATIC—Pertaining to the body.

SOMNAMBULISM—A deep state of hypnosis or a sleepwalking experience.

SUGGESTIBILITY—Attitude or mental set that makes one amenable to stimuli.

TRAUMA—A shock or injury.

UMBILICUS—The navel.

UNIOCULAR BLINDNESS—Blindness of one eye.

URTICARIA FACTICIA—Artificial rash.

VASAMOTOR—Pertaining to the contraction or dilation of a vessel.

VESICATION—A blister, or act of blistering.

BIBLIOGRAPHY

(BOOKS)

BAUDOUIN, C. *Suggestion and Autosuggestion.* Translated by E. and C. Paul, New York: Dodd, Mead & Co., 1922. 349 pages.

BRAMWELL, M. *Hypnotism: Its History, Practice, and Theory.* Philadelphia: Lippincott, 1928 (Revised Ed.). 480 pages.

BERNHEIM, H. *Suggestive Therapeutics: a Treatise on the Nature and Uses of Hypnotism.* Trans. by C. A. Herter. New York: Putnam's. 1900.

BRENMAN, M. and GILL, M. *Hypnotherapy.* Review Series, Vol. II, No. 3. 96 pages. Pub. of Josiah Macy, Jr. Foundation. 1944.

BRENMAN, M. *Self-Starvation and Compulsive Hopping with Paradoxical Reaction to Hypnosis.* In Press.

BREUER, J. and FREUD, S. *Studies in Hysteria.* Nervous and Mental Disease Monograph Series, 1936.

BROOKS, C. H. *The Practice of Autosuggestion by the Method of Emile Coue.* New York: Dodd, Mead. 1922.

BROWN, H. *Advanced Suggestion.* New York: William Wood and Company, 1919. 342 pages.

ESTABROOKS, G. H. *Hypnotism.* New York: Dutton, 1945.

HEYER, G. *Hypnosis and Hypnotherapy.* London: C. W. Daniel Company, 1931. 144 pages.

HOLLANDER, B. *Methods and Uses of Hypnosis and Self-Hypnosis.* London: George Allen and Unwin, Ltd. 1935. 191 pages.

HORSLEY, J. W. *Narcoanalysis.* London: Oxford University Press, 1943.

HULL, C. L. *Hypnosis and Suggestibility.* New York: Appleton-Century, 1933.

JANET, P. *Psychological Healing.* New York: Macmillan, 1925.

KARDINER, A. *The Traumatic Neuroses of War.* Psychosomatic Medicine Monograph III. Washington: National Research Council, 1941. 258 pages.

KLEIN, D. B. *The Experimental Production of Dreams During Hypnosis.* University Texas Bull., No. 3009, 1071. 1930.

LINDNER, R. M. *Rebel Without a Cause, the Hypoanalysis of a Criminal Psychopath.* New York: Grune & Stratton, Inc., 1944, 289 pages.

MILLER, H. C. *Hypnotism and Disease.* Boston: The Gorham Press, 1912. 252 pages.

MOLL, A. *Hypnotism.* Trans. by A. F. Hopkirk. London: Walter Scott, 1909.

MURRAY, H. A., Jr. *Explorations in Personality.* New York: Oxford University Press, 1938.

PRINCE, M. *The Unconscious.* (2nd ed.) New York: Macmillan, 1929.

QUACKENBOS, J. D. *Hypnotic Therapeutics in Theory and Practice.* New York: Harper. 1908.

ROTHENBERG, S. *Theories of Hypnosis and Its Use.* N. Y. State J. Med. 1928, 28:372-8.

SALTER, A. *What is Hypnosis?* New York: Richard R. Smith, 1944. 88 pages.

SATOW, L. *Hypnotism and Suggestion.* New York: Dodd, Mead & Co., 1923. 290 pages.

SCHILDER, P. and KAUDERS, O. *Hypnosis.* Translated by S. Rothenberg. Nervous and Mental Disease Monograph Series, 1927, No. 46. 118 pages.

SCHULTZ, J. *Injury to Health after Hypnosis.* Halle, 1922.

SPEYER, N. *Hypnotism and Treatment by Suggestion.* Liverpool, 1928. 135 pages.

STALNAKER, J. M. & RICHARDSON, M. W. *Time Estimation in the Hypnotic Trance.* 1930.

TUCKEY, C. L. *Treatment by Hypnotism and Suggestion or Psychotherapeutics.* London: Bailliere, Tindall and Cox, 1921. 413 pages.

WARREN, H. C. (Ed.) *Dictionary of Psychology.* Boston: Houghton Mifflin, 1934.

WINGFIELD, H. E. *An Introduction to the Study of Hypnotism.* (2nd ed.) London: Bailliere, Tindall & Cox, 1920.

WINN, R. B. *Scientific Hypnotism.* Boston: Christopher, 1939.

YELLOWLEES, H. *A Manual of Psychotherapy.* London: A. & C. Black, 1923.

BIBLIOGRAPHY

(ARTICLES)

AVELING, F., & HARGREAVES, H. L. Suggestibility with and without prestige in children. *British Journal of Psychology,* 12, 52-75. 1921.

BARRY, H. JR., MACKINNON, D. W., and MURRAY, H. A. JR. Studies in Personality. Hypnotizability as a personality trait and its typological relations. *Human Biology,* 3:1-36. 1931.

BARTLETT, M. R. Relation of Suggestibility to other personality traits. *Journal of General Psychology,* 15:191-196. 1936.

BASS, M. J. Differentiation of the hypnotic trance from normal Sleep. *Journal of Experimental Psychology,* 14:382-399. 1931.

BECHTEREW, W. V. What is hypnosis? *Journal of Abnormal Psychology,* 18-25. April 1906.

BECK, L. F. Hypnotic indentification of an amnesia victim. *British Journal of Medical Psychology,* 16:36-42. 1938.

BIRNIE, C. R. Anorexia nervosa treated by hypnosis in out-patient practice. *The Lancet,* 2:1331-32, December 5, 1936.

BRENMAN, M. Experiments in the hypnotic production of anti-social and self-injurious behavior. *Psychiatry,* 5:49-61. 1942.

BRENMAN, M. and KNIGHT, R. P. Hypnotherapy for mental illness in the aged: case report of hysterical psychosis in a 71-year-old woman. *Bulletin of the Menninger Clinic,* 7:5-6, 188-98. 1943.

BRENMAN, M. and REICHARD, S. Use of the Rorschach test in the prediction of hypnotizability. *Bulletin of the Menninger Clinic,* 7:5-6, 163-171. 1943.

BRICKNER, R. M. and KUBIE, L. S. A miniature psychic storm produced by super-ego conflict over simple posthypnotic suggestion. *Psychoanalytic Quarterly,* 5:467-87. 1936.

BROWN, W. Hypnosis in hysteria. Letter to the editor of *The Lancet,* 15:505, October 5, 1918.

BROWN, W. Hypnosis, suggestibility and progressive relaxation. *British Journal of Psychology*, 28:396-411. 1938.

CARLILL, H. Hypnotism. *The Lancet*, 1:61-66, January 5, 1935.

CASTER, J. E. & BAKER, C. S., JR. Comparative suggestibility in the trance and waking states—a further study. *Journal of General Psychology*, 7:287-301. 1932.

CONNELLAN, P. S. The treatment of repressed memories by hypnotism. *Bristol Medical-Chirurgical Journal*, 43:209-216. 1926.

CONNELLY, E. Uses of hypnosis in psychotherapy. *New Orleans Medical and Surgical Journal*, 88:627-32. 1936.

COPELAND, C. L. and KITCHING, E. H. Hypnosis in mental hospital practice. *Journal of Mental Science*, 83:316-329. 1937.

DAVIS, L. W. and HUSBAND, R. W. A study of hypnotic susceptibility in relation to personality traits. *Journal of Abnormal and Social Psychology*, 26:175-182. 1931.

DOLIN, A. O. Objective investigations of the elements of individual experience by means of the method of experimental hypnosis. *Arkh. Biol. Nauk.*, 36:28-52. 1934.

DONLEY, J. E. The clinical use of hypnoidization in the treatment of some functional psychoses. *Journal of Abnormal Psychology*, 3:148-160. 1908-09.

DORCUS, R. M. Modification by suggestion of some vestibular and visual responses. *American Journal of Psychology*, 49, 82-87. 1937.

DORCUS, R. M., BRINTNALL, A. K., & CASE, H. W. Control experiments and their relation to theories of hypnotism. *Journal of General Psychology*, 24, 217-221. 1941.

DREUGER, R. G. The influence of repetition and disuse upon rate of hypnotization. *Journal of Experimental Psychology*, 14, 260-269. 1931.

DYNES, J. B. An experimental study in hypnotic anaesthesia. *Journal of Abnormal and Social Psychology*, 27:87. 1932.

ERICKSON, M. H. The applications of hypnosis to psychiatry. *Medical Record*, 150. 60-65. 1939.

ERICKSON, E. M. Critical comments on Hibler's presentation of his work on negative after-images of hypnotically induced hallucinated colors. *Journal of Experimental Psychology*, 29, 164-170. 1941.

ERICKSON, M. H. Development of apparent unconsciousness during hypnotic reliving of a traumatic experience. *Archives of Neurology and Psychiatry*, 38:1282-1288. 1937.

ERICKSON, M. H. & ERICKSON, E. M. The hypnotic induction of hallucinatory color vision followed by pseudo negative after-image. *Journal of Experimental Psychology*, 22, 581-588. 1938. Concerning the nature and character of post-hypnotic behavior. *Journal of General Psychology*, 24, 95-133. 1941.

ERICKSON, M. H. Hypnotic investigation of psychosomatic phenomena: A controlled experimental use of hypnotic regression in the therapy of an acquired food intolerance. *Psychosomatic Medicine*, 5:67-70. 1943.

ERICKSON, M. H. and HILL, L. Unconscious mental activity in hypnosis, psychoanalytic implications. *Pschoanalytic Quarterly*, 13:60-78. January, 1944.

ERICKSON, M. H. The successful treatment of a case of acute hysterical depression by a return under hypnosis to a critical phase of childhood. *Psycholoanalytic Quarterly*, 10:583-609. October, 1941.

ERICKSON, M. H. and KUBIE, L. S. The translation of the cryptic automatic writing of one hypnotic subject by another in a trance-like dissociated state. *Psychoanalytic Quarterly*, 9:51-63. 1940.

ERICKSON, M. H. The use of automatic drawing in the interpretation and relief of a state of acute obsessional depression. *Psychoanalytic Quarterly*, 7:443-466. 1938.

ERICKSON, M. H. A study of clinical and experimental findings on hypnotic deafness: I. Clinical experimentation and findings. *Journal of General Psychology*, 19, 127-150. 1938.

A study of clinical and experimental findings on hypnotic deafness: II. Experimental findings with a conditioned response technique. *Journal of General Psychology*, 19, 151-167. 1938.

ERICKSON, M. H. An experimental investigation of the possible anti-social use of hypnosis. *Psychiatry*, 2, 391-414. 1939.

ERICKSON, M. H. Experimental demonstrations of the psychopathology of everyday life. *Psychoanalytic Quarterly*, 8, 338-353. 1939.

ERICKSON, M. H. The induction of color blindness by a technique of hypnotic suggestion. *Journal of General Psychology*, 20, 61-89. 1939.

ERICKSON, M. H. A study of experimental neurosis hypnotically induced in a case of ejaculatio praecox. *British Journal of Medical Psychology*, 15:34-50. 1935.

ESTABROOKS, G. H. Experimental studies in suggestion. *Journal of Genetic Psychology*, 36, 120-139. 1929.

ESTABROOKS, G. H. A standardized hypnotic technique dictated to a victrola record. *American Journal of Psychology*, 42, 115-116. 1930.

ESTRIN, J. Hypnosis as supportive symptomatic treatment in skin diseases: cases. *Urologic and Cutaneous Review*, 45:337-38. May, 1941.

FARBER, L. H. and FISHER, C. An experimental approach to dream psychology through the use of hypnosis. *Psychoanalytic Quarterly*, 12:202-216. 1943.

FERVERS, C. Hypnotic analysis with the patient in hypnotic state. *Der Nervenarzt*, 11:25-30. January, 1938.

FISHER, C. Hypnosis in treatment of neuroses due to war and to other causes. *War Medicine*, 4:565-76. 1943.

FISHER, V. E. and MORROW, A. J. Experimental study of moods. *Character and Personality*, 2, 201-208. 1934.

FRIEDLANDER, J. W. and GARBIN, T. R. The depth of hypnosis. *Journal of Abnormal and Social Psychology*, 33, 453-475. 1938.

GERRISH, F. The therapeutic value of hypnotic suggestion. *Journal of Abnormal Psychology*, 4:99. 1909.

GILL, M. M. and BRENMAN, M. Treatment of a case of anxiety hysteria by an hypnotic technique employing psychoanalytic principles. *Bulletin of the Menninger Clinic*, 7:5-6, 163-71. 1943.

GOLDWYN, J. "Hypnoidalization": its psychotherapeutic value. *Journal of Abnormal Psychology*, 24:170-185. 1929.

GRINKER, R. R. Conference on Narcosis, Hypnosis, and War Neuroses. Sponsored by the Josiah Macy, Jr. Foundation, New York. January, 1944. (Privately distributed).

HADFIELD, J. A. Chapter on "Treatment by Suggestion and Hypnoanalysis," Pages 128-149 in *The Neuroses in War*, edited by Emanuel Miller. New York: Macmillan and Company, 1940. 250 pages.

HART, H. H. Hypnosis in psychiatric clinics. *Journal of Nervous and Mental Diseases*, 74:598-609. 1931.

HIBLER, F. W. An experimental investigation of negative after-images of hallucinated colors in hypnosis. *Journal of Experimental Psychology*, 27, 45-57. 1940.

HULL, C. L. Quantitative methods of investigating waking suggestion. *Journal of Abnormal and Social Psychology*, 24, 153-169. 1929.

HULL, C. L. Quantitative methods of investigating hypnotic suggestion. Part I. Journal of *Abnormal and Social Psychology*, 25, 200-223. 1930.

HULL, C. L. Quantitative methods of investigating hypnotic suggestion. Part II. *Journal of Abnormal and Social Psychology*, 25, 390-417.

HULL, C. L., and HUSE, B. Comparative suggestibility in the trance and waking states. *American Journal of Psychology*, 42, 279-286. 1930.

HULL, C. L., PATTEN, E. F., and SWITZER, S. A. Does positive response to direct suggestion as such evoke a generalized hypersuggestibility? *Journal of General Psychology*, 8, 52-64. 1933.

HUSE, B. Does the hypnotic trance favor the recall of faint memories? *Journal of Experimental Psychology*, 13, 519-529. 1930.

HUSTON, P. E., SHAKOW, D., and ERICKSON, M. H. A study of hypnotically induced complexes by means of the Luria technique. *Journal of General Psychology*, 11, 65-97. 1934.

JENNESS, A. Chapter on Hypnotism. In *Personality and the Behavior Disorders*, edited by J. McV. Hunt. New York: The Ronald Press, 2 volumes, pages 466-502. 1944.

JENNESS, A. Facilitation of response to suggestion by response to previous suggestion of a different type. *Journal of Experimental Psychology*, 16, 55-82. 1933.

JENNESS, A. and DAMNS, H. Change of auditory threshold during reverie as related to hypnotizability. *Journal of General Psychology*, 17:167-170. 1937.

JENNESS, A., and WIBLE, C. L. Respiration and heart action in sleep and hypnosis. *Journal of General Psychology*, 16, 197-222. 1937.

JONES, E. The action of suggestion in psychotherapy. *Journal of Abnormal Psychology*, 5, 217-254. 1910.

KANZER, MARK G. The therapeutic use of dreams inducted by hypnotic suggestion. *Psychoanalytic Quarterly*, 14:313. 1945.

KLEIN, D. B. The experimental production of dreams during hypnosis. *University of Texas Bulletin*, 3009, 1-71. 1930.

KELLOGG, E. R. Duration of the effects of post-hypnotic suggestion. *Journal of Experimental Psychology*, 12, 502-514. 1929.

KOHNSTAMM, O. On hypnotic influence on disturbances of menstruation. *Die Therapie der Gegenwart*, 48:354-59. 1907.

KROGER, W. S., and FREED, S. C. The psychosomatic treatment of functional dysmenorrhea by hypnosis. *American Journal of Obstetrics and Gynecology*, 817-822. December, 1943.

KUBIE, L. S., and MARGOLIN, S. The Process of Hypnotism and the Nature of the Hypnotic State. *American Journal of Psychology*, 100:611-622. March, 1944.

KUBIE, L. S. Use of Induced Hypnagogic Reveries in the Recovery of Repressed Amnesic Data. *Bulletin of the Menninger Clinic*, 7, 6-7:172-82. September-November, 1943.

LEUBA, C. Images as conditioned sensations. *Journal of Experimental Psychology*, 26, 345-351. 1940.

LEUBA, C. The use of hypnosis for controlling variables in psychological experiments. *Journal of Abnormal and Social Psychology*, 36, 271-274. 1941.

LEVBARG, J. J. Hypnosis: a potent therapy in medicine. *New York Physician*, 14:18. 1940.

LIVINGOOD, F. G. Hypnosis as an aid to adjustment. *Journal of General Psychology*, 12:203-7. 1941.

LOOMIS, A. L., HARVEY, E. N., and HOBART, G. Brain potentials during hypnosis. *Science*, 83, 239-241. 1936.

LUNDHOLM, H. An experimental study of functional anesthesias as induced by suggestion in hypnosis. *Journal of Abnormal and Social Psychology*, 23, 338-355. 1928.

MESSERSCHMIDT, R. A quantitative investigation of the alleged independent operation of conscious and subconscious processes. *Journal of Abnormal and Social Psychology*, 22, 325-340. 1928.

MILBRODT, W., and KOHLER, A. Hypoanalytic therapy of alleged sciatica. *Die Medizinische Welt.*, 8:408. March 24, 1934.

MITCHELL, M. B. Retroactive inhibition and hypnosis. *Journal of General Psychology*, 7, 343-359. 1932.

MORGAN, J. J. B. Hypnosis with direct psychoanalytic statement and suggestion in the treatment of a psychoneurotic of low intelligence. *Journal of Abnormal Psychology*, 19:160-164. 1924.

MORGAN, J. J. B. The nature of suggestibility. *Psychological Review,* 31:6. 1924.

MUHL, A. M. Automatic writing combined with crystal gazing as means of recalling forgotten incidents. *Journal of Abnormal Psychology,* 19:264-73. 1924.

MUNIZ, A. L. A case of anxiety neurosis cured by hypnosis. *Revista Medica Cubana,* 47:135-142. February, 1936.

MUNIZ, A. L. Hysteria, mutism and blindness cured by psychoanalysis and hypnotism. *Revista Medica Cubana,* 48:675-678. July, 1937.

MUNIZ, A. L. Incoercible vomiting of pregnancy cured by hypnosis. *Revista de la Sanidad Militar,* Havana, 6:65-70. 1942.

NICHOLSON, N. C. Notes on muscular work during hypnosis. *Johns Hopkins Hospital Bulletin,* 31, 89-91. 1920.

NYGARD, J. W. Cerebral circulation prevailing during sleep and hypnosis. *Journal of Experimental Psychology,* 24, 1-20. 1939.

PATTEN, E. F. The duration of post-hypnotic suggestion. *Journal of Abnormal and Social Psychology,* 25, 319-334. 1930.

PATTIE, F. A. The genuineness of hypnotically produced anesthesia of the skin. *American Journal of Psychology,* 49, 435-443. 1937.

PATTIE, F. A. The production of blisters by hypnotic suggestion: a review. *Journal of Abnormal and Social Psychology,* 36, 62-72. 1941.

PATTIE, F. A. A report of attempts to produce uniocular blindness by hypnotic suggestion. *British Journal of Medical Psychology,* 15, 230-241. 1935.

PAVLOV, I. P. The indentity of inhibition with sleep and hypnosis. *Scientific Monthly,* New York, 17, 603-608. 1923.

PAVLOV, I. P. Inhibition, hypnosis, and sleep. *British Medical Journal,* 256-267. 1923.

ROSENOW, C. Meaningful behavior in hypnosis. *American Journal of Psychology,* 40, 205-235. 1928.

ROSENZWEIG, S., and SARANSON, S. An experimental study of the triadic hypothesis: reaction to frustration, ego-defense and hypnotizability. *Character and Personality,* 11:2, 1-19. December, 1942.

SALTER, A. Three Techniques of Autohypnosis. *Journal of General Psychology,* 24:423-438. 1941.

SARBIN, T. R., and MADOW, L. W. Predicting the depth of hypnosis by means of the Rorschach test. *American Journal of Orthopsychiatry*, 12:2, 268-70. April, 1942.

SARGENT, W., and FRASER, R. Inducing Light Hypnosis by Hyperventilation. *Lancet*, 235:778. 1938.

SCOTT, H. D. Hypnosis and the conditioned reflex. *Journal of General Psychology*, 4, 113-130. 1930.

SEARS, R. R. An experimental study of hypnotic anesthesia. *Journal of Experimental Psychology*, 15, 1-22. 1932.

SMITH, G. M. A phobia originating before the age of three— cured with the aid of hypnotic recall. *Character and Personality*. 5:331-37. 1937.

SPEYER, N., and STOKVIS, B. The Psychoanalytic Factor in Hypnosis. *British Journal of Medical Psychology*. 17:217-222. 1938.

STALNAKER, J. M., and RIDDLE, E. E. The effect of hypnosis on long-delayed recall. *Journal of General Psychology*, 6, 429-440. 1932.

STRICKLER, C. B. A quantitative study of post-hypnotic amnesia. *Journal of Abnormal and Social Psychology*, 24, 108-119. 1929.

STUNGO, E. Evipan Hypnosis in Psychiatric Outpatients. *Lancet*, April 19, 1941.

TAYLOR, W. S. Behavior under hypnoanalysis and the mechanism of the neurosis. *Journal of Abnormal Psychology*, 18:107-124. 1923.

TAYLOR, W. S. A hypoanalytic study of two cases of war neurosis. *Journal of Abnormal Psychology*, 16:344-355. 1921-22.

TRAVIS, R. C. A study of the effect of hypnosis on a case of dissociation precipitated by migraine. *American Journal of Psychology*, 36:207. 1925.

WELCH, L. The space and time of induced hypnotic dreams. *Journal of Psychology*, 1, 171-178. 1936.

WELLS, W. R. Experiments in waking hypnosis for instructional purposes. *Journal of Abnormal Psychology*, 18, 389-404. 1924.

WELLS, W. R. Ability to resist artificially induced dissociation. *Journal of Abnormal and Social Psychology*, 35, 261-272. 1940.

WELLS, W. R. The extent and duration of post-hypnotic amnesia. *Journal of Psychology*, 9, 137-151. 1940.

WELLS, W. R. Experiments in the hypnotic production of crime. *Journal of Psychology*, 11, 63-102. 1941.

WELLS, W. R. Hypnotizability versus suggestibility. *Journal of Abnormal and Social Psychology*, 25, 436-449. 1931.

WELLS, W. R. The hypnotic treatment of the major symptoms of hysteria: a case study. *Journal of Psychology*, 17:269-297. 1944.

WHITE, M. M. The physical and mental traits of individuals susceptible to hypnosis. *Journal of Abnormal and Social Psychology*, 25:293-298. 1930.

WHITE, R. W. Prediction of hypnotic susceptibility from a knowledge of subject's attitudes. *Journal of Psychology*, 3, 265-277. 1937.

WHITE, R. W. Two types of hypnotic trance and their personality correlates. *Journal of Psychology*, 3, 279-289. 1937.

WHITE, R. W. An analysis of motivation in hypnosis. *Journal of General Psychology*, 24, 145-162. 1941.

WHITE, R. W. A preface to the theory of hypnotism. *Journal of Abnormal and Social Psychology*, 36, 477-505. 1941.

WHITE, R. W., FOX, G. F., and HARRIS, W. W. Hypnotic hypermnesia for recently learned material. *Journal of Abnormal and Social Psychology*, 35, 88-103. 1940.

WHITE, R. W. and SHEVACH, B. J. Hypnosis and the Concept of Dissociation. *Journal of Abnormal and Social Psychology*, 37:3, 309-328. July, 1942.

WHITE, R. W. Hypnosis Test. (Pages 453-461 in *Murray's Explorations in Personality*), New York: Oxford University Press. 1938.

WIBLE, C. L., and JENNESS, A. Electrocardiograms during sleep and hypnosis. *Journal of Psychology*, 1, 235-245. 1936.

WILLIAMS, G. W. The effect of hypnosis on muscular fatigue. *Journal of Abnormal and Social Psychology*, 24, 318-329. 1929.

WILLIAMS, G. W. A comparative study of voluntary and hypnotic catalepsy. *American Journal of Psychology*, 42, 83-95. 1930.

WILLIAMS, G. W. Suggestibility in the normal and hypnotic states. *Archives of Psychology*, 19, No. 122. 1930.

WILLIAMS, G. W. A study of the responses of three psychotic groups to a test of suggestibility. *Journal of General Psychology*, 7, 302-309. 1932.

YOUNG, P. C. An experimental study in the normal and hypnotic states. *American Journal of Psychology*, 36, 214-232. 1925.

A Personal Word From Melvin Powers
Publisher, Wilshire Book Company

Dear Friend:

My goal is to publish interesting, informative, and inspirational books. You can help me accomplish this by answering the following questions, either by phone or by mail. Or, if convenient for you, I would welcome the opportunity to visit with you in my office and hear your comments in person.

Did you enjoy reading this book? Why?

Would you enjoy reading another similar book?

What idea in the book impressed you the most?

If applicable to your situation, have you incorporated this idea in your daily life?

Is there a chapter that could serve as a theme for an entire book? Please explain.

If you have an idea for a book, I would welcome discussing it with you. If you already have one in progress, write or call me concerning possible publication. I can be reached at

(213) 875-1711 or (213) 983-1105.

Sincerely yours,

Melvin Powers

12015 Sherman Road
North Hollywood, California 91605

MELVIN POWERS SELF-IMPROVEMENT LIBRARY

ASTROLOGY

_____ASTROLOGY: HOW TO CHART YOUR HOROSCOPE *Max Heindel*	3.00
_____ASTROLOGY: YOUR PERSONAL SUN-SIGN GUIDE *Beatrice Ryder*	3.00
_____ASTROLOGY FOR EVERYDAY LIVING *Janet Harris*	2.00
_____ASTROLOGY MADE EASY *Astarte*	2.00
_____ASTROLOGY MADE PRACTICAL *Alexandra Kayhle*	3.00
_____ASTROLOGY, ROMANCE, YOU AND THE STARS *Anthony Norvell*	4.00
_____MY WORLD OF ASTROLOGY *Sydney Omarr*	5.00
_____THOUGHT DIAL *Sydney Omarr*	3.00
_____ZODIAC REVEALED *Rupert Gleadow*	2.00

BRIDGE

_____BRIDGE BIDDING MADE EASY *Edwin B. Kantar*	5.00
_____BRIDGE CONVENTIONS *Edwin B. Kantar*	5.00
_____BRIDGE HUMOR *Edwin B. Kantar*	3.00
_____COMPETITIVE BIDDING IN MODERN BRIDGE *Edgar Kaplan*	4.00
_____DEFENSIVE BRIDGE PLAY COMPLETE *Edwin B. Kantar*	10.00
_____HOW TO IMPROVE YOUR BRIDGE *Alfred Sheinwold*	2.00
_____INTRODUCTION TO DEFENDER'S PLAY *Edwin B. Kantar*	3.00
_____SHORT CUT TO WINNING BRIDGE *Alfred Sheinwold*	3.00
_____TEST YOUR BRIDGE PLAY *Edwin B. Kantar*	3.00
_____WINNING DECLARER PLAY *Dorothy Hayden Truscott*	4.00

BUSINESS, STUDY & REFERENCE

_____CONVERSATION MADE EASY *Elliot Russell*	2.00
_____EXAM SECRET *Dennis B. Jackson*	2.00
_____FIX-IT BOOK *Arthur Symons*	2.00
_____HOW TO DEVELOP A BETTER SPEAKING VOICE *M. Hellier*	2.00
_____HOW TO MAKE A FORTUNE IN REAL ESTATE *Albert Winnikoff*	3.00
_____INCREASE YOUR LEARNING POWER *Geoffrey A. Dudley*	2.00
_____MAGIC OF NUMBERS *Robert Tocquet*	2.00
_____PRACTICAL GUIDE TO BETTER CONCENTRATION *Melvin Powers*	2.00
_____PRACTICAL GUIDE TO PUBLIC SPEAKING *Maurice Forley*	3.00
_____7 DAYS TO FASTER READING *William S. Schaill*	3.00
_____SONGWRITERS RHYMING DICTIONARY *Jane Shaw Whitfield*	5.00
_____SPELLING MADE EASY *Lester D. Basch & Dr. Milton Finkelstein*	2.00
_____STUDENT'S GUIDE TO BETTER GRADES *J. A. Rickard*	2.00
_____TEST YOURSELF—Find Your Hidden Talent *Jack Shafer*	2.00
_____YOUR WILL & WHAT TO DO ABOUT IT *Attorney Samuel G. Kling*	3.00

CALLIGRAPHY

_____ADVANCED CALLIGRAPHY *Katherine Jeffares*	6.00
_____CALLIGRAPHY—The Art of Beautfiul Writing *Katherine Jeffares*	5.00

CHESS & CHECKERS

_____BEGINNER'S GUIDE TO WINNING CHESS *Fred Reinfeld*	3.00
_____BETTER CHESS—How to Play *Fred Reinfeld*	2.00
_____CHECKERS MADE EASY *Tom Wiswell*	2.00
_____CHESS IN TEN EASY LESSONS *Larry Evans*	3.00
_____CHESS MADE EASY *Milton L. Hanauer*	3.00
_____CHESS MASTERY—A New Approach *Fred Reinfeld*	2.00
_____CHESS PROBLEMS FOR BEGINNERS *edited by Fred Reinfeld*	2.00
_____CHESS SECRETS REVEALED *Fred Reinfeld*	2.00
_____CHESS STRATEGY—An Expert's Guide *Fred Reinfeld*	2.00
_____CHESS TACTICS FOR BEGINNERS *edited by Fred Reinfeld*	2.00
_____CHESS THEORY & PRACTICE *Morry & Mitchell*	2.00
_____HOW TO WIN AT CHECKERS *Fred Reinfeld*	2.00
_____1001 BRILLIANT WAYS TO CHECKMATE *Fred Reinfeld*	3.00
_____1001 WINNING CHESS SACRIFICES & COMBINATIONS *Fred Reinfeld*	3.00
_____SOVIET CHESS *Edited by R. G. Wade*	3.00

COOKERY & HERBS

_____CULPEPER'S HERBAL REMEDIES *Dr. Nicholas Culpeper*	2.00
_____FAST GOURMET COOKBOOK *Poppy Cannon*	2.50

_____ GINSENG The Myth & The Truth *Joseph P. Hou*   3.00
_____ HEALING POWER OF HERBS *May Bethel*   3.00
_____ HEALING POWER OF NATURAL FOODS *May Bethel*   3.00
_____ HERB HANDBOOK *Dawn MacLeod*   3.00
_____ HERBS FOR COOKING AND HEALING *Dr. Donald Law*   2.00
_____ HERBS FOR HEALTH—How to Grow & Use Them *Louise Evans Doole*   3.00
_____ HOME GARDEN COOKBOOK—Delicious Natural Food Recipes *Ken Kraft*   3.00
_____ MEDICAL HERBALIST *edited by Dr. J. R. Yemm*   3.00
_____ NATURAL FOOD COOKBOOK *Dr. Harry C. Bond*   3.00
_____ NATURE'S MEDICINES *Richard Lucas*   3.00
_____ VEGETABLE GARDENING FOR BEGINNERS *Hugh Wiberg*   2.00
_____ VEGETABLES FOR TODAY'S GARDENS *R. Milton Carleton*   2.00
_____ VEGETARIAN COOKERY *Janet Walker*   3.00
_____ VEGETARIAN COOKING MADE EASY & DELECTABLE *Veronica Vezza*   2.00
_____ VEGETARIAN DELIGHTS—A Happy Cookbook for Health *K. R. Mehta*   2.00
_____ VEGETARIAN GOURMET COOKBOOK *Joyce McKinnel*   3.00

GAMBLING & POKER

_____ ADVANCED POKER STRATEGY & WINNING PLAY *A. D. Livingston*   3.00
_____ HOW NOT TO LOSE AT POKER *Jeffrey Lloyd Castle*   3.00
_____ HOW TO WIN AT DICE GAMES *Skip Frey*   3.00
_____ HOW TO WIN AT POKER *Terence Reese & Anthony T. Watkins*   2.00
_____ SECRETS OF WINNING POKER *George S. Coffin*   3.00
_____ WINNING AT CRAPS *Dr. Lloyd T. Commins*   3.00
_____ WINNING AT GIN *Chester Wander & Cy Rice*   3.00
_____ WINNING AT POKER—An Expert's Guide *John Archer*   3.00
_____ WINNING AT 21—An Expert's Guide *John Archer*   3.00
_____ WINNING POKER SYSTEMS *Norman Zadeh*   3.00

HEALTH

_____ DR. LINDNER'S SPECIAL WEIGHT CONTROL METHOD   1.50
_____ HELP YOURSELF TO BETTER SIGHT *Margaret Darst Corbett*   3.00
_____ HOW TO IMPROVE YOUR VISION *Dr. Robert A. Kraskin*   2.00
_____ HOW YOU CAN STOP SMOKING PERMANENTLY *Ernest Caldwell*   2.00
_____ JOY OF WALKING *Jack Scagnetti*   3.00
_____ MIND OVER PLATTER *Peter G. Lindner, M.D.*   3.00
_____ NATURE'S WAY TO NUTRITION & VIBRANT HEALTH *Robert J. Scrutton*   3.00
_____ NEW CARBOHYDRATE DIET COUNTER *Patti Lopez-Pereira*   1.50
_____ PSYCHEDELIC ECSTASY *William Marshall & Gilbert W. Taylor*   2.00
_____ REFLEXOLOGY *Dr. Maybelle Segal*   2.00
_____ YOU CAN LEARN TO RELAX *Dr. Samuel Gutwirth*   2.00
_____ YOUR ALLERGY—What To Do About It *Allan Knight, M.D.*   3.00

HOBBIES

_____ BEACHCOMBING FOR BEGINNERS *Norman Hickin*   2.00
_____ BLACKSTONE'S MODERN CARD TRICKS *Harry Blackstone*   3.00
_____ BLACKSTONE'S SECRETS OF MAGIC *Harry Blackstone*   2.00
_____ BUTTERFLIES   2.50
_____ COIN COLLECTING FOR BEGINNERS *Burton Hobson & Fred Reinfeld*   2.00
_____ ENTERTAINING WITH ESP *Tony 'Doc' Shiels*   2.00
_____ 400 FASCINATING MAGIC TRICKS YOU CAN DO *Howard Thurston*   3.00
_____ GOULD'S GOLD & SILVER GUIDE TO COINS *Maurice Gould*   2.00
_____ HOW I TURN JUNK INTO FUN AND PROFIT *Sari*   3.00
_____ HOW TO PLAY THE HARMONICA FOR FUN AND PROFIT *Hal Leighton*   3.00
_____ HOW TO WRITE A HIT SONG & SELL IT *Tommy Boyce*   7.00
_____ JUGGLING MADE EASY *Rudolf Dittrich*   2.00
_____ MAGIC MADE EASY *Byron Wels*   2.00
_____ STAMP COLLECTING FOR BEGINNERS *Burton Hobson*   2.00
_____ STAMP COLLECTING FOR FUN & PROFIT *Frank Cetin*   2.00

HORSE PLAYERS' WINNING GUIDES

_____ BETTING HORSES TO WIN *Les Conklin*   3.00
_____ ELIMINATE THE LOSERS *Bob McKnight*   3.00
_____ HOW TO PICK WINNING HORSES *Bob McKnight*   3.00
_____ HOW TO WIN AT THE RACES *Sam (The Genius) Lewin*   3.00

_____ IMPOTENCE & FRIGIDITY *Edwin W. Hirsch, M.D.*		3.00
_____ SEX WITHOUT GUILT *Albert Ellis, Ph.D.*		3.00
_____ SEXUALLY ADEQUATE MALE *Frank S. Caprio, M.D.*		3.00

METAPHYSICS & OCCULT

_____ BOOK OF TALISMANS, AMULETS & ZODIACAL GEMS *William Pavitt*		4.00
_____ CONCENTRATION—A Guide to Mental Mastery *Mouni Sadhu*		3.00
_____ CRITIQUES OF GOD *Edited by Peter Angeles*		7.00
_____ DREAMS & OMENS REVEALED *Fred Gettings*		2.00
_____ EXTRASENSORY PERCEPTION *Simeon Edmunds*		2.00
_____ EXTRA-TERRESTRIAL INTELLIGENCE—The First Encounter		6.00
_____ FORTUNE TELLING WITH CARDS *P. Foli*		2.00
_____ HANDWRITING ANALYSIS MADE EASY *John Marley*		3.00
_____ HANDWRITING TELLS *Nadya Olyanova*		5.00
_____ HOW TO UNDERSTAND YOUR DREAMS *Geoffrey A. Dudley*		2.00
_____ ILLUSTRATED YOGA *William Zorn*		3.00
_____ IN DAYS OF GREAT PEACE *Mouni Sadhu*		3.00
_____ KING SOLOMON'S TEMPLE IN THE MASONIC TRADITION *Alex Horne*		5.00
_____ LSD—THE AGE OF MIND *Bernard Roseman*		2.00
_____ MAGICIAN—His training and work *W. E. Butler*		3.00
_____ MEDITATION *Mouni Sadhu*		4.00
_____ MODERN NUMEROLOGY *Morris C. Goodman*		3.00
_____ NUMEROLOGY—ITS FACTS AND SECRETS *Ariel Yvon Taylor*		3.00
_____ PALMISTRY MADE EASY *Fred Gettings*		3.00
_____ PALMISTRY MADE PRACTICAL *Elizabeth Daniels Squire*		3.00
_____ PALMISTRY SECRETS REVEALED *Henry Frith*		2.00
_____ PRACTICAL YOGA *Ernest Wood*		3.00
_____ PROPHECY IN OUR TIME *Martin Ebon*		2.50
_____ PSYCHOLOGY OF HANDWRITING *Nadya Olyanova*		3.00
_____ SUPERSTITION—Are you superstitious? *Eric Maple*		2.00
_____ TAROT *Mouni Sadhu*		5.00
_____ TAROT OF THE BOHEMIANS *Papus*		5.00
_____ TEST YOUR ESP *Martin Ebon*		2.00
_____ WAYS TO SELF-REALIZATION *Mouni Sadhu*		3.00
_____ WHAT YOUR HANDWRITING REVEALS *Albert E. Hughes*		2.00
_____ WITCHCRAFT, MAGIC & OCCULTISM—A Fascinating History *W. B. Crow*		5.00
_____ WITCHCRAFT—THE SIXTH SENSE *Justine Glass*		3.00
_____ WORLD OF PSYCHIC RESEARCH *Hereward Carrington*		2.00
_____ YOU CAN ANALYZE HANDWRITING *Robert Holder*		2.00

SELF-HELP & INSPIRATIONAL

_____ CYBERNETICS WITHIN US *Y. Saparina*		3.00
_____ DAILY POWER FOR JOYFUL LIVING *Dr. Donald Curtis*		3.00
_____ DOCTOR PSYCHO-CYBERNETICS *Maxwell Maltz, M.D.*		3.00
_____ DYNAMIC THINKING *Melvin Powers*		2.00
_____ EXUBERANCE—Your Guide to Happiness & Fulfillment *Dr. Paul Kurtz*		3.00
_____ GREATEST POWER IN THE UNIVERSE *U. S. Andersen*		4.00
_____ GROW RICH WHILE YOU SLEEP *Ben Sweetland*		3.00
_____ GROWTH THROUGH REASON *Albert Ellis, Ph.D.*		4.00
_____ GUIDE TO DEVELOPING YOUR POTENTIAL *Herbert A. Otto, Ph.D.*		3.00
_____ GUIDE TO LIVING IN BALANCE *Frank S. Caprio, M.D.*		2.00
_____ HELPING YOURSELF WITH APPLIED PSYCHOLOGY *R. Henderson*		2.00
_____ HELPING YOURSELF WITH PSYCHIATRY *Frank S. Caprio, M.D.*		2.00
_____ HOW TO ATTRACT GOOD LUCK *A. H. Z. Carr*		3.00
_____ HOW TO CONTROL YOUR DESTINY *Norvell*		3.00
_____ HOW TO DEVELOP A WINNING PERSONALITY *Martin Panzer*		3.00
_____ HOW TO DEVELOP AN EXCEPTIONAL MEMORY *Young & Gibson*		4.00
_____ HOW TO OVERCOME YOUR FEARS *M. P. Leahy, M.D.*		3.00
_____ HOW YOU CAN HAVE CONFIDENCE AND POWER *Les Giblin*		3.00
_____ HUMAN PROBLEMS & HOW TO SOLVE THEM *Dr. Donald Curtis*		3.00
_____ I CAN *Ben Sweetland*		4.00
_____ I WILL *Ben Sweetland*		3.00
_____ LEFT-HANDED PEOPLE *Michael Barsley*		3.00

_____MAGIC IN YOUR MIND *U. S. Andersen*		4.00
_____MAGIC OF THINKING BIG *Dr. David J. Schwartz*		3.00
_____MAGIC POWER OF YOUR MIND *Walter M. Germain*		4.00
_____MENTAL POWER THROUGH SLEEP SUGGESTION *Melvin Powers*		2.00
_____NEW GUIDE TO RATIONAL LIVING *Albert Ellis, Ph.D. & R. Harper, Ph.D.*		3.00
_____OUR TROUBLED SELVES *Dr. Allan Fromme*		3.00
_____PSYCHO-CYBERNETICS *Maxwell Maltz, M.D.*		2.00
_____SCIENCE OF MIND IN DAILY LIVING *Dr. Donald Curtis*		3.00
_____SECRET OF SECRETS *U. S. Andersen*		4.00
_____SECRET POWER OF THE PYRAMIDS *U. S. Andersen*		4.00
_____STUTTERING AND WHAT YOU CAN DO ABOUT IT *W. Johnson, Ph.D.*		2.50
_____SUCCESS-CYBERNETICS *U. S. Andersen*		4.00
_____10 DAYS TO A GREAT NEW LIFE *William E. Edwards*		3.00
_____THINK AND GROW RICH *Napoleon Hill*		3.00
_____THREE MAGIC WORDS *U. S. Andersen*		4.00
_____TREASURY OF THE ART OF LIVING *Sidney S. Greenberg*		5.00
_____YOU ARE NOT THE TARGET *Laura Huxley*		3.00
_____YOUR SUBCONSCIOUS POWER *Charles M. Simmons*		4.00
_____YOUR THOUGHTS CAN CHANGE YOUR LIFE *Dr. Donald Curtis*		3.00

SPORTS

_____ARCHERY—An Expert's Guide *Dan Stamp*	2.00
_____BICYCLING FOR FUN AND GOOD HEALTH *Kenneth E. Luther*	2.00
_____BILLIARDS—Pocket • Carom • Three Cushion *Clive Cottingham, Jr.*	3.00
_____CAMPING-OUT 101 Ideas & Activities *Bruno Knobel*	2.00
_____COMPLETE GUIDE TO FISHING *Vlad Evanoff*	2.00
_____HOW TO WIN AT POCKET BILLIARDS *Edward D. Knuchell*	3.00
_____LEARNING & TEACHING SOCCER SKILLS *Eric Worthington*	3.00
_____MOTORCYCLING FOR BEGINNERS *I. G. Edmonds*	2.00
_____PRACTICAL BOATING *W. S. Kals*	3.00
_____RACQUETBALL MADE EASY *Steve Lubarsky, Rod Delson & Jack Scagnetti*	3.00
_____SECRET OF BOWLING STRIKES *Dawson Taylor*	3.00
_____SECRET OF PERFECT PUTTING *Horton Smith & Dawson Taylor*	3.00
_____SECRET WHY FISH BITE *James Westman*	2.00
_____SOCCER—The game & how to play it *Gary Rosenthal*	2.00
_____STARTING SOCCER *Edward F. Dolan, Jr.*	2.00
_____TABLE TENNIS MADE EASY *Johnny Leach*	2.00

TENNIS LOVERS' LIBRARY

_____BEGINNER'S GUIDE TO WINNING TENNIS *Helen Hull Jacobs*	2.00
_____HOW TO BEAT BETTER TENNIS PLAYERS *Loring Fiske*	4.00
_____HOW TO IMPROVE YOUR TENNIS—Style, Strategy & Analysis *C. Wilson*	2.00
_____INSIDE TENNIS—Techniques of Winning *Jim Leighton*	3.00
_____PLAY TENNIS WITH ROSEWALL *Ken Rosewall*	2.00
_____PSYCH YOURSELF TO BETTER TENNIS *Dr. Walter A. Luszki*	2.00
_____SUCCESSFUL TENNIS *Neale Fraser*	2.00
_____TENNIS FOR BEGINNERS *Dr. H. A. Murray*	2.00
_____TENNIS MADE EASY *Joel Brecheen*	2.00
_____WEEKEND TENNIS—How to have fun & win at the same time *Bill Talbert*	3.00
_____WINNING WITH PERCENTAGE TENNIS—Smart Strategy *Jack Lowe*	2.00

WILSHIRE PET LIBRARY

_____DOG OBEDIENCE TRAINING *Gust Kessopulos*	3.00
_____DOG TRAINING MADE EASY & FUN *John W. Kellogg*	2.00
_____HOW TO BRING UP YOUR PET DOG *Kurt Unkelbach*	2.00
_____HOW TO RAISE & TRAIN YOUR PUPPY *Jeff Griffen*	2.00
_____PIGEONS: HOW TO RAISE & TRAIN THEM *William H. Allen, Jr.*	2.00

*The books listed above can be obtained from your book dealer or directly from
Melvin Powers. When ordering, please remit 50¢ per book postage & handling.
Send for our free illustrated catalog of self-improvement books.*

Melvin Powers
12015 Sherman Road, No. Hollywood, California 91605

Notes

Notes

Notes